No Day without a Line

No Day without a Line

FROM NOTEBOOKS

Yury Olesha

Edited, Translated from the Russian,
and with an Introduction by
Judson Rosengrant

NORTHWESTERN UNIVERSITY PRESS / EVANSTON, ILLINOIS

Northwestern University Press
Evanston, Illinois 60208-4210

Printed in the United States of America

ISBN 0-8101-1382-1

Library of Congress Cataloging-in-Publication Data

Olesha, I͡Uriĭ Karlovich, 1899–1960.
[Ni dni͡a bez strochki. English]
No day without a line : from notebooks / Yury Olesha ; edited, translated from the Russian, and with an introduction by Judson Rosengrant.
p. cm. — (Studies in Russian literature and theory)
Translation first published: Ann Arbor : Ardis, c1979.
Includes bibliographical references.
ISBN 0-8101-1382-1 (pbk. : alk. paper)
1. Olesha, I͡Uriĭ Karlovich, 1899–1960—Biography. 2. Authors, Russian—20th century—Biography. I. Rosengrant, Judson, 1941– . II. Title. III. Series.
PG3476.037Z5213 1998
891.78′4203—dc21 98-17688
[B] CIP

The paper used in this publication meets the minimum requirements of the American National Standard for Information Sciences—Permanence of Paper for Printed Library Materials, ANSI Z39.48-1984.

Contents

vii Introduction

1 No Day without a Line

Childhood 3

Odessa 39

Moscow 99

The Golden Shelf 136

The Extraordinary Intersection 198

223 Notes

Introduction

YURY OLESHA was born in the southern Russian city of Elizavetgrad in 1899, the same year as Ernest Hemingway and Vladimir Nabokov, but moved with his family to the cosmopolitan port of Odessa in 1902.[1] His parents were middle-class Polish Catholics, and although his father had owned an estate with his brother in Elizavetgrad and was still officially a member of the gentry, he worked in Odessa as a tax inspector in a vodka distillery. His job was not, however, a very demanding one; indeed, it seems to have been largely a sinecure, for according to Olesha he spent most of his time playing cards and drinking at his club, activities that eventually consumed the proceeds from the sale of the estate and that were otherwise the cause of family distress. The Oleshas also had a daughter, Wanda, who was two years older than her brother and who died in 1919 of typhoid, a common disease in the collapse and privation that accompanied the 1917 revolution and ensuing civil war.

Olesha's upbringing, as may be inferred from his notebooks, his other published autobiographical writings, and his thinly disguised autobiographical stories and sketches, was quite conventional. His family, though never well-off, were loyal members of prerevolutionary Russian society with aspirations and pretensions consistent with their attenuated gentry status. Like many children of his time and class, Olesha began his education at home, although not with private tutors of the kind described, for example, by his wealthy Petersburg coeval Nabokov[2]—that would have been far beyond the Oleshas' means—but with his beloved grandmother, who shared a room with him in the family's succession of modest central Odessa apartments and who taught him arithmetic and gave him his first lessons in reading and writing Russian, a language he seems to have learned on a substratum of early childhood Polish. In 1909, at the age of ten, Olesha was enrolled in Richelieu Gymnasium in Odessa, an eight-year institution whose rigorous pre-university curriculum included, besides a thorough grounding in Russian language and literature and Old Church Slavonic, training in foreign languages (Latin,

French, and German), what might now be called the social sciences and humanities (history, law, and introduction to philosophy), science (physics and geography), mathematics, and religion. He graduated in 1917 with a perfect record of fives, a commendation for good behavior, and a gold medal in language and literature, the last award entitling him to university admission without the customary examinations.

After Richelieu Gymnasium Olesha entered the University of Novorossiya (now Odessa State University), where he studied law. Then in 1919, at the height of civil strife in the Ukraine and after a bout of his own with the typhoid that had killed his sister, he left the university and a discipline that must by then have seemed fairly irrelevant to become a Red Army volunteer, serving as a telephonist in a coastal artillery battery. At the same time, he began work as a propagandist, or "poet-agitator" as he would later call it with characteristic irony, writing newspaper articles and short plays and pamphlets for the Bureau of Ukrainian Publications, an adjunct of ROSTA, the Russian national telegraphic agency. Having like so many other idealistic young people thus lent his allegiance to the Bolsheviks and their confident assurances of a brave new world of economic justice, Olesha decisively broke with the conservative sympathies of his family, who would eventually flee to nonsocialist Poland.

While still a student at Richelieu, Olesha began to write verse. It was by his own later estimate derivative and mannered, composed under the sway of the great symbolist Alexander Blok and the minor "ego-futurist" Igor Severyanin, but especially the latter, whose mellifluous and beautifully performed poetry was then extremely popular in Odessa, as elsewhere in the country. Olesha's first published effort, a ballad called "Clarimonda," appeared in 1915 in the Odessa newspaper *The Southern Herald.* After graduating from Richelieu, Olesha gave more serious attention to verse and began to take an active part in Odessa literary life. He was associated with several other ambitious young people, among them the already accomplished poet Eduard Bagritsky and the future novelist Valentin Kataev, in a literary circle called the Green Lamp, named after a similar group to which the youthful Pushkin had belonged. Besides providing a congenial forum where young men and women might read and discuss their work, the Green Lamp arranged public readings and, from time to time, colloquia with local scholars or with older writers who lived or had sought refuge in Odessa or were passing through on their way into emigration—men like the poet Maximilian Voloshin or the novelists Alexei Tolstoy and Ivan Bunin. During this time, Olesha was also linked to another, perhaps more politically engaged literary circle, the Poets' Collective, whose notable membership included the young satirist Ilya Ilf.[3]

In 1921 Olesha moved to the Ukrainian industrial city of Kharkov, where he continued to work as a propagandist for the Bureau of Ukrainian

Publications and where he began to experiment with fiction. "The Angel," his first published story, appeared in the Kharkov newspaper *Proletarian* in 1922. The same year Olesha moved again, this time to Moscow, then reasserting itself as the country's capital and preeminent intellectual center. There he joined the staff of the popular transportation newspaper the *Whistle,* beginning what would become his true apprenticeship.

> I began at the *Whistle* not as a journalist, incidentally. I served in what was called the "information section," and my job consisted of stuffing envelopes with letters written by the section head to the various addresses of the worker correspondents. I wrote in the addresses. Before that I'd already had something of a poet's calling, but since I'd embarked it in Odessa, and I'd come from Odessa, the provinces, to Moscow, the capital, I had to start everything all over again. That's why I took the job of sealing envelopes.
>
> Once—I don't remember anymore what the reasons were—the section head, Ivan Semyonovich Ovchinnikov, suggested that I write a verse satire based on a letter from one of the worker correspondents. And I wrote the satire . . . There was something in it about the Moscow River, about a certain captain, about a riverboat and its captain who stopped his boat not where he was supposed to according to the schedule, but where his sweetheart lived. As it seems to me now, the satire wasn't badly done.
>
> "How shall I sign it?" I asked my section comrades. "Eh? What do you think? I need a name that's interesting but still has an industrial tinge . . . Help me out."
>
> "Sign it 'Chisel,'" said Grigorievich, one of my colleagues, fat and amiable.
>
> "Well, why not?" I agreed. "That's not bad. I'll sign it 'Chisel.'"[4]

Olesha's efforts as "Chisel" quickly established him as a leading member of an editorial staff that included several of the most talented young writers of the day, men who would make lasting contributions to twentieth-century Russian literature—most importantly the novelist and playwright Mikhail Bulgakov, but also Olesha's fellow Odessans Valentin Kataev, Kataev's brother Evgeny Petrov, and Petrov's longtime coauthor Ilya Ilf, who had moved to Moscow as well.[5] Olesha became famous as "Chisel," his column enjoying great success with the paper's readership, who responded to its accurate portrayal of working life and to its amusing sallies against the corruption and inefficiency that were impeding the establishment of the new transportation system. Olesha's warm recollections in *No Day without a Line* of his work at the *Whistle* may strike some readers as sentimental and, given the dissolution of the revolutionary élan and idealism of the 1920s and early 1930s in the developing Stalinist national psychosis, perhaps even as historically disingenuous, yet there can be no doubt that the pride he took in his contributions as "Chisel" was genuine, or that the group that gathered under the paper's initially tolerant auspices constituted an extraordinarily stimulating professional environment, at once indifferent to doctrine, socially involved, and imbued with the individualist and experimentalist predilections of artistic modernism.[6] Ultimately two collections of Olesha's satirical verse were published: *Chisel* in 1924 and *Salute* in 1927. Sending his friend and colleague Bulgakov a copy of the first volume, he wrote, "Mishenka, I'll never write abstract lyrical verses. Nobody needs them. A poet must write satirical poems so that his lines may have practical value for people who earn seven rubles [a week]. Don't be angry, Mishunchik; you're a good humorist (Mark Twain, too, was a humorist). Within a year I'll give you yet another *Chisel.* Fondly, Olesha."[7]

Yet despite this endorsement of the social value of his work as "Chisel" and despite the wide public attention that work brought him, Olesha in fact began almost immediately after his arrival in Moscow to devote himself as well to literature of a more "abstract" and "lyrical" kind, not to poetry, certainly, but to fiction and drama, and moreover fiction and drama of a stylistically sophisticated and ideologically skeptical variety that could hardly have been calculated to appeal to the ordinary working people whose practical needs he had so earnestly championed in the note to Bulgakov. Olesha remained at the *Whistle* for some time, however. Like his colleagues at the paper and like many other fellow travelers in the tumultuous artistic and political life of the 1920s, he seems, perhaps inevitably, to have been unsure of the proper place of literature and of his own relation to it. Thus, simultaneously with his emergence as a writer of avant-garde prose and drama that were fundamentally if not explicitly at odds with the premises and emerging social arrangements of the new epoch, he continued to work as a "poet-agitator" on behalf of those premises and arrangements, finally ending his relationship with the *Whistle* in 1932—although without ever fully resolving (either then or later) the inner conflict between his moral and intellectual need to set himself apart in the independent stance of the modern and especially Russian writer, and his heartfelt desire to be included, to participate as an active and respected member of the community engaged in building the recently proclaimed Soviet world.[8]

The middle 1920s through the early 1930s was Olesha's most productive period. The classic short novel *Envy,* which he may have begun as early as 1922 while still in Kharkov, was published in 1927 in the influential "thick" journal *Red Virgin Soil.* It came out as a book the next year, and in 1929 it was staged at the Vakhtangov Theater in Moscow in the author's own adaptation as *The Conspiracy of Feelings.* In 1928 Olesha also published his popular "novel for children," *The Three Fat Men,* begun during his early years at the *Whistle.* This portrayal of a revolution in the innocent terms of fantasy became a favorite almost at once. It has been performed as a play (the first time in 1930, adapted by Olesha and produced by Konstantin Stanislavsky at the Moscow Art Theater); it has been presented as a ballet, an opera, and a radio drama; it has been filmed four times (three times in animated versions); and it continues to be reprinted in large editions, since its imagination and wit are by no means limited to the period of its creation nor necessarily colored by Soviet ideology. In 1931 Olesha's only original play, *The List of Assets,* was staged by Vsevolod Meyerhold at his theater in Moscow. During this period Olesha also published a number of short stories and novelle of very high quality, of which the best and most frequently anthologized in Russian and translation are "Liompa" (1927), "Love" (1928), "The Chain" (1929), and "The Cherry Stone" (1929). Like the rest of Olesha's fiction of the 1920s, these works are marked by an exuberantly imagistic style, philosophical commitment, and a whimsical sense of fantasy. Most of them were collected in a volume called *The Cherry Stone,* published in 1931. Two collections of pamphlet size also came out at that time: *Love* in 1929 and *Notes of a Writer* in 1931.

However generically diverse, the writings of this period, roughly 1924 to 1932, bear a common stamp. Their guiding theme is the familiar romantic and modernist one of conflict between the impulses of individual imagination, especially its conventional epitome, artistic imagination, and the unconcern, mundane imperatives, or oppressive social constitution of the larger community. To be sure, by the 1920s this theme had a well-established Russian tradition, but in Olesha's hands and as a response to the severe stresses of Soviet life, it acquired special dimensions. In order to indicate their nature and to clarify the underlying conceptions that arguably influenced the subsequent development of his career, let me take a brief look at "The Cherry Stone." As one of Olesha's best stories and one of his most typical, it will stand very well for his writings of the 1920s and early 1930s.

Despite its amusing play with narrative conventions, abrupt intersecting of symbolic planes, and self-mocking tone, "The Cherry Stone" treats the theme of the conflict between the worlds of imagination and society (or between artist and society) with great seriousness, presenting it in direct, almost allegorical form. The story's hero and narrator, the young man Fedya, is a sensitive, dreamy, ineffectual person who sublimates his unrequited love for the young woman Natasha (herself drawn to a virile, decisive man of action) in art, symbolized by a cherry stone, a seed that will, like artistic imagination, eventually produce something of grace and beauty but whose significance and power are for the time being merely potential. The story defends what it calls the "invisible land" of imagination, a realm where things happen differently than in the world of "everyday reality," and that in the story's view is properly subject only to the laws of private sensation and perception as they emerge from the unpredictable circumstances of individual formation and identity. It argues, in other words, for the place of art and nonutilitarian beauty in a world of five-year plans, usurping materialism, and ruthless social reorganization, a world governed by people like Natasha's unreflective man of action. It argues, too, for the authority of the artist's own subjective vision, for the integrity of his particular manner of seeing and interpreting the world, however jejune or insubstantial or irrelevant that vision may at first appear to be.

Of course, Fedya's cherry stone and the beautiful fruit-bearing tree it will produce in time, given hospitable conditions and a place to grow, are not the only symbols in the story. Natasha herself may be understood to represent a new Russia too much attracted to positivist ideals of social utility, a Russia that must be reminded of the spontaneous, undirected nature of creative imagination and of the importance of art—that it is not a childish or self-indulgent pastime, but an essential human activity with its own claims and requirements. "The Cherry Stone" thus dramatizes the situation of the artist in the new world of overrationalized social organization. Yet the story does not merely present the artist's situation; it also suggests something of the distinctive nature of his vision, and by extension it also intimates, in a paradoxical inversion of its own antiutilitarian stance, a view of the purpose of art, of its cognitive and social value.

Fedya sees the world as an ever shifting kaleidoscope of surface phenomena—as a realm where function may be ignored or even negated, and where the ordinary is capable of startling transformation by an imagination free to follow its impulses and insights where it will. His is a mode of seeing that is fundamentally lyrical, since it is concerned with personal sensation and feeling, and it is also one that finds its most natural expression in the barely mediated associative juxtapositions and epistemic shifts of metaphor and simile. And, of course, it is a mode the character shares with his creator, since the subjective aesthetic ideology and corollary metaphorical technique presented in and by the story clearly originate in Olesha's sense of his own gifts and from the dilemma of his public and private situation as a Russian writer, a dilemma that he had in common with many of his generation but that he seems to have felt with special poignancy.

As the Danish Slavist Nils Nilsson has observed in regard to this interrelation of style and meaning, Olesha's

> is not only a world of unusual perspectives and optical illusions, but also—and for the most part just because of them—a world of startling metaphors. An object loses its firm contours, becomes material pliable to the will of the imagination, which starts to form new things out of it. But this is not all; there is a further stage. As often happens with the imaginations of children, the metaphor itself becomes true, is materialized. It is not just a simple comparison, made in passing. We witness a fantastic metamorphosis.[9]

And in fact there is in "The Cherry Stone," as in a great deal of Olesha's writing, a tendency to realize metaphor—to present the image produced by the comparison as being quite as "real" as its constituent terms. Olesha never implies, however, that his new images must have a deeper, mystical significance. Though his technique may derive from theirs, he is not a symbolist invoking some more resonant world beyond our own, nor, on the other hand, is he, like a nineteenth-century realist, much interested in using imagery as an instrument of character revelation or thematic development, although his figures may, of course, serve these ends as well. Rather, he is a realist of the senses, a hedonist of color and form, who uses imagery to deflect and confound ordinary ways of seeing, thereby inviting the reader to regard his own world more attentively, to look at things with a fresh eye, to see them as they might be said to exist beyond their incorporation in a priori epistemological and linguistic systems or in received or imposed social and political systems. In Olesha's view, it is the purpose of art "to make the world new," to re-present it in what he regards as the unsullied and immediate aspect of childhood. And art does this by employing a subversive language whose basis is metaphor and whose result is the disruption of the automatic identification of things with their functional categories. Thus, by providing an instrument for breaking through mental and linguistic stereotypes that channel our perceptions and lead us to view the world in predetermined, derivative ways, art permits us once again to see the thing qua thing. Art returns us to the world "as it is," to see it as we did when we were still "cognitively innocent," when we were still children new in the world and able to respond to it directly without preconceptions. In a key passage in "The Cherry Stone," Fedya becomes aware of an anthill and suddenly realizes that he has not actually seen one since childhood.

> The last time I had seen an anthill was about twenty years ago. Oh certainly it had happened to me to step on anthills many times in those twenty years, many times indeed. And probably I saw them, but seeing them I didn't think, "I'm walking on anthills." Rather, the word "anthill" merely detached itself and that was all. The living image was at once dislodged by a handy term.
>
> But then I remembered: the anthills had come into view all of a sudden. One . . . Oh, there's another! Then, look! Look, another! And the same thing happened this time. Three anthills appeared, one after the other.
>
> From my height I couldn't see the ants; I could only make out a certain restlessness of form that might just as easily have been taken for something motionless. And my sight was perfectly willing to be deceived: I looked, and I was quite ready to believe it wasn't the ants that were swarming in great numbers over the anthills, but the anthills themselves crumbling like dunes.[10]

From a normal adult perception content merely to identify or name a phenomenon of no special interest or importance, we pass to that of the artist who, like the child, finds that phenomenon exceedingly interesting in itself, and who offers us a simile, "crumbling like dunes," whose effect, beyond the sheer pleasure of the phrase, is to convey his delight in an immediate perception, a reconnection with the primeval materiality of being, and thus vicariously to renew for us some part of the surrounding world.

Leaving aside the questions raised by this aesthetic theory (the validity of the child-artist identification, the adequacy of defining art as a kind of articulate sensuous response and of reducing its means to a special figurative use of language, the absence of criteria other than originality and vividness for judging the power of new semantic configurations, or, for that matter, the theory's evident debt, perhaps via the formalist critic Victor Shklovsky, to the ideas of Henri Bergson), there are two basic and opposing principles governing the form and themes of "The Cherry Stone." First is an emphasis on the objective world of things ("the living image"), and second is the celebration of unbridled fancy, of that realm wherein the objective world is allowed to undergo strange transformations ("my sight was perfectly willing to be deceived"). One might be tempted to argue that these principles lie at the source of Olesha's grasp of the world, that they are the mainspring of his art, had they not been placed in opposition to each other in the context of a highly sophisticated, indeed, a "cognitively corrupted," polemical allegory whose own method subverts at least part of its claim for the authority of innocence. But whatever the case, the story's aesthetic does allow Olesha to concentrate on the material surfaces of the world and to avoid, beyond making a strong theoretical claim for autonomy, the more provocative issues of value and meaning that would have brought him into direct conflict with the prevailing, increasingly monolithic state-decreed moral, social, and aesthetic order.

Following the publication in 1932 of a bitter fragment called "Something from the Secret Notebooks of Fellow Traveler Sand," Olesha's contributions as a serious literary artist were, no doubt as a matter of both private and public policy, considerably diminished. In 1934 he gave a celebrated speech before the First Congress of Soviet Writers in which he eloquently argued in defense of an independent literature and for the principle of artistic autonomy, especially as that principle involved the necessity of the artist to choose his own themes, to deal with material congenial to his own sensibility and originating in own personal experience, even if that experience had prerevolutionary roots, as in his case it most certainly did. Following the 1934 speech, and until 1954 when the political climate at last improved, Olesha worked, but clearly not as he wished. Despite the fact that his early prose was twice reprinted (in 1935 and again in 1936), his themes were no longer deemed appropriate or interesting by the official arbiters of taste and public meaning. Like many others, he found partial recourse in such minor genres as the sketch, the biographical reminiscence, and journalism (including occasional politically loyalist literary criticism). He also wrote short fiction of markedly inferior quality for popular magazines, translated Turkmen and Ukrainian authors, and from 1934 to 1942 wrote or collaborated on some eight screenplays.

After the German invasion of the Soviet Union in 1941, Olesha was evacuated with the Odessa Film Studio to Ashkhabad in Turkmenistan, where, in addition to his duties as a screenwriter, he resumed work as an agitator and propagandist, going on the radio some fifty times in the latter capacity. In 1946 he returned to Moscow, where he and his wife lived in extremely difficult conditions, moving from one friend's apartment to another's, since their own residence had through carelessness or bureaucratic fiat been reassigned during the war. Olesha continued to work, but much less frequently, given not only the precariousness of his own personal situation but also the harsh and largely indiscriminate repression that accompanied the state's abrupt reassertion of control over the arts after the war and that continued ever more brutally until Stalin's death in 1953. Finally, in 1954, Olesha and his wife were given a modest apartment in the writers' building on Lavrushinsky Lane across from the Tretyakov Gallery in central Moscow, and there, at last freed from substantial material worry and able in the considerably relaxed post-Stalinist climate to write more or less as he pleased, he began work on *No Day without a Line.* He devoted himself to that project for the rest of his life, taking time out for such other things as a revision of the Russian translation of Halldór Laxness's play *The Silver Moon* (1955), the preparation for publication of the first collection of his prose to appear in the Soviet Union in twenty years (1956), a screenplay called *A Girl in the Circus,* and stage adaptations of Dostoevsky's *The Idiot* (1958) and Chekhov's "Belated Flowers" (1959). On May 10, 1960, perhaps on the verge of his most interesting work, he died of a heart attack.

No Day without a Line, first published in 1965 and then again in a slightly revised and expanded version in 1974, has been reprinted many times.[11] It was Olesha's last and perhaps his favorite project. Despite his other literary activity, he worked on it constantly, indeed, as the title suggests, almost daily, accumulating over the six- or seven-year period before his death a large quantity of new writing but also of reworked older things, including, in some cases, material from as far back as the 1920s.[12] But because he died without finishing the book, without even indicating a plan by which its various components might be assembled, it is something of an editorial curiosity and presents difficult, or at least complex, critical problems. For *No Day without a Line* is Olesha's only in the sense that he wrote its parts; its design belongs to its editors. And their task ultimately required independent conclusions, since it was impossible to say what he wanted the finished product to look like. The folders in his archive consisted of a disparate collection of unpaged and mostly undated fragments, sometimes thematically linked and sometimes complete in themselves. Since the fragments could not simply be placed in the order of their composition—there was no way of determining that—it was necessary to divine their relationships from internal evidence, arranging them, say, by the chronology of the events mentioned, or according to the different topics discussed, or by some other principle or set of principles, but in any case one inherent in the text and not imposed from without. This task was begun by Olesha's widow, Olga Suok, and by her brother-in-law and Olesha's close friend Victor Shklovsky (and, for a short time, by the younger critic Arkady Belinkov), whose solution was first to sort the fragments into rough thematic categories, such as "controlling images" ("botanical" or "animal," for example), "family," "Richelieu Gymnasium," "the circus," "literary figures," "critical comments," and so on. Since Olesha sometimes repeated himself (evidently seeking more accurate or expressive formulations), it was necessary for the editors to select the best from those fragments dealing with the same subject, and since he sometimes left whole sections unfinished, either in the sense that they were not completely polished (were still in progress) or had simply been abandoned as unpromising, it was necessary to omit material. Fragments were also omitted if they touched on the living or were otherwise sensitive by the relatively liberal but still by no means permissive Soviet editorial standards of the early 1960s. In most cases, however, the fragments were complete and finished, and, as their author had certainly intended, ready for and capable of publication; indeed, a number of them had already been published in the 1950s under Olesha's own supervision in newspapers and magazines and in his *Selected Works*.[13] After Suok and Shklovsky had completed their labors, the textual scholar Mikhail Gromov proceeded with the editing. His method was intuitive: he worked not according to a plan based on close stylistic and contextual analysis of the fragments themselves, but sought rather to arrange them in a fashion that would reflect what he viewed as their inner logic. Although the result is not without its dubious decisions, it is, in the absence of authorial instructions, at least a cogent alternative.[14]

In book form, then, *No Day without a Line* consists of a series of fragmentary texts usually no longer than a few paragraphs. These texts are in large part discrete units, carefully written and artfully composed, in which an image or scene is developed, a precise recollection delineated, or an idea entertained. Occasionally, they form a series of reflections on a common autobiographical, biographical, or critical theme (for example, Olesha's memories of his gymnasium years, his recollections of Mayakovsky, or his discussions of Tolstoy and H. G. Wells). These texts have been combined by the editors in large sections or chapters: "Childhood" and "Odessa," dealing primarily with Olesha's childhood and school years and the period following his graduation from Richelieu Gymnasium; "Moscow," memoirs of his arrival in Moscow in the early 1920s and his apprenticeship as a professional writer at the *Whistle,* including vivid portraits and sketches of several of the principal literary figures of the day, as well as reflections on literature and the arts; "The Golden Shelf," devoted mainly to highly personal yet acute criticism and reminiscence; and finally "The Wonderful Intersection," an evocation of contemporary Moscow and an occasion for observations on life and literature, including musings on the author's mortality and several obituaries of figures close to Olesha in one way or another. These five sections or chapters, despite their more or less chronological arrangement, are basically thematic groupings. Of course, they are sufficiently broad that much in them might easily be rearranged or redistributed without significantly altering the effect.

And Olesha seems to have had definite ideas about what that effect was to be, even if he never indicated how it was to be achieved. In a letter written to his mother in 1954, for example, he remarked, "I am, by the way, now writing a book of memoirs, at least in form, although it goes much deeper than memoirs. Odessa during my childhood figures in it, so that I find myself in the sphere of childhood and of closeness to you . . ."[15] And *No Day without a Line* itself is rife with comments on the nature of the enterprise—its themes, its style, its lack of narrative extension. These features no doubt had their origin in Olesha's decision to write the way he did, to take up something every day about his own life, or about what he was thinking and reading, and finish it on the spot. The book's journal or notebook character was thus not accidental; it too grew by a daily accretion of entries:

> I once happened to give special heed to the ancient dictum that no writer may have a day in which he fails to write at least a line. I resolved to start following that rule and then and there wrote my first "line." The result was a brief and as it seemed to me an altogether finished fragment. The same thing happened the next day, and day by day thereafter I began to write these "lines."

Olesha presumably chose to write in this way because, at the time, it was the only way he could. He required a form that was concise, that would allow him to concentrate on a single idea or theme without having to elaborate or generalize—that would give him the freedom to exercise his talent in the manner best suited to it from moment to moment. Such a form was necessary for several reasons. First, the actual writing of *No Day without a Line* was to have for Olesha a kind of therapeutic value. He had not been writing easily or well for many years, and, if the numerous references in the text to painful stylistic difficulties are to be believed, his skills had atrophied. He needed a form that would permit him in regular daily exercises to reestablish his control of language (and at the same time of the more distant territories of memory), yet that would not burden him with structural problems. Second, it was a form that followed not only from his sense of the current state of his own talent, but also from his views about the nature of modern literature.

> Contemporary things in prose can have value appropriate to the contemporary psyche only if they're written in one sitting. Reflections or recollections of twenty or thirty lines—say at the maximum a hundred lines—that's the contemporary novel.

> The epic seems to me neither necessary nor, as a matter of fact, even possible. Big books are now read in intervals—on the subway, even on its escalators—so why then should a book be large? I can't imagine anyone reading for a long time—all evening, say. First, there are millions of television sets. Next, you've got to read the papers. And so on.

One need not entirely agree with these ideas to recognize that the pace and complexity of modern life might indeed encourage writing that is brief and unelaborated and thus easily grasped by the distracted reader. But more to the point—and this brings us to a third reason for the fragmentary nature of *No Day without a Line*—such writing, polished yet notational, was especially congenial to Olesha's own sensibility. As a discerning American student of his work has made clear, he "had always preferred to write in small forms, to move from careful observation of one object to another without making explicit the relation between them. He had always been aware that his work 'grows by the accumulation of separate fragments, one could almost say of strophes.'"[16] Moreover, such writing was very well suited to someone who had from the outset taken a kind of lyrical interest in physical reality—in its colors, sounds, shapes, textures, and smells. As Olesha declares in *No Day without a Line* in the context of a vivid evocation of light and color in relation to an early childhood experience, "These notes are all attempts to restore life. I want to distraction to restore it sensuously."

But the representation (or restoration) of a past reality, be it sensuous, psychological, social, or historical, must be filtered through and inevitably transformed by memory. And it will be transformed all the more if that reality belongs to the remote past and the rememberer is an artist, that is, someone with a highly developed sense of the interrelation of form and meaning and a greater willingness and capacity that most of us have to engage in the aesthetically motivated selection, coordination, and presentation of recollected experience. As Lydia Ginzburg put the issue, "the writer's own point of view reshapes the material [of memory], and imagination ineluctably strives to fill in the gaps—to retouch, to render more dynamic, to bring to a conclusion."[17] It is perhaps in unspoken reaction to this inevitable fact that Olesha tends in the various renderings of his past, and especially in "Childhood" and "Odessa," to limit himself to impressions of detail, striving thereby to recapture the childhood experience in its own pristine terms and to avoid wherever possible adult interpretation. At the beginning of "Odessa," he remarks, "I too would like to pass back through my life as Marcel Proust managed in his day." What he means, far from comparing himself to Proust, is that he wants the past to be reborn in the integrity of the original moment, to live again in the incarnations of art. He would like, in the terms of the above discussion of "The Cherry Stone," to return to the child's primordial grasp of the world. He would like to recall its essential, uncategorized immediacy, and to represent that recollection in a way that substitutes freshness and intensity for conventional narrative development with its subordination of concrete event to an abstract of system of meaning, whether the author's psychological, social, or historical formation (Olesha is chary of these), or the acquisition of the values and attitudes he may regard as constituting his adult identity (a subject about which he avoids direct reflection).

Yet even though in presenting his childhood and adolescent years Olesha does indeed limit himself to a very great degree to impressions of detail (often exhibiting an astonishing attention to the quality of each moment), it is only a tendency; he obviously cannot avoid adult retrospection entirely, nor would we want him to do so. One therefore finds in the passages devoted to his early years an alternation of point of view in which the childhood or adolescent perception is subjected to adult commentary. Sometimes this is simply unavoidable for what might be called rhetorical reasons: the narrative may require background information necessary to the reader's comprehension. But sometimes it has a larger purpose, as Olesha frankly uses the episode in question to elicit an autobiographical theme, to indicate, in other words, a possible relation between past and present. Thus we find in these passages shifts of focus in which the field is suddenly enlarged. For example, in an unusually long fragment describing the bombardment of Odessa by the battleship *Potyomkin*, or, rather, in one describing Olesha's reaction to that event, he observes, "I was six years old. I want to give myself an account of what I felt and understood at the time." He then proceeds to record the impressions of a very small child whose parents' sympathies were with the czar. "In attempting to grasp what was threatening me, I came to the conclusion that evil people like bandits undoubtedly wanted to rob and kill everybody, and that very likely the worst things would be done to children, whom those bandits especially hated." But toward the end of the fragment he says, "Just think, at the moment I was experiencing bewilderment and fear, somewhere on a deck flooded with sunlight naval gunners with little mustaches were peering through artillery sights and disputing with each other amid the streaming ribbons of their caps." The rather conventional child's view is replaced by a no less conventional adult version in which the sympathy has shifted: the attention is no longer on the dangerous activity of the sailors, but on their color and drama. They are, to be sure, still perceived in subjective terms, but much less frighteningly so. The childish figure of the "bandit" is superseded by another of almost cinematic variety (perhaps derived from Eisenstein's famous 1925 film) in which the sailors are depicted as brave and dashing figures whose activity had in fact been quite "innocent": the battleship had not wished "to hit the city—it had aimed at the Municipal Theater where a military council presided over by General Kaulbars was in session—but it missed, and both shots fell on Odessa." What began as an event filled with "bewilderment and fear" has by the end of the passage acquired a kind of cozy historical glamour. That event—the *Potyomkin* mutiny and the 1905 revolution of which it was a part—has only secondary importance, however. The real subject is Olesha's imaginative response, its different degrees of objective derivation and subjective modulation, its particular location at the intersections of form and meaning and of past and present that lie at the foundation of all autobiography and memoir.

In another fragment describing Olesha's first impressions of Richelieu Gymnasium, where he had been taken by his grandmother to be enrolled in the beginning class, the following occurs.

> My grandmother had brought not a professional writer but a little boy like the others. And the little boy didn't see all that the writer remembers now. Perhaps none of it happened. No, of course it happened. Certainly, it was autumn and the leaves were falling . . . Certainly, they did creak as they sailed past, rubbing their sides together like ships. And like ships they described circles—two or three rings of a spiral—as they floated by me to settle gently on the asphalt, on the edge where a large number of them already lay, an entire perished fleet. Occasionally, a gust would turn some of them in a different direction . . . No, the boy did see it, and the writer, drawing on other recollections, now merely remembers what the boy brought by his grandmother actually saw.
>
> That means she did in fact bring a writer, a poet, albeit a very small one. And where's the border really? At what point did the boy begin to see? At what point was he merely a boy and then suddenly a poet? For on that morning he unquestionably did look and he did see.

Olesha is openly concerned here with the genesis of artistic identity, and, as in all autobiographical writing where "the Child is father of the Man," the link between childhood and adult perception is crucial. But that relationship can never, in Olesha's view, be completely clear, for it is a cumulative one without precise demarcations. Indeed, it may be that "child" and "man" is a false distinction. Rather, a life should perhaps be regarded not as first one and then the other, but as a continuum in which adult consciousness is potential in the child's view of the world, and the child's view is latent in adult perception. "Child" and "man" (or "imagination" and "rationality," if you will) are then coexistent terms of alternating dominance. Their relationship reaches explicit equilibrium in the artist, for it is the artist, as we shall once again recall from our discussion of "The Cherry Stone," in whom the child's perception is not allowed to fade as it does in most of us, but in whom it is maintained in all its vitality, becoming a source of his art. And therefore *No Day without a Line,* however much it is concerned with the depiction of separate moments, and however effective it is in conveying the mood and texture of episodes that at first glance seem to lack larger significance, is nevertheless much more than a miscellany of études, sketches, or brief reminiscences and recollections. Its purpose is the representation of a life, not in its cumulative development, but in its remembered totality: "Let not the reader think that this book, however much it may appear to be made up of separate pieces on disparate themes, is only drawn out lengthwise. No, it is rounded. If you like, it even has a subject, a very interesting one. Someone has lived and survived till old age." That subject, the life of a man and an artist, is conveyed in *No Day without a Line* by the accumulation of bits and pieces that in themselves have, like the tesserae of a mosaic or the shards of a stained-glass window, only the apparent significance of color and shape, but whose effect when combined is a whole that far exceeds their mere sum. And, paradoxically, the precise combination of these pieces may be unimportant, for however they are combined, the resulting figure will possess the same meaning, the same unique underlying identity. The accumulation of the book's fragments, although seemingly random and without clear motivation, was nevertheless governed by a deep purpose, and that was the reestablishment of the author's link with his past and therefore with himself. Each fragment, whether autobiographical, biographical, or critical, returns a part of that past to the active present. It is reborn in the artful manipulations of language, and so in the process is he.

The present edition of *No Day without a Line* differs from the 1979 Ardis edition that preceded it in three ways.[18] First, it is a collation of both the 1965 and 1974 Russian versions of Olesha's text, although I have taken the liberty of omitting some passages that seemed obviously defective and of rearranging others (notably those pertaining to Dante and Dostoevsky) in what the internal textual evidence clearly suggests is their proper placement and order.[19] Second, the translation is a new one, and I hope more sensitive to the distinctive qualities of Olesha's style and more accurate in rendering the richness of his text—its nuances and levels. Third, the notes, based on my own research in America and Russia, are much more extensive and detailed than in the Ardis version, or, as far as that goes, in any other edition of the text. The notes are intended to serve a variety of readers, from nonspecialist to specialist, and will thus for some perhaps contain too much information altogether, while for others perhaps too much that will seem superfluous or merely obvious. My own sense, however, is that the notes are essential to the translation, for they not only help to clarify the implication of Olesha's original in sometimes surprising ways but also to shed new light on many of the biographical, historical, and intellectual contexts of his extremely interesting career.

Punctuation in the translation naturally follows American conventions, although Olesha's use of *points de suspension* to indicate an incomplete or undeveloped thought has been retained. This device should never be taken to mean that text has been omitted.

I have used two systems of transliteration. All personal and place names, whenever they have not simply been translated, are given in the popular system (J. Thomas Shaw's System I), with the customary exception of those that may already be familiar to the reader in another form or that have common English equivalents: thus, "Tchaikovsky" and not "Chaykovsky," "Alekhine" and not "Alekhin," "Alexander" and not "Aleksandr," and so forth. I have likewise opted for a simplified version of Russian street names, avoiding the unnecessary, in English, feminine ending: thus, "Deribasovsky" and not "Deribasovskaya," and so on. On the other hand, all bibliographical references in the commentary and in the introduction have, for the convenience of the reader who may wish to consult the original Russian sources, been given in a simplified Library of Congress notation (Shaw's System II). It is hoped that this somewhat awkward procedure will satisfy the needs both of those who have some Russian and of those who do not and who might be distracted by extraneous phonetic information in the text itself.

I have sought in the translation itself to produce English marked by the same discipline, clarity, and freshness I find in Olesha's supple, expressive Russian, and to be as accurate as possible in conveying his various meanings. But it has been my guiding principle that the sine qua non of good literary translation is a constant awareness of the need to maintain a balance between respect for the otherness of the original and naturalness in English. Taken absolutely, these two values—fealty to the original language and allegiance to one's own tongue—are irreconcilable. Understood contingently, making the constant adjustments of diction, tone, syntax, and style required by the text at each of its innumerable points, they may reach a kind of reciprocity in which each version seems to inform the other and the translation stands, in some paradoxical way, on its own yet is still an authentic and convincing representation and interpretation of the truly autonomous original. When such kinship occurs, it may of course be as much a matter of luck as of will, labor, and trust—trust in the unique qualities of the original and in the capacities of one's own language, of the instrument at one's disposal. As regards Olesha's remarkable original and the resources of contemporary English, I think we are very fortunate, indeed, and I hope his new readers will agree.

No Day without a Line

Childhood

BEFORE OFFERING this book to the reader's attention, I want to tell the story of its origin. This is necessary because the book is an unusual one—mere fragments—and could prove not only incomprehensible but even irritating.

The book came into being as a result of the author's conviction that he had to write . . . Even if he didn't know how to write as others do.

I once happened to give special heed to the ancient dictum that no writer may have a day in which he fails to write at least a line.[1] I resolved to start following that rule and then and there wrote my first "line." The result was a brief and as it seemed to me an altogether finished fragment. The same thing happened the next day, and day by day thereafter I began to write these "lines."

I believe the one work I could write that would be meaningful to people and needed by them is a book about my own life.

Last year the rumor spread that I had written an autobiographical novel.

As I was passing through the restaurant of the Writers' Club, Tarakhovskaya, the author of children's verses and, of course, adult epigrams, suddenly raised her face to me and asked,

"Is it true you've written an autobiographical novel?"

I said it wasn't, and she was distressed. You could see in her face that she was distressed.

"Oh dear, but they say it's such a wonderful autobiographical novel!"

And it began to seem a pity even to me that I hadn't written that novel. I parted with her very tenderly and gratefully.[2]

I recall only the one instance. But I heard about my novel on all sides.

Obviously, if they credit the rumor and help spread it themselves, then they want me to write such a novel. And maybe I should, if that's what my contemporaries want. They've merely indicated the form—an autobiographical novel . . . That shows, by the way, a grasp of the nature of my writings.

Shall I try it?

Well, here's the beginning.

I was walking to school along the city's main street, which was called Deribasovsky, walking past the shops and their windows—all, by the way, very dressed up and rich-looking—past the sycamores, the green benches, and the clock in front of Barzhansky's shop, a clock so large in diameter and hung so low that in truth you could walk past it.

The clock repair shop of Iosif Barzhansky.

The clock above the street.

Its hands seemed to me as large as oars . . . No, that's all . . .

I shall now express a thought that may, at the very least, seem foolish, but I request understanding.

Contemporary things in prose can have value appropriate to the contemporary psyche only if they're written in one sitting. Reflections or recollections of twenty or thirty lines—say, at the maximum a hundred lines—that's the contemporary novel.

The epic seems to me neither necessary nor, as a matter of fact, even possible.

Big books are now read in intervals—on the subway, even on its escalators—so why then should a book be large? I can't imagine anyone reading for a long time—all evening, say. First, there are millions of television sets. Next, you've got to read the papers. And so on.

Let me write fragments without finishing them—at least I'm writing! Even so, this is literature of a kind, in a sense perhaps the only kind. Perhaps it's impossible for a psychological type like myself in a historical period like the present to write otherwise. Yet if he writes and to some extent knows how to write, then let him write, even this way.

It may appear to some that in these fragments I'm pursuing some kind of individualistic nonsense, that somehow I want to place the emphasis on myself, on my own relation to the world. That isn't so. I want us to write well. And it's my hope that one way or another I can be of help in that regard. This book is by no means an attack on anyone at all.

The chief characteristic of my soul is impatience. I recall being hobbled my whole life by anxiety that there was something that needed to be done before I could rest easy. That anxiety assumed various forms: I supposed the "something" to be a novel waiting my attention, or a good apartment that had to be obtained, or the reissuance of identity papers, or a reconciliation with somebody or other, when in reality the important thing that needed to be taken care of before I could rest easy was life itself. This may be reduced to the paradox that the most difficult thing in life is life itself: wait, I'll die, and then at last I shall live.

Nevertheless, I was always an optimist and very fond of life. Even now I recall the pleasure I felt inhaling the scent of freshly painted green stable signs on which I had traced in whitewash with my own hand the names of the horses over whose stalls the signs were to be placed. The oil paint infused my body with a sense of well-being. Probably what smelled was the turpentine. But the horses? Did I see them? I don't remember. I didn't even notice the horses. I saw only the meadow-colored signs and the white letters raised almost like little sausages above the flatness of the planks. I completed the task like a devotee, like a boy who has been allowed to do something intensely wished for . . .

Nothing written should perish. But I wrote in pencil on the oilcloth next to an inkstand and in somebody else's house at that, I wrote on little sheets of paper I immediately crumpled up, I wrote on cigarette boxes and on the wall. I didn't just scribble but wrote with considerable polish, working on my style. It would be good to recall what I wrote.

I remember a passage about Edgar Poe—how he was picked up in a park and carried off with the edge of his cloak dragging on the ground. I remember apropos of the letters of Van Gogh how modest he was, how in his modesty he tried to convince his brother that after all he too could take up painting—it's easy! I remember something about how it was my cherished dream to be able to do somersaults. And there are many other fragments. Somewhere in my papers is Herschel, climbing up to his observatory with a guest,[3] and then my schoolboy astonishment at learning that Latin is none other than the language of the ancient Romans. Still earlier is a passage about the death of my classmate Volodya Dolgov from scarlet fever and our going to the funeral—how it seemed as we walked down a lane that the church was coming toward us. And there's something about a window open in winter through which a flapping curtain blows in a way somehow reminiscent of sobbing—an image of death. And there are many more passages, pictures, sketches, thoughts, and figures.

One should preserve everything. That's what a book is for.

Sometimes the thought occurs to me that the fear of death may be nothing more than a recollection of the terror of birth. And indeed there was a moment when, rending my mouth in a cry, I became detached from some kind of integument, and slipping into surroundings unfamiliar to me fell into the palm of somebody's hand . . . How could that not have been terrifying?

If I really am to begin writing a book about my life, then the first chapter ought to be devoted to the amazing circumstance that I wasn't always the same but changed in size. And it wouldn't hurt to recall that at one time I didn't even exist.

Sometimes I think of a certain day when a certain young woman made her way to an encounter with a certain young man. I know neither the season when that day occurred nor the place . . . I see neither the young woman nor the young man. Nevertheless, because they met on that day which swirls like smoke in my fancy, I happened to emerge into the world.

What if that encounter had never taken place? Would I still have had to make my appearance from a different set of parents? And would I have been I?

Naturally, I don't remember being born, that is, the moment of birth. It would in fact be silly even to take up this question, were it not for our abiding astonishment that we can't remember that moment and our desire to do so, to draw nearer in our memories, if only a little.

What really is our first memory? Probably what we take as the first is far from being so. Perhaps our first memories have remained in the form of those nightmares that sometimes visit us in the middle of a deep sleep when we awake in a panic and can't remember anything of what was happening, even though our hearts are beating so fast and with such a pounding that it's obvious something awful was taking place the very second we managed to wake up. It can't be that those first impressions of the world weren't frightening: our first moments of independent breathing, our first sensation of our own weight, our first visual, aural, and tactile sensations . . . My brain was already working, and clearly my organs of memory were too, so it's impossible that nothing of those first moments has remained. Certainly, something has remained but in very tenuous form, in the form of fragments, shapeless fragments that exist not as pictures, but as a kind of . . . I can't even define it . . . as a kind of continuous howl in the depths of consciousness.

The astonishing act of memory. We recall things for reasons utterly unknown to us. Tell yourself, "Now I'll remember something from childhood." Close your eyes and say this. Something completely unexpected will be recalled. The participation of the will is excluded here. A picture lights up, switched on by something like engineers in the back of your mind. Damn it, there isn't any will in me! Rather, it's beside me! How little, therefore, does it influence the whole me! How little do I, who am conscious and possessed of desires and a name, occupy a place in the whole me that has neither desires nor name! I'm almost next to myself. I speak, yet my whole self belongs in that moment to nature, and nature is unaware that as I speak I'm sitting on a couch in my study. I'm an electrical something in the current of matter, in the current of electricity running through the entire universe.

One of the desires most firmly fixed in us is that of recalling our first impression of the world in which we've begun to live.

I make a constant effort to remember it . . . Sometimes it seems to me that I've succeeded, that there it is, my first impression. I'm soon convinced, however, that the impression I've seized upon is hardly the first one I saw clearly. All its signs tell me it made its appearance to an already more or less discriminating consciousness of the external world. But the first impression? Just what was the first? Will I ever recall it? Is it possible to recall it?

Science says that in infancy we see the world tipped over on its side. If that's true, then it means I too saw the world that way. I don't recall that picture of a tipped-over world, so it follows that my first impression of the world has vanished forever. I must therefore be content with the later ones, regarding them as if they were the first.

I'm eating watermelon under a table and wearing a girl's dress. The red slices of watermelon . . . That's what stands before me as my earliest memory. Before that all is darkness, darkness unrelieved.

The first thing I remember clearly is being carried from a bath. I was held by a woman whose old curls hung down limply . . . Who was she? An aunt? How can I remember what kind of curls she had? How can I know they were old? Or even more, that they were limp? That's something I invent now, on the spur of the moment. But why do I invent just that and not something else? Why do those pictures come into being at the same time? There's a reason for it. Obviously, with some part of my conscious mind I caught hold of those images that now seem invented.

I was born in 1899 in the town of Elizavetgrad, now called Kirovograd. There's nothing I can say about that town that might lend it substantial character. I lived there for only a few years of early childhood, after which I found myself residing in Odessa where my parents had moved. Much later, when already a youth, I visited Elizavetgrad, but even then I saw only its southern provincial streets and their sunflowers. A cock crowed, the sunflowers gleamed white and yellow—that's the whole of my impression of the town where I was born.

Of my father, I know that before I was born he had been a landowner. His property was of respectable size, wooded, and called "Youth." He and his brother had sold it for a substantial sum, which over the next several years the two of them lost at cards. Echoes of that tragedy filled my childhood. I remember a family quarrel accompanied by the threat of gunshots, a quarrel resulting, as I recall, from the loss of the balance of the money . . . In Elizavetgrad, however, we were still well off. We rode behind our own trotter and lived in a large azure apartment. My father, whom in those years I naturally called "Papa," drank and played cards at the club. "Club" was one of the chief words of my childhood:

"Papa's at the club."

The consensus was that my father should have avoided alcohol; it had a bad effect on him. And truly I do remember an episode when he put me on a windowsill and aimed a revolver at me. He was drunk, and Mama fell down on her knees, pleading with him to "stop that.". . .

That revolver figures more than once in my recollections. Not because my father was distinguished by any particular tendency to murder—nothing of the sort. It was just that in those days such weapons were for the first time readily available to ordinary people, that is, to people not directly connected with the military. The revolver became a kind of elegant trifle, a toy sold in shops. To a certain extent, it's always in a man's nature to take offense, and when a thing like a revolver is nearby, why not reach for it, especially if all you have to do is open the night table?

So there I stood on the windowsill, my father aiming at me. It was a joke, of course, but one thing was clear. My father shouldn't have drunk. That fact was known to his associates at the club and to his other acquaintances and to his mother-in-law, his aunts, and the rest of his family. When sober, Papa was considered the sweetest, the most charming, the most delightful of people, but let him drink and he turned into a beast.

I can say I remember my father as very young. Probably he wasn't yet thirty when I realized he was my father. I don't recall what he looked like. I remember a fragment from what my parents called his "name day." I was in a doorway, and Papa was coming out of the room I wanted to enter. The table within was heaped with multicolored sweets—chocolates in unusually fancy paper wrappers. Papa returned, took something from the table, and handed it to me. Standing before me, as I now recall, was a young man youthfully bending his shoulder, his soft hair clipped short . . .

I remember my mother just as vaguely. She drew well and was called "Raphael." It's true I never saw any of her pictures, so as far as her drawing or being called "Raphael" is concerned, that may be a different memory, somehow cast up to me from another's life.

Although there's no real picture of it in my memory, it's nevertheless beyond dispute that my mother was beautiful. Talk of it swirled about my childish head, and before me now is a photograph of her from those years. She's wearing a beret, a woman with brilliant gray eyes, a young woman who has been offended by something, who has been crying, but who is now quite cheered up.

Her name is Olga.

When I was a child everybody said I looked like my father. But when I came to see that the mirror reflected no one else but me—when I learned, if one may put it this way, to look into the mirror—I saw that on the contrary it was my mother I resembled and not my father. I mentioned this discovery and they laughed at me. The opinion that I resembled my father had become so firmly established that, I repeat, they laughed at me. Yet however many times I looked in the mirror, each time told me that I was right: out of my face gazed the face of my mother. Out of my face soiled with the unclean thoughts of boyhood, the beautiful face of my mother. I don't know why I was the only one in those years who saw that resemblance, but I really was the only one. Little by little, however, the others began to exclaim,

"Why, he looks like his mother!"

And others recognized that, besides the resemblance to my father, a resemblance to my mother had begun to emerge. That was several years later, when I started to change from a boy into a youth . . . The more secretive, the closer to first love grew the life of my soul, the more conspicuously the resemblance to my mother shone through. The more convinced I was that I stood on the bewitching threshold of another existence, one linked to a woman, the longer my mother's nose, lips, and eyes lingered on my face.

And thereafter, once having entered life, I couldn't imagine myself as other than resembling my mother.

By the Old Style I was born on February 19, the same day the emancipation of the serfs was celebrated in czarist Russia.[4] I saw something festive in that coincidence. It was, in any case, nice to think that on your birthday banners were hung and illuminations put up.

I received presents from morning on. I remember the bluish smoke of cap pistols, I remember decals of a very special quality, and I remember a gold five-ruble piece—just imagine!—given to me by my grandmother. For a long time it was kept in a little leather purse. That mighty golden circle amid the rather dirty folds of the leather called forth terribly complicated and obscure feelings. Embossed on it was a little image of the czar with a clean, shiny forehead. At that time five rubles was a very large amount. It could have been the basis for the most splendid of dreams, like buying a bicycle or going abroad . . . I don't remember the fate of that coin. I think it may have been borrowed by the adults and never returned.

What were illuminations? They were lanterns made of crude glass, one strip red, another green, a third yellow. Actually they weren't strips but facets, and I think the lanterns had six of them. Inside, stuck in a socket with jagged edges, a candle burned. The light was very murky, passing as it did through glass that had been stained in sheds. Nonetheless, when the lanterns were hung by the dozens on wires stretched among the trees it meant something, at least to the soul of a child.

Nothing compares with the grief I experienced as a four-year-old in connection with the departure home of a cousin who had been visiting us. His name was Volodya, and he was the student of an institute that had granted him the right to wear on his shoulders little curved rectangular boards of metal and velvet with large bright gold letters and numbers. He was blond, rather plump, and had a cauldron-shaped, though handsome head. But these are later impressions. At the time I perceived only the splendor of a certain kind of existence, a splendor I obviously couldn't analyze, but one in which I took both physical and spiritual pleasure, rejoicing with every particle of my being as in a gift from the gods, as in an immense share at my disposal of something enchanting, something of which there is much in paradise, but that only comes to us in the form of a single, fleeting smile or of anything that suddenly flies into our memories from life.

The barber shop on Uspensky Street. It was somehow off the beaten track. You even reached the doorway over cobblestones through which grass was growing.

Grass grew between the cobblestones and the cobblestones were blue. How long has it been since I've seen a cobblestone, since I've held one in my hands? They were always warm, and they always covered your hands with dust, which you removed by slapping your palms together.

My father said to the barber, with whom he had some mysterious though friendly bond,

"Give my heir a haircut."

I was, most likely, a very small boy and still being taken for haircuts. After that phrase, I crossed the rug to the chair and the mirror, next to which the barber waited all in white, like a wafer.

"Give my heir a haircut."

It was distressing for me to hear that. And somehow shameful. And for some reason I remember that distress to this day. What sort of heir was I? An heir to what? I knew Papa was poor. Then what was I heir to? My father alone, a repetition of him?

It was just a word used in a given situation and not Papa's own. It was customary then to speak of one's son as an heir. But an heir to what? I was alone then, alone in the world, and I'm alone now.

He cut my hair, that wafer-barber, and to this day I remember how cold my head felt after the haircut, how wide my collar became, and how the barber's two fat fingers, like a pair of tubes, reached down inside my collar in order to pull out, as it must have seemed to them, the rest of my hair.

She came from Siberia and her name was Galka. Obviously, she was still very young. I remember something in dark tones, a single strand of dark hair.

It was winter in Odessa and above all an exceptionally cold one. I remember windows with snow on the other side of them. My gymnasium student sister wasn't permitted to go to school that morning.[5] We sat in the dining room, dark despite the snow beyond the windows (which looked out onto a wall), and busied ourselves with some sort of children's handicraft. I think we were making a theater. I had a piece of wallpaper that made my palms and fingers taste bitter and columns of colored pencils. On the wallpaper I drew fir trees covered in snow, snowdrifts, a road . . .

My Siberian aunt good-naturedly took part in those handicrafts with my gymnasium student sister.

I don't recall that we ever had a Christmas tree. Our delight in Christmas trees was always connected with the one at some friend's home rather than with our own. There in someone else's house were dancing, children, candies, and cakes. Actually, I think I may be swiping this from poems and stories I've read . . . In any case, we received gifts at home too—books, large expensive ones.

Of course, the fragrance of the needles is forever, as are the soft needles themselves. They were allowed to litter the parquet and accumulate in ever increasing numbers in the corner under the tree. They flowed into other rooms, mingling with the glass ornaments that had, like giant tears, also fallen to the floor. It all ended with the tree's being carried from the house, heaved over the shoulder like a carcass.

After Kataev and Pasternak, there's not much you can add to descriptions of Christmas trees and Christmas.[6]

Mr. Orlov and his daughter were invited to a Christmas party, and there, as the children were dancing, the tree toppled over, as a result of which Orlov's daughter was burned to death. The day she was buried, he went to the circus. We children were horrified when we heard that, but the adults justified Orlov. They said he grieved deeply and that was why he had gone to the circus. One of my strongest impressions is of Orlov at the circus after his daughter's funeral. And it seems to me now that I can still see his slightly bowlegged figure in the first row above the yellow arena, a mustache under his nose and over it the little circles of his pince-nez.

This probably was first love. There was a little girl I wanted to imitate. She somehow bent her body first one way, then the other, adjusting, one assumes, some part of her clothing. I made the same movement, although by myself and without necessity.

I was, I think, five years old. The girl was very likely older, but not by much. I don't recall her first name. I do her last one: Arkharova.

I remember twilight on a street in front of the fence of a little garden near where Gymnasium No. 3 used to stand, an area that to me was wonderful—not quite out of town yet already close to the sea, an area where there were villas with roses and parrot cages on their balconies.

It was twilight, but we children were still outside. Our parents were probably nearby, but we didn't associate with them. We kept to ourselves as children do. And Arkharova was with us. What was she like? No, I shall never draw her face out of that twilight. But I didn't need to see her face then. My feeling was based on other premises. What I required, for example, was to bend just like her, first to the right, then to the left, in order to straighten my clothing . . .

I remember a balustrade sunk in the grass . . . Perhaps it was the railing of a terrace? It was said that an old lady with many cats lived there. I saw neither the old lady nor her cats. We didn't go near her house. It grew particularly ominous in the twilight when the possibility the old lady and her cats might suddenly appear was most terrifying. One of the windows at the bend of the plinth gleamed dully above the garden as after a rain . . .

In the end it's not important what I've achieved in life; what's important is that I've lived every moment of it.

Once when I was a small boy and had just gone to bed, I suddenly heard very close to me a sound, muffled yet quite distinct, that was exactly repeated over and over. I began to pull at the blanket and the sheet, convinced that from their folds a beetle or some little toy or machine would fall. I looked under the pillow, but there wasn't anything there . . . I lay down, and the sound returned. And then suddenly it disappeared, and then it came back again.

"Grandma," I asked my grandmother with whom I shared a room, "did you hear that?"

No, she hadn't heard anything. And then suddenly, as if from outside of me, came the realization that what I had heard was the beating of my own heart. That realization neither surprised nor frightened me. The recognition that it was quite proper for a heart to be beating inside me came quietly and gently as if I had known it for a long time, although I was in fact just encountering it for the first time.

Once my father brought home a monkey he had either purchased or obtained as a gift.

We were little and went to bed early, and my father had most likely brought that gift or purchase from the club, so that as far as we were concerned the monkey was something that had arrived together with the sun and the morning. It seems to me now that the monkey was dressed in some kind of garment—blue trousers?—but more likely he was wearing only his fur, a tiny golden beast. There was some joke connected with him: either

Papa had become his master while drunk, or the monkey had come into his possession through a bet. In a word, as a result of something he himself didn't understand, the little beast was humiliated, mocked, and insulted.

We never saw him in anybody's arms. It was beyond comprehension how Papa had ever managed to get him home. The monkey was always at a distance, one insurmountable to us, not being gymnasts, and one that increased by the corners of open windows, then immediately by whole clumps of trees, then all at once by an entire street . . . He moved away from us in immense arclike leaps, and just when it seemed that the building custodian was about to capture him in the vicinity of the chimney, suddenly from a neighboring street a delighted cry would be heard,

"A monkey! Look, a monkey!"

No one can recall that picture from my childhood with me anymore. No one at that time older than I can tell me how the story of the monkey ended. For me, the so-called bird's-eye view of roofs and chimneys evokes in my memory a different little picture. Or not a little picture but an enormous one framed by the sky itself in which high, high up where it is very hard to look, almost as hard as looking at the sun, there looms the golden point of a balloon.

As a child I never once succeeded in flying a kite. True, I didn't ask anyone for help. I knew that you needed a certain connection of string to the kite's snout, so to speak, a connection called a tether, but exactly how that connection was supposed to be made, I had no idea. Meanwhile, on the condition of that unfortunate tether depended whether the kite would take off or merely bump along the ground, horned in that moment like some billy goat.

And my nonflying kites did resemble billy goats. They had tiny horns—the tips of the struts protruding through the torn surface of the paper. The kite's tail seemed like the beard of a particularly ornery and stupid goat.

Those sufferings of mine took place on Mikhailovsky Field.

It's possible I'm about to describe my very first visit to the theater.

We, that is, my sister and I, were invited to the theater by the wealthy Orlovs to see *The Children of Captain Grant*.[7] The play was being performed with resounding success at the Odessa Municipal Theater. I don't remember everything in sequence, only the moment when sitting in something called a "box" I glanced around and saw a golden wall illuminated from below, a wall that suddenly began to seem to me to be not a wall at all, but a sunny summer garden through which figures dressed in what looked like exotic Turkish clothing were walking. That was the curtain. It's still not the theater. It's only the curtain.

Today, July 30, 1955, I begin to write the history of my time. When did it begin, my time? If I was born in 1899, then the Boer War had already begun, the Art Theater had been founded in Russia, Chekhov was at the height of his fame, and the newly crowned Nicholas II was sitting on the throne . . .[8] What about technology? Obviously, they still didn't know of the torpedo with which you could blow up a battleship by surprise without coming near it. The torpedo became famous later on, during the Russo-Japanese war.[9] So did the machine gun, used for the first time by the Japanese and called a *mitrailleuse* . . .

And so my time began around the same time the torpedo and machine gun made their appearance. The destruction of battleships at sea, their black silhouettes listing and sending searchlight beams into the dark expanse of night, that's what's pasted in the corner of almost the first page of my life. "Tsushima," "Chemulpo," those are the words I heard as a child.[10]

The torpedo seemed a terrible invention, a diabolical thing, the ultimate the brain dedicated to evil could imagine.

"The Whitehead torpedo."[11]

Someone had spoken that phrase in my hearing or perhaps a book told it to me . . . The torpedo glided beneath the surface, striking inexorably, implacably, and in the middle of the dark blue night a battleship rolled over on its side, sending up beams of white light in supplication.

That's the beginning of the history of my time. For me, it bore the names "Mukden" and "Lyaoyan," or was called "Won't Papa have to go to war?"[12]

When I was little, the world still paid a great deal of attention to fireworks. Hardly a holiday passed by without complete apotheosis by rocket, Roman candle, cascade, and firecracker . . . Polished spectacles employing that varicolored exploding, shooting, and blazingly spinning material were arranged in honor of current or historic events. I remember a great fireworks display on the occasion of the loss of the Russian heavy cruiser *Varangian* in the war with Japan.

Arriving at the fireworks site the next day on a gray morning, you could still see its skeleton: sticks, wire, and twine. And in that skeleton you could recognize the outline of the ship that had the night before amidst shooting blue and green rockets spun round in a crimson fire of the so-called pinwheel variety and then burned up in the sight of all.

You could also find empty rocket cylinders, dark blue tubes with a burnt smell that you very much wanted to bring back to life. But they were dead, just empty cardboard tubes that made a tapping noise and rolled when you kicked them with the tip of your shoe . . .

Somewhere in basements hid the pyrotechnists—Germans, probably, who knew how to do that sort of thing. I never saw a pyrotechnist, the last fabulous figure before the advent of the aviator.

On an overcast summer day, and all the more summery for that, since the foliage was especially vivid against the gray background, I stood with my grandmother in the park above the panorama of the port and the sea stretching out to the horizon and watched something new and interesting for us taking place in the port itself. My attention was fixed chiefly on a horse, a black horse led by its bridle. Certainly the word "coffin" figured in our remarks to each other, since we were watching a funeral procession, although I don't remember a coffin. Probably there was a catafalque too and even a caisson, since the funeral was a military one, but I looked only at the horse. I didn't realize then that it was the custom to lead a soldier's battle mount behind his coffin, and seeing it for the first time, I was utterly absorbed by the spectacle. At that distance I could make out neither the horse's eyes nor its lips nor even its mane, like hair in relief. I saw only the horse's moving silhouette, or not even its silhouette, but rather a quilted image of one, a quilted image in muffled black.

"General Kondratenko," my grandmother repeated over and over.

They were burying General Kondratenko whose remains had been brought from Manchuria where he had fallen in the war with Japan.[13]

The funeral cortege soon disappeared from view. Out of sight, it proceeded from the port to the city and then along the street that afterward was renamed "Kondratenko." Grandmother and I remained in the park amidst the gray, I would say full, round air cleaved by the sharp leaves of one kind of tree, yet receiving on the contrary even greater roundness and fullness from the catkins of another kind that were falling everywhere upon it—tiny, tiny catkins gathered in pendants and cream-colored corollae with a triangular presence of green.

"General Kondratenko," my grandmother repeated over and over.

The palace of the commander-in-chief was on Nikolaevsky Boulevard, on the corner of the boulevard and the arc at its entrance, that wonderful arc of magnificent buildings in Russian empire style.[14]

The palace was one of those buildings, the one at the very end of the arc—or was it the beginning? No, the arc had neither beginning nor end.

At the palace's entrance paced a sentry who sometimes entered a striped sentry box. That's the sort of antiquity I'm familiar with—striped sentry boxes!

I was walking with one of the adults. Maintaining my distance, I glanced over at him. Was he looking at the sentry? And at the box? Of course he was.

"The palace of the commander-in-chief," the adult said.

Like children, adults too are impressed with things like sentries and commanders-in-chief.

I was the son of an excise official and our family was petit bourgeois, so I perceived the mutiny on the battleship *Potyomkin* as an act monstrous in its horror.[15] When the *Potyomkin* came to Odessa and dropped anchor, everyone in our family was seized with fear, including me.

"It will raze Odessa!" Papa said.

To our family, the *Potyomkin* was in rebellion against the czar, and although we were Poles, we were for the czar, who we thought would one day grant Poland its autonomy. The figurative expression "leaving no stone in place" was also being used, which especially affected me, since it was easy to imagine one stone removed from another and falling down next to it.

I don't remember the battleship's arrival off the shore of Odessa or its dropping anchor. I saw it from the boulevard. It lay in the distance, white, elegant, with several tall smokestacks like all military vessels of the day. The sea was deep blue and the battleship was milky white, and in the distance it looked quite small, as if it hadn't sailed there but had been set down on the deep blue surface. It was summer, and I watched from Nikolaevsky Boulevard near where Pushkin's monument stands and where in that season the red flowers of the African canna bloomed in beds that hissed beneath the streams of their sprinklers.

I was six years old. I want to give myself an account of what I felt and understood at the time. Naturally I had no idea why a mutiny had taken place on the battleship, although I did know it was against the czar. As I've said, what I felt was fear.

The events taking place in the city were termed "disorders." The word "revolution" wasn't used.

In trying to grasp what was threatening me, I came to the conclusion that evil people like bandits undoubtedly wanted to rob and kill everybody, and that very likely the worst things would be done to children, whom those bandits especially hated.

It's amazing, but I actually heard shots fired by the *Potyomkin*! There were two from powerful nine-inch guns. One shell fell on the corner of a building on Nizhinsky Street. I don't remember where the other one landed. Afterward I saw a picture of the damaged building in *The Grainfield.*[16]

Both shells hurtled over my head, two rumbling noises that made me duck. Until then I'd never heard gunfire. It seemed that above me something very long was flying that had begun very far away and that had no intention of ever coming to an end. Just think, at the moment I was experiencing bewilderment and fear, somewhere on a deck flooded with sunlight naval gunners with little mustaches were peering through artillery sights and disputing with each other amid the streaming ribbons of their caps . . .

At home were fear and conversation almost in a whisper. Then came the spectacle of transporting the body of the dead Vakulenchuk to the waterfront, to Platonovsky Pier, I think.[17] I heard the name Vakulenchuk then; it isn't something I remember from later on. It was spoken in our dining room, although it got no further than the ceiling.

The dead sailor lay in the port. That threatened us with disaster. It was a hot summer. The chestnut trees were in bloom and cherries were on sale. I had been sent for cherries just as the *Potyomkin* fired its two shots at the city. It didn't want to hit the city—it had aimed at the Municipal Theater where a military council presided over by General Kaulbars was in session—but it missed, and both shells fell on Odessa.[18]

Among those terrified the *Potyomkin* might bombard the city, we fled to the station at Vygoda—still one of those closest to Odessa but already in the steppe and the domain of German colonists.[19] After the short train trip, we rode in a *britzka*. That was my first encounter with the endlessness of the steppe, with its heat and lilac hue. I rather disliked it. I probably got those impressions through a haze of nausea caused by the *britzka*'s swaying back and forth under the noonday sun, by anxiety, and by the disruption of my normal eating schedule. The horses' bobbing croups, their tails swinging back and forth and the breech strap wandering over their rumps, the flies moving through the air with the *britzka* as though stationary, stationary like chandeliers, the black rectangles of the fields on the horizon—how could that not have seemed like sickness or have produced nausea?

The state of unfamiliarity, nausea, and anguish continued even after I found myself next to a window in one of the German peasant cottages . . . There, beyond the window and just as nauseatingly as everything else I'd seen, chickens were conducting their business. First they walked slowly about, holding their white feet out in front of them, then suddenly upon seeing something, they broke into a run, then they started walking again, then they ran, then they walked, then they ran again . . . And the heat sang, it rang and it spoke, it opened and closed its eyes . . .

The village lived a life of its own. It may not even have been aware that Odessa was besieged. Lethargic, hulking, terrifying people named Friedrich, Bruno, Eustace, Friedrich, Eustace lived there. They came up to the window and peered in at us, quite unabashed, whispering to each other and prodding each other with their elbows. Somewhere behind me in the depths of the room lay Mama with her lady's coiffure; somewhere else lay Papa.

But to make up for it were the evenings! Oh, the evenings were wonderful! Oh, so wonderful!

They sat me on a young stallion with a nasty temper. It made those two boys laugh that I couldn't ride horseback. They wanted me to fall, for the horse to bolt and throw me, for me simply to be done away with. Of my entire ride on that stallion, I recall only the animal's long, narrow neck literally running out from under my hands . . . I slid first to one side, then to the other. There wasn't any saddle. I sat on the horse's sharp spine, which made me suffer, and I suffered too because I was causing the horse pain.

The two boys, one taller than I was, the other shorter—a chubby but brave and manly lad who stood several rungs higher than I on the ladder of heroism—ran after me, ran on either side of me, ran ahead of me, waiting for me to fall off.

The stallion, recently cut, dashed in the direction of the herd, which was visible as a shadow undulating on the horizon. It was clear that eventually he would throw me, but I held on, though shouldn't I have tried to escape that body, that alien body that hated me and sensed my weakness?

Somehow I managed to dismount. The instant I did so, the horse sprang proudly back, lashing me with the loose reins, and galloped away, scattering the earth and suddenly flashing its golden croup . . . The boys burst into laughter, and I was ashamed. I was neither a warrior nor a man, but a coward, a thinker, a good-natured soul, an old man, dung . . . There in that twilight hour in the steppe near Voznesensk, my character was defined for all time.

Into my mind from one and the same sphere come the sailor Gross, the year 1905, the port fire, General Kaulbars, a trip to Manheim,[20] the gymnasium headmaster, and football. Into my mind come various insects that crawled about the park (several with scutes so heavy they seemed exhausted by their weight), naval officers with black and gold cruciform daggers who strolled with ladies in sea-foam white hats, and Maestro Davinhof, who conducted the boulevard cafe band while seated on a white horse.

Into my mind come the lilac-colored flowers—little lilac cypresses whose name I never managed to learn—that descended the slope to a meadow on our right as Papa and I and a third person walked in the direction of Arcadia on our way somewhere, either to a hospital to visit someone, or to a private house that turned out to be full of sunlight and broad glass doors standing across our path.[21]

I heard the explosion of a bomb thrown into Ditman's Cafe in Odessa by an anarchist in 1905. All exchanged frightened glances in that instant: I, Grandma, Papa, Mama, my sister, and two other people who were visiting us. The noise first erupted from below, then subsided and seemed to spread. True, it all took but a tenth of a second.

Everything in my recollections of that period is mixed up. A policeman in a theater hacked an army officer to death with his saber. The officer was buried with garlands bearing the inscription "For What?"

The police officer Panasyuk was killed. It was raining. There was a pogrom. First news about it. Then the news spread. A pogrom, a pogrom . . . What, a pogrom? A pogrom, a pogrom . . . And then a woman from next door, a lady, ran into our living room and asked us to hide her family.

You were ordered to hang an icon on your door if you were Christians. The next morning on Theater Lane I saw an indoor icon above the entrance to a dry grocer's shop—between the sill of a second-story window and the lintel over the door. The day was gray and gloomy after a rain.

Once when I had gone out onto our iron back-door balcony and was looking in the direction of the courtyard, I saw Papa coming toward our stairway on his way back from somewhere.

He whom I was used to seeing with a mustache no longer had one; he had shaved it off. His face now looked fat and fleshy, a fleshy red face under a straw boater.

It produced a sensation. "Karl Antonych has shaved his mustache!"

That development was discussed for a long time by our family and neighbors, indeed, by the whole courtyard and any acquaintances who happened to drop in. Papa could barely tear himself away from the mirror, and when we children gathered round, he puffed out his cheeks and made faces in order to look even funnier.

Golden childhood. But was it really so golden? What about the proximity to a still recent nonexistence? Or helplessness before the measles and scarlet fever? Or the need to study, go to school, and learn lessons? Or the cough to which everyone attended? Or the aversion to certain kinds of food that were precisely what you needed to eat? Eggs, for instance. Once at the base of a wall I saw a broken egg from which the ghost of a nestling flowed. Could I have eaten eggs after that?

In the so-called tobacco shops where they sold stamps and gymnasium notebooks, you could also buy rockets. They cost a ruble, I think. In appearance, they were dark blue tubes attached to little sticks like those used to support flowers. By means of the stick, the missile was stuck in the ground. It had a fuse, a twisted little black tail protruding from the bottom of the tube. To launch the rocket you lit the fuse, although I never saw that done. I saw only the holiday, only the fire and rejoicing, only the flourish of the rocket's peacock tail. I heard only the rocket's ignition and the whistling sound it made as it took off, a sound that filled the absolute silence of the dark blue velvet night, then lost itself aloft in a high-flying, glowing point . . . Only that, only their enchantment did I know of rockets, but the rocket itself I never held in my hands.

There was a tobacco shop next to the entrance to our building, just to the left of our gate. The owner's name was Isaac.

"Go to Isaac's!"

Or,

"Doesn't Isaac have any?"

On the sign over Isaac's shop in huge letters as big as chairs was the single word "Tobacco." It was the standard sign for shops of that kind—

after the Turkish model, no doubt, since Turkey wasn't very far from Odessa—and quite beautiful, I would say.

Isaac stood behind a fairly high, narrow bureau from which he took stamps after opening the lid. The stamps were kept in a safe place; they were something on the order of cash or foreign currency. There was a small dark blue picture of the czar on them. They cost seven kopecks. Little children were often sent for stamps. How long and how well I have remembered that price, remembered just that price: seven kopecks.

Isaac was round-faced and affable with a silky young tuft of beard. His store was small, just a shop, really, a tobacco shop, but it was clean and the lacquered wood of its counter and bureau gleamed. Entering it, you sensed at once how much Isaac and his wife Manya loved their shop and wanted their customers to enjoy coming there.

Childhood memory has preserved Manya too.

She was a languorous young woman with untidy but stylish hair who spoke in a Jewish lilt—affectionately, ending almost every phrase on an inquiring note.

"Ye-es? For arithmetic? With li-ines?"

Though it was called a tobacco shop, besides everything connected with smoking (as was always the case in those days), its stock included notebooks, stamps, writing accessories, multicolored sheets of glazed paper for pinning to desks, and decals, which, by the way, were usually kept in sheets in large notebooks with the dark purple spots of the untransferred decals still intact. All this, as I say, was in addition to the tobacco products. The latter consisted of Russian cigarettes, cans of tobacco, and cigarette papers with cardboard mouthpieces for home manufacture. But of course the best thing about the tobacco shop was that you could also buy rockets there.

"Isaac," I once asked, "do you sell rockets too?"

Although only a boy, I still called Isaac by his first name as did everyone else.

"There are Roman candles," he said. "They're the same as rockets and cost a ruble."

How startled I was to hear that name. Why "candle"? And why "Roman"?

"Which ones are they?"

"How should we know which o-nes?" Manya replied. "You were given five rubles on your name day, and you want to spend it on ro-ockets? Isaac, did you he-ar, his grandmother gave him five ru-ubles!"

The whole courtyard knew about that gift. At the barber's where I'd been sent to get a haircut, I had on the orders of Georges, the owner, even opened my coin purse, also given to me by my grandmother, and taken out the gold coin for everyone present to look at.

I went up one step and then the next (there were two in all) and entered the store. That it was brightly lit I could tell from the street as I drew near it, since its windows and door could be seen quite far off in the form of radiant yellow planes blocking my path. Once inside I fully appreciated the quality of its illumination: the store was simply awash in light. Indeed, it suddenly began to seem like a bath; everything within could have been taken for items floating on still untouched bath water: soap, sponge, toys . . . Nevertheless, it was a grocery store.

Shopping at that store was called "shopping at the German's."

I was forbidden to go into the courtyard.

"He plays with those ragamuffins."

I was the son of a father who was addressed as "sir" and saluted by the policeman. Although poor, my father was still a gentleman. I wasn't allowed to play with children who, as they said then, didn't belong "to our circle"—with the ragamuffins, that is.

Once, after the midday meal when I thought my father was asleep, I decided to go out into the courtyard anyway. I didn't do it straight off, but in order to soften the offense, as it were, first got some water from the tap in the kitchen, cold water from a dark blue enamel cup with white spots that naturally looked like a dark blue cow. To this day I recall the needlessly melancholy taste of the water. Then I went out onto the front-door landing.

Hardly had I taken a few steps away from it than I was called back by my father who was leaning out the window. I had to return since my father ordered me to, and when I got back inside I was given a thrashing, if by that it's possible to mean the punishment whereby you aren't beaten with a birch rod but simply spanked with an open hand on a bare bottom.

My father was very cross, probably because he had, as happens in a similar story by Chekhov,[22] lost at cards that day, although there may have been some other reason. I recall lying almost suspended in the air in the pose of a swimmer and being loudly smacked on the behind.

That's all I remember. For me, the best things in the story are that I considered it necessary to soften the offense and that the cup resembled a dark blue cow.

I was subjected to corporal punishment from my father another time, while traveling with him and Mama in a second-class sleeper on the then czarist railroad from the Crimea.

We were in the Crimea, we were in the Crimea! There on a veranda a shaggy artist in a pince-nez clipped his poodle, which emerged shivering, slimmer, and more naked from his hands, and there in the moonlight in Alupka Vorontsov's palace[23] shone white with its marble lions that seemed to be wiping their muzzles, lions on which they put me astride, which made my sex organ hurt, although I didn't mention that to anyone . . .

We were in the Crimea, we were in the Crimea!

Children's toys were sold at Kolpakchi's shop on Ekaterininsky Street. The magic lanterns attracted the most attention; looking at them, you were simply paralyzed with astonishment. A glass plate with a picture on it was always inserted in them—with a commercial purpose, as if saying, "See how this is done." The pale, hazy plate made of dull glass that . . . No, that's a very unclear description! It was loaded, that magic lantern, and "loaded" is just the word, for if you had lit the lamp inside it in some suitably dark location, you would have put the lantern into action at once. The plate would have appeared on the wall as a luminous pink, green, and carmine picture from some fairy tale familiar to all children.

The magic lantern was the kind of toy you shouldn't even dream about. Probably it was very expensive. It stood glowing in its black chamber like a sort of cock gazing down at everyone. We didn't dream about it. We bought caps instead. We already had the pistols; they had been purchased for our name days—one in the fall, another in the spring, a third in the summer. They were black, probably made of brass, and smelled of burning from being frequently fired—articles exceedingly yet pleasantly heavy to the hand of a child. The caps were sold in tiny round boxes of wrinkled cardboard with a yellow or at least damp color. They lay in the box in a pink little mound requiring painstaking description.

They used to sell large sheets of paper on which were printed pictures of a destroyer in different views, so to speak, so that it was possible, by cutting out and gluing the pictures together along the lines indicated for that purpose, to come out in the end with a three-dimensional model. I never succeeded in achieving that final result or even in coming close to it, although it wasn't terribly difficult. The pictures looked extraordinarily appetizing. It seemed all you had to do was take a pair of scissors and in an hour or so there, reclining on the table before you as if in dock, would be the gray hull of a destroyer . . . But how to reach that point. My ability and patience were only sufficient, perhaps, for cutting out the block of a gun turret. After that everything got crumpled up and spread out on the table in the form of paper balls that stuck to your hands or dangled in clusters from your arms . . . And of course you cried and wanted to be pitied.

Obviously, there was always a desire in me to create by myself, to invent everything by myself without having to submit to any blueprint whatever.

When at a very young age I drew what I thought were Russian soldiers in combat with the Japanese, it didn't at all occur to me that what I was drawing was wrong; I was convinced that the lines taking shape beneath my pencil did in fact represent soldiers.

Adults looking at my drawings didn't at all see what I saw. It even seems to me that I caught amused glances among them. Moreover, I remember to this day noticing then that the bent knee of one of the shooting soldiers was merely a right angle—two lines joined in a right angle. In short, I had an insight that told me I was drawing rubbish . . .

There was a notebook approximately the size of a postcard, though more square than a postcard, a thick, heavy booklet that was almost a small book.

On the basis of adult perception, it now seems to me that the notebook consisted of two dozen or so rather thick pages on each of which was an engraving of one or another well-known picture.

In fact, I'm almost sure that on one of those pages there was an engraving of David's *Tennis Court Oath.*[24]

Yes, they were undoubtedly engravings: I remember the thin parallel lines, the images' gray masses, that darkness of the entire field into which it was pleasant and alluring to look and suddenly recognize among the obscure, swirling events some path illuminated by a distant sun, a path along which a child walked.

Engravings then. A whole little book of engravings.

But why give a child such a gift on his name day? Are engravings really that interesting?

I liked to cut armor out of cardboard. Best of all turned out hip guards in the form, as you might suppose, of a kind of belt with a notch below the stomach. The design was successful, although the business went no further than the fitting, when my hips were fully enveloped in what was really cardboard but looked like a knight's hip armor. It was necessary, of course, to fasten the hip guards to your waist somewhere to keep them from falling down. But that was impossible, since you can't really sew cardboard. And there ended what was in essence a game of arms.

I remember to the point of hallucination a moment when I was engaged in that game. It was twilight in the dining room—our dining room on Grechesky Street that looked out onto the wall and the Orlovs' window—and I was holding in my hand some cardboard that shone light blue in the twilight. My goodness, I have only to extend my hand and the cardboard will reappear and the instant repeat itself!

The carpenter worked by the entrance to the cellar where the sun still reached. The sun is very important here; it gilded the shavings. And how strong the bond between them and the sun always was. How lovingly the sun caressed them. Sometimes, when you weren't looking directly at them but were absorbed in conversation, it would seem that a nymph had suddenly appeared next to the carpenter's bench.

I don't remember what the carpenter was working on. What's important is that a friendship arose between us. I was a boy no taller than his bench, and to me the carpenter seemed old. In all probability, he'd been a soldier in the war with Japan. Everything then was still alive with its echoes. He wore a mustache, and a cross was visible through the opening of his dark blue polka-dot shirt. The fact that he drew on the boards delighted me, as did the thick pencil he put in his mouth to moisten. His straightedge flew continually up and down, and it too was yellow—like matches, like the soldier, like the sun . . .

While working in the basement, the carpenter made for me something like a model of a soldier's rifle, or rather an outline of one cut from slightly yellowish white pine. It's hard for me to describe the joy I felt when I first took that object in my hands. It had everything it was supposed to have: a butt that fit comfortably underneath my cheek, a long stock with part of the barrel extending beyond it, a sight, and the hint of a bolt with a hammer-cocking mechanism . . . True, none of it had the powerful blue-black of a real rifle. On the contrary, it was pale in color and even had traces of the lines drawn on it with the carpenter's thick pencil. All the same, I had the sense of actually possessing a rifle.

I don't remember what preceded the event that played itself out in the next moments, but no sooner had I taken aim at something there in the basement than an older boy appeared on the threshold, a boy quite unknown to me whose face I didn't even see, who took the carpenter's gift from my hands and departed with it just as if it had been his own, without even looking back, apparently without even admitting the thought that I might try to protest.

Thus, for no more than an instant, I was the possessor of that thing that seemed so splendid to me. There on the threshold of the cellar where the sunlight lay in rectangles, fate played on me a kind of amazing practical joke.

As often happens with children, I could have put out an eye, although it's a very good thing I didn't! I do, however, remember the sudden blow of a long splinter that resulted in a flash of light before my eyes, and I screamed,

"My eye! My eye's been put out!"

I didn't feel any special anger toward the one who had, as I supposed, put out my eye. I wasn't angry at anyone in particular, nor indeed angry at all, and I certainly had no sense that my companion was in any way at fault. It had happened and that was all. That scene took place in the courtyard by the spigot, and within a few minutes I was at the pharmacy, where they put a thick bandage over my eye with soft doughlike contents that simultaneously gave off a pleasant and disgusting odor.

I was a boy, a son, who had nearly lost an eye. I was a very potent childhood figure. I was talked about at the barber's, at the custodian's, at the Greek butcher's, in wealthy apartments and in poor ones. Fathers home from work were told about me, as were relatives just arrived from other cities.

I and the boy who had almost put out my eye decided to conceal the true circumstances of the affair: I'd been running and had simply bumped into something. The truth got out, however, and the boy's mother, pressing me to her breast and bending over me her bonnet of yellow hair, gazed tenderly at me and called me a good boy. But I don't remember being guided by any particularly noble motives. It was just simpler not to tell on my friend, for if I had, there would have been moralizing, and that would have had an adverse effect on our subsequent possibilities of playing in the courtyard and enjoying our freedom.

My eye remained intact, and I soon forgot to rejoice every day that I had two eyes complete with irises, with pupils that changed diameter, and with eyelashes that led a life quite independent of my own, that perhaps sometimes even engaged in conversation while extending out over my eyes like branches, for sometimes it really did seem from below that they extended out in front of me like branches . . .

These notes are all attempts to restore life. I want to distraction to restore it sensuously.

In an attic almost set on fire by the sun, I stood in front of two boys who forced me, a very small child, to repeat certain obscene words after them. I did so, and they made me repeat the words over and over. During this they howled with laughter. The attic, and this invariably happened in attics whenever we got into them in the summer, almost burned and smoked. Yes, yes, in the corners where the building was a little ramshackle, where you could see whole piles of the sun, smoke floated—dark blue smoke.

The courtyard smelled of rosin. The odor came from an open shed where barrels stood with contents unknown to us children. The odor seemed to us not so much pleasant as in some way serious, on the basis of which it was forgiven its lack of pleasantness . . . The odor was yellow, yellow as the sunlight lying on the stones in the courtyard and on the bricks of the wall was yellow, yes, a sunny, yellow odor. Around the courtyard walked the languorous Vitya Koifman with her full lips and untanned, pleasingly pale face.

Later we climbed a ladder at the risk of falling and saw through temporary doors recently cut in the wall of the outbuilding under construction the inside of an already completed room, it too bathed in yellow light.

"You'll fall," Vitya Koifman called out to me from below, lifting her face which I saw flat below me, as if I were sitting in a palm tree looking down at a Negro woman who had just come running from the village. "Watch out, you'll fall!"

While calling this, she laughed, as if it would be funny if I did fall. She laughed because I was a boy and she was a girl and a certain embarrassment had emerged between us. That embarrassment was a friend rather than a foe. It was enjoyable to be together and feel that embarrassment. It told of much and did much, so that it was very likely the kindliest friend of those years.

When I was little, Chinese often came into the courtyards to sell silk. They still wore pigtails. Traditional Chinese dress in those days consisted of broad dark blue trousers, a short dark blue jacket, black slippers turned up at the ends, and a pigtail. The latter was black, shiny, and stiff, as if it had through great effort been fashioned from tar. The Chinese was handsome, narrow-eyed, and manly in spite of his pigtail, or perhaps because of it—a kind of exotic, fairy-tale manliness.

He came into the courtyard with a bundle suspended from an iron measuring rod that rested on his shoulder. The bundle thus lay on his back. The bundle's clean, trim appearance, its elegant compactness, and its great weight bound up in shapely form were very attractive . . .

Once I received several wonderful gifts on my name day. It's unlikely they were Russian toys, so much did they differ from everything else that filled the corners of my nursery. About one of them there was no hesitation: Japanese grass, it was called, and that wasn't just its name but in fact what it was.

"A glass of warm water," somebody said.

"Yes, certainly . . ."

A glass of warm water appeared, its surface unsteady for a moment. Everyone was standing around the table. It was still a name day, its climax in fact, when the rooms were filled with the light blue smoke and gunpowder smell of shooting from a cap pistol. The name day of a boy who, on that occasion, never stopped being the center of circles of people and things.

The glass of warm water was taken from a woman's hand and set down on the table, thereby enlarging the circle of things by one glass of water. But the boy never released his grip on his pistol. He was surrounded, too, by ringlets of caps . . .

A gentleman with a black beard, whose last name may have been Makeev, held in his hands a little box no bigger than a matchbox from which he pulled, just as from a matchbox, a little drawer . . .

The one among the adults I most wanted to be like was Richard Gross.

I came home, and there at the table, sitting and drinking tea like everyone else, was the one I most wanted to be like.

No sooner had I entered the room than I noticed his white sailor's jumper. From its collar, which lay so handsomely on his shoulders, his white neck grew like a splendid stalk.

My sister, playing with her thoughts, words, and eyes, wanted him to regard her as lively, intelligent, and appealing (which in fact she was) and expressed her doubt about his ever having been to any particularly remote and wonderful countries, implying that he had invented it all in order to make himself more interesting . . . He laughed, which had a charming effect, since he laughed like a victor, like a kind, handsome man who had in fact done what he said, and not only did he affirm the truth of his words but even promised to visit a remote and wonderful country in the near future.

A few days later he disappeared. And then a postcard suddenly arrived with a gelatin-coated image of a port with palm leaves and steamship smoke-stacks.

The postcard was addressed to my sister—still a girl!—and on the reverse side where messages were written, there was a message for her:

"Richard was in Bombay!"

And the postcard really was from Bombay.

The three of us—my grandmother, my sister, and I—came back as we had left, came back from the park where we had gone for a walk just as we did every day. Nothing unpleasant had happened . . . Yet all the same I stood dumbfounded in the middle of the room I had just entered, my heart filled with a feeling till then unknown to me.

There in the park Grandma had read to us a tale about a dragon and a prince who was seeking the water of life and death.

"Dragon" in Polish is *smok*.

It guarded the road leading to the water of life and death, that *smok*. Oh, how clearly I hear that word echoing across unbelievable distances—*smok*. How distinctly I see myself almost glancing back at that word flying around me.

Grandma was busy with something of her own—perhaps she was darning or sewing—while I was leafing through a book whose only meaning for me was that sometimes I saw images in it that puzzled me to the point of trembling. I didn't know how to read, but I still knew that those spaces covered with black marks were meant for reading. I knew they were pages and letters and that people read them.

Later on, when I was old enough to understand a good deal more, I found in our house the book whose pages I had been turning. That book—and perhaps, reader, you yourself know it—was a supplement to *The Grainfield* that had come out at the turn of the century, something on the order of a collection of historical materials that summed up what had gone before. It was called *The Nineteenth Century*. It isn't difficult to imagine how many remarkable images were in it if the book summed up a century like the nineteenth.

When I note my inability to write, I have in mind the putting together of sentences. It's very hard for me to write a sentence in one stroke, so to speak, especially if it's meant to define an abstract idea. The sentence suddenly breaks in two, and I'm left hanging, holding onto some piece of a subordinate clause . . .

I console myself with the fact that I'm a Pole and that Russian is, after all, alien to me and not my native tongue. It's possible that that in fact is the reason.

I remember once when my father wanted to check on my progress in reading Russian. (My grandmother taught me, and my father acted in this instance as a kind of supreme judge.)

"Iván!" my father shouted, getting angry. "Iván!"

I pronounced the name with the accent on the first syllable in the Polish manner, a language in which the final syllable is never stressed.

"Iván!"

"Ívan," I repeated.

"Iván! Iván! Iván!"

No, I still pronounced it "Ívan." As if afraid he would end up striking me in a fury, my father broke off the examination, and I started to cry. I was still a little Pole, and it was hard for me to change a tune I had acquired with my blood.

An inexpensive, one-volume edition. A large-format book, thick, with a dilapidated binding. It's easy to picture that binding: turning back its front cover, you saw tiny latticed veins of calico . . .

The book was called *Pushkin*. I still couldn't read, and I still didn't know what "poet," "verses," "composition," "writer," "duel," or "death" meant. I only knew that it was Pushkin.

What's the first book I ever read? Probably one in Polish called *Baśnie ludowe* (Folk Tales). I remember its smell—musty, I would say now—and the separated corner of its cardboard binding. And I remember the violet and green cloaks of the grizzled kings and the little black tails that hung from their ermine mantles . . . It was a history of Poland in popular sketches—about Piast, Bolesław Chrobry, and Bolesław Krzywousty.[25] It has seemed to me ever since that pictures can hum. Those pictures certainly could.

I remember not joy but confusion the day I was given Krylov's fables to read.[26] It was a smallish book from Wolf's well-known Golden Library with a red and gold binding. Depicted on the cover in a golden oval were a boy and girl bent forehead to forehead reading a book. Even now I remember how truly metallically the gold in that oval shone.

The fables were well illustrated—graphically and realistically, yet with great transparency. Bears, peasants, foxes, geese. Printed under each picture, or on both sides of it, or on the page next to it were verses that to my amazement were called fables. I read one, then another, then a third, and I was overwhelmed with a tedium I can still recall. In the first place, they were written in a language entirely unlike anything I was used to hearing. In the second, they concerned animals that behaved sometimes like animals and sometimes like people, but that always talked like people. One sensed the muddle at once. Then in the same way a lion would converse, for example, with a fox. So that one sensed a geographical muddle, as well . . . The presence in the pictures of lions, elephants, and snakes encouraged one to expect events. And not merely events, but terrible, mysterious, even savage ones. Yet when I started to read I found not events but some sort of boring account about how musicians can't finally ever sit down and play. My child's imagination couldn't understand why it was necessary to enlist a creature like a lion if not to have him tear somebody apart or have somebody rescued from his clutches.

Those unreal lions, bears, and foxes symbolizing human qualities had nothing whatever in common with the beasts of the fairy tales of Hauff, say, or the Brothers Grimm . . .[27]

A narrow door led to the store through a rather thick wall, and that made the moment of entry particularly appetizing, if one may put it that way. I think there was even a little bell that tinkled whenever the door was opened . . .

It was a bookstore, and in the room next to it was a small library of Polish books you could borrow.

The books were Polish, the owner of the shop and the library was Polish, his wife was Polish, they sold Polish pictures—everything, in fact, was Polish, even the smell that was somehow like that of the Roman Catholic church standing next door on Ekaterininsky Street.

My mother had sent me to the store for a book. I passed through to the little library and asked the owner's wife, an old woman, if they had the book my mother wanted.

"*The Leper*," I said, giving the novel's title.[28]

No, *The Leper* never did turn up at the library. It was always out on loan. When a friend told her the novel's story, my mother's tears flowed . . .

"No, boy, *The Leper*'s already been checked out."

The rows of books were piled on top of each other up to the ceiling—different kinds of books, new ones, worn ones, some in bright, non-Russian dust jackets. The books gave off an odor that remains in my memory as one of the most pleasant I've ever known, although to tell the truth it was rather moldy and mousy.

"We have Żuławski's *On the Silver Sphere*.[29] Take it, your mama will be pleased." I took *On the Silver Sphere*. A look at the dust jacket told me the novel's action obviously took place on the moon: the large lunar sphere, depicted by the artist as indeed made of silver, rose above the horizon, and several people, standing exhausted among the bushes and casting long shadows, gazed at it sadly.

On the way out, I stopped to look at the postcards sold there and displayed with their faces turned toward the customer by means of some kind of wire device. People collected postcards in those days, and they were therefore manufactured with special art, using pure colors and good cardboard . . . The reproductions were glossy and sharp in every detail. For example, a fire . . . A large building, already reduced to a skeleton, stood black against the blazing background, and the clusters of sparks and the little golden helmets of the firemen, though the size of pinheads, were still visible when I turned back at the door to look at them for the last time.

"*On the Silver Sphere*?" Mama asked. "What's this? Some sort of rubbish, no doubt. You should have got *The Leper*."

"But they didn't have *The Leper*," I said.

"This is rubbish."

But the light blue dust jacket with its silver moon and long shadows caught her attention, and she asked not so much me as herself,

"What's this?"

And opening the book, she began to read.

"No, it's not bad," she said after a moment. "It's not bad, not bad. An inventor who . . . No, it's not bad."

It turned out to be a sad book about a group of people who had flown to the moon and lost all possibility of returning to the earth, for which they continued to yearn . . .

Once my parents came back from the theater with a very strong impression of the performance they had just seen. They immediately began telling me about it.

"A clock strikes," Mama said, "and Death enters. Oh, it's horrible! He has a scythe! Yes, yes, a scythe, and . . ."

I was no longer listening, since the image of Death with a scythe had overwhelmed my imagination. By the time I freed myself of the image, Mama was already finishing her account of the passage she was recalling, although I had managed to hear with half an ear, so to speak, other terrible things about a pope who hadn't wanted to follow Death, who had resisted, but whom Death had dragged off anyway, laughing maliciously.

"No, you'll come! He's resisting! Ha, ha, you'll come! You'll come!"

My parents pronounced the play's name with special significance, as if it were also frightening in some way.

"*Dante Alighieri*," Mama said all of a sudden, and it made my skin crawl. All the same, I wanted to hear it again, and I asked,

"What was it?"

And Mama repeated the name.

When I asked her to explain what it meant, she couldn't. It evidently wasn't very clear to her either. Obviously, the performance had been adapted from *The Divine Comedy*, and the figure of Dante moving through the terrors of Hell had never been named by the other characters in the play while on stage . . . And that was why it was hard for Mama, as an unschooled spectator, to connect the name of the play with that figure. That was why she couldn't tell me it was the name of a poet.

Papa, who was the Commerce Association librarian, used to let me climb into the armchair—into that splendid olive leather armchair about which all Odessa was talking—and read whatever I liked and as much as I liked.

And sometimes he would even order ice cream for me.

My feet in the armchair, I read Kuprin and gobbled ice cream. I read his "Seasickness."[30] Since I was innocent, I didn't understand the secrets of that story, but I did grasp with particular fullness the luxury of life, if only because I sensed without any doubt the inevitability of eventually comprehending the secret of which books spoke, and ice cream, and the armchair, and the mountains of sunset beyond the window—whole mountains of sunset.

It has been a long time since I've read the stories of Conan Doyle. Where are they? In books frayed by the years, books that only turn up at a friend's house by chance.

I remember my sister's delight in retelling their plots.

"The hound of the Baskervilles," she said, staring into my eyes with her own open wide, "was a dog, you see, that . . ."

I don't remember anymore what the dog did. I think one of the terrifying things, one of the mysteries, was that the breath from its muzzle glowed in the dark.

When I was a boy, I received as an award for passing from one grade to the next a book called *The Great Hero Suvorov.* It was a large, expensive book with a beautiful, sturdy binding, almost silken, on which there was a picture, predominantly carmine, of a speeding warrior carrying a lance—a Cossack. It pleased me very much, that book. It was most likely put together in a patriotic spirit that downplayed the Frenchmen Masséna and Macdonald and other young heroes and lauded the fierce old man Suvorov.[31]

I remember being able to draw a straight line vertically or horizontally with a pen or a pencil on paper without using a ruler. Each time the line was absolutely straight and parallel either to the bottom of the paper or to its side.

My father, giving me some register to divide, said,

"Here's a ruler for you."

And I remember saying,

"I don't need one."

My father started to get angry. Then I drew a line underneath a column of figures, and he was so amazed, I remember, that he said nothing at all. He merely raised his eyebrows.

That indeed was youth, strength, the future.

Now, however, I can't even draw a straight thought, as is obvious from this passage.

The cold spells still hadn't completely gone, and a kind of wariness therefore still remained in the world, even though it was already clean and dry. And amidst that tidiness of nature—if only in the courtyard where I passed my school vacation—Easter drew near.

A few days more and thick towers of freshly baked Easter cake would lie across the beds, cake whose touch reminded your palms of sand. A few days more and hyacinths would appear in the house . . .

The Easter table was decorated with long-stemmed hyacinths in holders. The hyacinths were pink and violet with blossoms that looked like little boats, a whole cavalcade of little boats dropping down toward the flower pot. A whole cavalcade of pink or violet boats descending in a spiral, looping the stem in spirals . . . Is that right or not?

We were Catholics, so it wasn't entirely our Easter. Our Easter was in Warsaw, in Paris, in Rome. Nevertheless, we had a church, and wax blood on the forehead of Christ, and the suspension of daily and spiritual routines that is characteristic of a great holiday. The true masters of the situation were the Orthodox, of course. They had bells that emitted gigantic bursting bubbles of sound, they had multicolored eggs, and they had the triple Easter kiss . . . They had soldiers in black dress tunics with red shoulder boards and housemaids with snow-white handkerchiefs in their hands, they had Kulikovo Field with its menagerie. Actually, Kulikovo Field belonged to everyone.[32]

At Lanzheron you could get to the sea not only by the road; you could also run down the bluffs.[33]

They were overgrown with high weeds, those bluffs, and strewn with rubbish, and dangerous dogs slept there that would suddenly leap out at you. Nevertheless, they led down to the sea, which literally beyond some broken box would suddenly build its rumbling cubes, its parallelograms, its ovals, its canopies, all in sparkling turquoise and sometimes in beams of light of such length that some, appearing but for a hundredth of a second, would make you cry out.

Tin cans and old shoes and calendar sheets floated there too, leaping first up onto the shore, then immediately off again . . . You might also see a saddle, its rawhide seaweed spread out in the water.

Once after running down a bluff, I saw some acrobats bathing and practicing their routines. Several young people were doing splendid somersaults, tossing each other up onto their shoulders where, their calves bowed, they turned head over the other's heels. Each turn ended with two feet again upon the sand, the golden sand which pushed up between their toes.

Their clothing, ordinary trousers and shirts, lay in little heaps on the sand. After they had trained for a while, they would run into the sea. All of this was accompanied by cries, the shrill cries you hear only at the seashore on a hot day.

It was clear they weren't first-class acrobats from a large circus. The latter would have been surrounded by things excellent in color and form—dressing gowns and beach umbrellas—and multicolored bottles would have been piled on the sand . . . No, those youths and boys were, if not amateurs, then an indigent street troupe akin to those that in my childhood would perform in courtyards with a barrel organ, or akin to that ball, that blue back, and that young woman upon the ball painted by Picasso.[34]

So I've completely lost the ability to write. Authorship in the sense of writing a sequence, a run of lines one after the other, is becoming unattainable. I compose individual lines. That's possible if you're writing verse, but prose, articles, and drama can't be created that way. I don't compose sweeping forward but write as if looking back. I don't compose by shading in, constructing, and pondering. I recollect, as if what I'm intending to write had already been written, had been written but somehow scattered, and I want to gather it together again, gather the pieces into a whole. In a word, I must either untangle this knot, as they say, or end the whole business.

Farewell, road to Lanzheron, farewell!

There at its very beginning like part of a viaduct stood an arch faced not in fine white marble but in plaster. There under its limestone vaults little booths were huddled, or rather just things for sale: kvass, gingerbread, perhaps cheap rockets.

Farewell, road to Lanzheron, farewell!

Carrying an oblong cardboard box, the group moved quickly across the gravel. By their gesticulating, rapid shuffling, and the way they all talked at once, you had the sense that their consciences weren't clear, that they were swindlers.

In front of them waited a bare wooden table surrounded by a throng of children, among whom I too was standing.

They came up to the table, where one of them sat down on a stool and took from his pocket a tablet with perforated sheets for tearing out. The others busied themselves with the box, which was now standing on end. After a few moments, we saw a doll emerge from it and come to a halt in a walking position. The sun shone brightly on the doll. It was ordinary—expensive, it's true, but ordinary—with wide blue eyes, rather spread-out arms, and flaxen curls. Its articulation was a bit squeaky, as we could hear, its eyelashes were velvet dashes, and its tulle dress was, as it seemed to me, translucent on its rose-colored body.

I don't know how the little girls viewed the doll, although probably with delight. The boys naturally regarded it with revulsion, although they still wanted to win it. It might be sold or traded; it was valuable property.

And so the doll was raffled. I'll never forget how one of the swindlers stood up with a blue and red pencil in his hand to explain the conditions of the lottery, which consisted of guessing the doll's name. Whoever guessed naturally won, although for the privilege of guessing you had to pay five kopecks.

Five kopecks was a lot. For five kopecks you could buy a large portion of ice cream and waffles, a round sandwich you could eat for a long time. A glass of kvass, for example, cost only two kopecks.

I managed to catch a show of the carnival variety. Thus I saw balls being thrown at the hinged cardboard figure of a Japanese soldier, causing it either to topple head over heels or . . . I don't remember what. In a word, something unfortunate happened to the soldier that made you laugh. I also saw a post, really a very tall mast, climbed for prizes concealed at the top. There on a little platform so hard to reach lay a watch, I believe. Also connected with a mast was a stunt that excited the public imagination of the day—the leap from the top. That mast or pole was about ten stories high, and below it, where the leap was aimed, was a trench filled with water . . . The stunt was unquestionably dangerous, if only because at the time the technique for diving into water from great heights was not very highly developed. Yet what dives they were! The acrobat leaped into what was little more than a shallow ditch. And he bade farewell to his wife, that daredevil. Yes, just so, he bade farewell to his wife. In the center of the huge crowd surrounding the scene of action, two small figures stood, one in a circus cloak, the other in the russet garments of a madonna. As they embraced, they briefly rested their foreheads on each other's shoulders . . . I think a little military band played as well. I remember the vast size of the crowd, its hum. It was annoyed by the wait, indeed, was afraid the jump might be called off, that Death, already hovering aloft in the gray sky full of May rain, would be forced to depart. A banner fastened to the mast, a banner flying in that same gray sky, slightly distracted the crowd . . .

"He's saying good-bye!" rumbled through the crowd . . . "He's saying good-bye to his wife!"

Those in back couldn't see, but it was clear now that they wouldn't be cheated, that the jump would take place, that Death would not, after all, be forced to fly back home. There it is, there! With its scythe! And, truly, its scythe did flash.

Or rather, it wasn't its scythe but the lightning that flashed. Nevertheless, the acrobat was prepared to die.

First, I'll describe a shooting gallery. How two gentlemen shot at bottles. Then at a little ball. And then how they went for beer. And how I wanted to be grown up . . . Why did I want to be grown up? Didn't I like childhood? What didn't I like about it?

Most often the gentlemen shot at bottles. By means of some sort of mechanical device, the bottles moved across the wall in the background, one after another in single file, somehow suggesting living creatures of a rather threatening sort. The gentlemen shot at the moving bottles and that gave the latter even more the illusion of being alive. Sometimes it was enjoyable to think they were being punished, those living and somehow dissatisfied creatures.

The word "shooting gallery" included everything all together. It was located on the left as you entered the park, indeed, was almost pushed out into the blue expanse of the sky and sea. Half the shooting gallery was lit, the half reached by the sunshine as it fell through the wide open doors. The bottles and most of the figures shone in the summer twilight. The gentlemen were shooting slender Monte-Cristos with faceted black barrels. The shots cracked. It smelled of gunpowder—sweet, with a touch of iron . . .

As a child, when that was exactly what I most wanted to do, I never once got to shoot. I only watched others do it, and I could have watched for hours. First the gravel rustled under their approaching feet, then two gentlemen exchanging friendly banter appeared at the threshold. It wasn't, strictly speaking, a threshold, but more like a border—the border between warmth and coolness. The two men—and most often there were two—came to a halt.

"Shall we?"

"All right, let's."

They tossed away their cigarettes, which fell on the lawn at the very edge of blueness, and hardly had they reached for them than the loaded Monte-Cristos, shapely as deer antlers, were already in their hands.

"Well?" said the first.

"Well?" said the other.

Mount Zhevakhov could be seen from the boulevard in the form of a not-too-distant yet bluish ridge. But it was far away, although not so much in a geographical as in an everyday or domestic sense—what possible reason could you have for going there?

A train pulled by a small locomotive called a steam engine went in the mountain's direction. A small, boldly whistling steam engine with five or six green cars . . .

What a marvelous thing the freedom of recollection is. How charming that it comes when it likes, that we can in no way make ourselves remember one thing and not something else. Ha, ha, obviously, there's an exact law for the generation of memory, but we'll never understand it, not on your life!

I remember our going out to sea on the yacht *Infatuation*. There were three of us: the celebrated Odessa syphilologist Egor Stepanovich Glavche, his adopted son Andronka, and me, the little boy Yura.[35] That yacht ought to be described at some length. She was flat—you barely sat above the water line—long, flat, narrow, and swift. No, this description is so poor it breaks off by itself. The memory won't come, so we'll just describe how on our way back to Odessa, which we'd left in the morning, the city's lights burned in the distance, how it seemed that they moved from place to place, then disappeared, then flared up again, and how that field of light seemed to breathe and move . . . No, apparently this recollection won't come off either.

How gently the sea murmured and coursed through your fingers as you dipped them in the water, the dark sea water that ran to meet you just below the gunwale the distance of an elbow—or two elbows, since you were leaning on your forearms . . .

That evening Dr. Glavche took Andronka and me to an exhibit. He was dressed in a brilliant black, so-called alpaca jacket, a white vest, gray pinstriped trousers, and on his head he wore a stiff hat made of straw, a so-called boater. In those years, that was dandified yet perfectly proper attire. Dr. Glavche's hair was clipped short, and he had a black beard that was neither long nor bushy—a black triangle with its point turned upside down. His speech was smooth and carefully enunciated. He wore a pince-nez, as nearsighted people did then instead of the eyeglasses that are used today.

From his pocket he would take a pure white handkerchief with which, after removing his boater, he would sometimes wipe his crown, not black but gray, since his hair was close-cropped. He was solidly built, even portly, and his little white collar gleamed.

The summer evening was bright and smelled of flowers that were especially noticeable at dusk—lilies and white roses, weightless in the twilight. In the distance, the lighthouse beacon shone at even intervals, first red, then green. The regular alternation was probably caused by the rotation of a lamp with different lenses, but either because I didn't know that or because I didn't think of it, it was possible to imagine that the lighthouse was somebody standing with his back to you who turned around and glanced at you first with a red eye and then with an emerald one.

We set out for the exhibit on foot. It was in the park not far from the center of town. We walked with Dr. Glavche in the middle and Andronka and me on either side. Dr. Glavche was in fine spirits, joking and snapping his fingers in various ways and playing with his cane. Everything promised an evening of wonders.

That world was completely different. A small plateau of park covered with flower beds was separated from the descent to the port—indeed, simply from the port itself with its steamships, sea, breakwater, and lighthouse—by an old reddish stone wall with arches in it. From the wall and the age-old deposits on its stones grew flowers that gently swayed in the breeze. The gravel beneath the wall never stopped rustling. Those who wished to look at the sea came and left. Children played there . . .

In Odessa we sailed the sea in dories. They were large, heavy boats with no keel and a flat bottom—something like a cart lifted from its wheels and thrown into the sea. They were crudely painted in red and dark blue and set in motion by means of huge, heavy oars secured to the oarlocks with a strength sufficient, at least, for tethering oxen. There was always a lot of water in the bottom of those boats, pools in which rags, the red remains of shrimp, or a bottle swam. The dory skimmed over the waves. There was something of the Greek myths about the appearance of those boats. I remember to this day, as if I had only just seen it, the brown pearlike calves of the fishermen as they ran behind a boat they were launching in order to leap into it once it was afloat.

Another boat was called an "Ace." It was a little shell. But with a keel. Its ribs were visible from the inside, grayish white like bones. Two oars, the left one a little closer to the bow, the right one nearer to the stern—an ambling gait.

Usually it waited for us in the port in the very same place not far from a whole forest of piles. It was moored to a bollard on the pier. The rope brushed the water again and again, and as it and the water parted, it seemed that they kissed. We hauled the boat to the pier and walked onto it. It heeled over, first to one side, then to the other. We picked up the oars, which at first seemed unusually round.

Oh yes, it had a rudder too. From the rudder to the helmsman ran lines he held in each hand. They were held in the palm from behind the back, since as everybody knows, the helmsman sits with his back to the rudder.

Usually we rowed in the port. The port was enormous, a virtual sea, especially for two boys in an "Ace." A steamship standing at anchor was, as we rowed beneath it, no less than a wall to us. Yes, a gigantic wall, rusty brown at the bottom, cleaner toward the top, and elegantly clean at the very top.

Going down the left side of French Boulevard away from Gymnasium No. 3, you would suddenly come to a lane . . . In it were the bleak colors, the dingy, cattle-brown colors of a pen, one of whose boards sagged as though leaning its belly against the passerby. At the same time, the lane gleamed with the deep blue of the sea visible in the distance. And so you wanted to turn into it . . . But I was always hurrying somewhere, always hurrying. And so I never did turn into that lane. I think it looks the same today. The fence still sags, and in the distance, above the daisies and broad burdocks, the sea is still visible.

Odessa

I TOO would like to pass back through my life as Marcel Proust managed in his day.

Where does he begin? I don't remember. I think with a magic lantern and the movement of its luminous, transparent, iridescent image on the wall, then on the door, then on the door handle—an image of the knight Golo that merges with the door handle, and so on. Or with a walk in which they, the children, go with their father what seems to them a very great distance from home . . . They find themselves in some quite unfamiliar place, and then their father, as if taking a visiting card from his pocket (or a magician a playing card?), suddenly pulls from the darkness the wicket of their own house.[1]

Where shall I begin? My memory continually draws me back to that day in early fall when I arrived at the gymnasium with my grandmother to take the examination for the preparatory class. Perhaps with that?

To be honest, I'm still writing all this more like a professional writer than someone who is merely recalling something and passing it on. Recalling what? Life? That day they caught a thief on Deribasovsky? I ran toward shouting in a courtyard, and there, almost crucified, a young man was being held, very pale, handsome, and dressed like everyone else. I've thought ever since that thieves are handsome and insane . . . That took place on a block near the top of the steep incline where Deribasovsky began its descent to the port but was still very clean, smart, and elegantly paved with non-Russian stones; where there were large, well-to-do houses with high arches at their entrances; and where the Pathé company building stood with its neon cock that turned on and off in the evenings.

I think I've grown dull. Maybe it's sclerosis. Creative thoughts about a future play are in order, however. The dullness consists of the fact that no thoughts of an unusual or higher nature have occurred to me for some time. But did I really ever have such thoughts? If you consider the mental processes of a Hegel or Freud, then my thinking is like a conversation in the subway about "how can I get from here to there or maybe there" and no higher.

I should write a story about a soul that has been cast into the world in terror but that seeks optimism, a story about myself, beginning after all with my first visit to the gymnasium.

My grandmother taught me Russian and arithmetic. Remembering that now, I can't understand why, in a family where there were both mother and father, it happened that the lessons connected with my proposed enrollment in the gymnasium preparatory class were entrusted to my grandmother, an old woman, a Pole, in fact, who wasn't entirely literate in Russian and who confused Russian stress.

I copied from books, took dictation, and studied the four rules of arithmetic. I don't remember how the lessons went. My recollections are only of details: sitting at the dining room table facing the window and the door to the balcony, or my grandmother's temple with her dry hair tucked behind her ear . . .

My grandmother brought me to take the entrance examination for the preparatory class at Richelieu Gymnasium in Odessa.[2] I remember our waiting outside under trees from which the leaves were falling. They floated in the air, those yellow-red autumn leaves, and it seemed that they creaked as they sailed past. I didn't think then that they creaked like ships; that occurs to me now. But perhaps I did think of it then.

Over and over, we followed first one leaf and then another drifting nearby.

If you had examined them flat, some of them would have looked like Gothic cathedrals.

They drifted down upon us from the blue sky, catching on the windowsills and changing direction.

Everything that day happened amid the falling leaves, everything, including our odyssey.

With her poetic soul, Grandma understood all the beauty of what was happening. How suddenly sad it became to see her face.

Many other boys besides me had been brought to take the examination. They were divided into groups: those who like my grandmother and me were standing under the trees and almost leaning against their trunks, those who were sitting on the benches or waiting next to them, and those . . . Is it necessary to have three examples? All right, let there be three: those who were walking around the courtyard with their adult brothers or their fathers—small, intelligent boys wearing eyeglasses full of gleaming microreflections of the autumn, the grounds, and the city.

My grandmother had brought not a professional writer but a little boy like the others. And the little boy didn't see all that the writer remembers now. Perhaps none of it happened. No, of course it happened. Certainly, it was autumn and the leaves were falling . . . Certainly, they did creak as they sailed past, rubbing their sides together like ships. And like ships they described circles—two or three rings of a spiral—as they floated by me to settle gently on the asphalt, on the edge where a large number of them already lay, an entire perished fleet. Occasionally, a gust would turn some of them in a different direction . . . No, the boy did see it, and the writer, drawing on other recollections, now merely remembers what the boy brought by his grandmother actually saw.

That means she did in fact bring a writer, a poet, albeit a very small one. And where's the border really? At what point did the boy begin to see? At what point was he merely a boy and then suddenly a poet? For on that morning he unquestionably did look and he did see.

It isn't entirely clear to me now why my grandmother's assistance was required. I was, you see, sufficiently grown up to have gone by myself, even if I was a boy with all the characteristics of his age: a passion for wandering off, for example. Most likely, my grandmother had been sent to keep track, so to speak. Whatever the reason, that day, which has remained vital and radiant in my memory as few others have, is bound to my grandmother. Indeed, it simply belongs to her; it is her day, the day of her remembrance.

I don't remember how we got to Richelieu Street. Probably we first went down Grechesky (after coming out of the house, since we lived near the corner of Grechesky and Polsky), then turned onto Richelieu, then from Richelieu at the place dominated by the theater we turned onto Deribasovsky, and then after going all the way down Deribasovsky, we turned right on Sadovy where the post office dominated and where at the end of the street the gymnasium stood. There was probably no other way to go. Since I've already brought up what was dominant on which street, I ought to say that on Deribasovsky it was the giant clock of Barzhansky's shop. It hung, if one may put it this way, right in your path, so that by lifting your head you could actually see the big hand of the clock making its jump to the next minute.

And so we reached the gymnasium building, an old-fashioned two-story yellow affair with small windows in its thick walls, built perhaps during the reign of Paul I, when Odessa was still a very young city.[3] Or rather we reached the corner, since the building stood on the corner of Sadovy and Torgovy. And it seems to me now that I am there for the first time in my life.

"You'll have to go that way, into the courtyard," the doorman said. "If you're here for the examination, you'll have to go into the courtyard."

And he held up his hand to indicate the direction, although he was in fact pointing at a wall—clear to himself, no doubt, but to Grandma and me, quite incomprehensible. His arm in its sleeve, which even sagged under the weight of its braiding, looked to me almost like the arm of Peter the Great.

"That way," the doorman repeated, now pointing to the far end of a corridor at some windows in which trees were moving.

We pretended to understand and returned to the street. If we hadn't been nervous, it would have been easy to figure out in the end just where the doorman was directing us, even if it was through a wall, but we wandered around on the street, irritated with each other. The business got straightened out when we saw what were apparently another grandmother and grandson walking confidently toward the end of the street, and we set off behind them.

"Are you going to the examination too?" Grandma asked.

The grandmother in front didn't hear, but the grandson looked back, and it was clear that they too were going to the examination: his face was scared, with a frozen smile.

"What?" the boy asked.

"Are you going to the examination?" Grandma asked again.

"Yes, yes, to the examination," the other grandmother replied, a diminutive woman in a pleated white collar, although she probably wasn't a grandmother at all but an aunt. She didn't invite us to join them, but on the contrary quickly took the boy by the hand and walked on in even more solitary fashion, so that the four of us continued on our way as if to different destinations.

We opened a door in a large wooden gate and, stepping over the threshold, found ourselves in a kind of corridor open to the sky but a corridor between two walls nonetheless. The corridor was paved with asphalt and extended about twenty paces from the doorway to a courtyard also completely covered with asphalt, although above it there was no narrow strip of sky as over the corridor but a broad expanse of blue reaching far above the trees. Then we entered the courtyard, which was square-shaped—an asphalt courtyard slightly bluish from wear . . . Acacias had been planted around its perimeter, and from them, as from all the trees that day, leaves were falling.

Trees, and beneath them boys. Boys, grandmothers, mothers, fathers, older brothers. The trees dropped their leaves, the leaves accumulated beneath the trees, and the boys stood on the leaves under the trees, leaning against their sloping trunks, which seemed to soar upward far away.

Finally I too was called. A last glance at my grandmother left under a tree and I was already on the iron stairway. One, two, three, and the stairway's iron rumbling ended, then a door and a hallway . . . And then I found myself with several other boys in a not-very-large room, indeed, a rather small one, even narrow, although it did have three windows. Was it a classroom? Yes, it was! Beyond the windows I could see the street, the houses on the other side, and the tops of the trees, just as yellow as the one under which I'd left my grandmother. The classroom was brightly lit. Here and there quadrangles of light lay in patches or were broken apart as they fell in corners or upon the desks. But I was seeing the desks for the first time . . . Were they school desks? Yes, they were! Until then, I'd only heard about them from my sister who had started school before me. At the desks boys were sitting.

I was so nervous it was difficult for me to make out what was going on. Oh, how nervous I was! An examination was in progress. In front of the blackboard—my sister had told me about it too: Oh yes, the blackboard. Is that it? Yes, it is!—in front of the blackboard that, although coated with chalk dust, even wrapped in a chalky cloak, was indeed black and that extended the whole length of the wall, two figures were standing, one old and the other young. The old one was the teacher giving the examination; the young one was the boy being examined. The old one wore a uniform with a double-breasted jacket covered in chalk dust and in his hand he held a piece of chalk; the young one wore a sailor jacket.

Nothing will alter my conviction that during the examination for the preparatory class at the gymnasium when, nearly dropping the chalk from my hand, I was ready to accept the fate looming before me in all its horror that I'd failed the examination because I couldn't solve the problem, a miracle occurred: I solved it.

I was about eleven when I started the gymnasium. A mere eleven years lay between me and nonexistence in the world, yet already I wore a visored uniform cap, a double-breasted jacket, and a leather belt with a metal buckle in the middle of my stomach. Already I was standing in front of a geographical atlas of the two hemispheres and gazing at the lilac polygons of the colonies and the shell of Madagascar and reading and understanding the words "Great Britain" . . . Already I was writing German Gothic letters and thinking of the heroes of history who had lived before me—before my eleven years. How did I perceive the circumstance that I'd only been alive a short time, that I'd only begun to live? I didn't perceive it. Rather, others told me I was little. I myself, I repeat, neither felt it nor reflected upon it. I didn't think about the fact that it was possible for me to be something other than I was. If I did want to be grown up, I didn't think about physical changes but about the possibilities that are given to adults, such as not having to prepare lessons or being free to eat as many eclairs as you like. I was a human being, just a human being, not knowing of myself that I was little and had only recently come into the world, or that I was growing, learning, acquiring understanding, and the like. Quite so, I was just a human being.

I didn't like it when they made me wear a hood. It made me feel smaller than I was, weaker and sicklier. Even now I can feel its nap on my cheeks and lips. It was coarse, that nap, and it made you almost want to spit, or at least blow it away from your cheeks on frosty, windy days.

I think there were other hoods as well with gold braid.

Sickness was always hovering near us schoolboys. I remember sitting with one of my classmates on an iron step near the top of the covered stairway that led to our hallway—the door of which was still closed, since being diligent boys we had arrived before the rest—and counting those among our comrades who were out with the measles. It was dark in that little nook, almost as dark as night, and a bit frightening: perhaps the Measles herself was sitting next to us in a kerchief out of whose oval her cheekbones protruded like two stones.

I can't restore to memory exactly when I had the measles myself, whether during my gymnasium years or earlier. In that era, they protected your eyes and closed the shutters in the daytime. I lay in the large dining room of our apartment on Grechesky Street, an uncomfortable, uselessly broad room looking out onto a wall. I lay on a bed placed next to a closed folding door on the other side of which, I knew, were the foyer and the entrance. I was being treated by Dr. Gartenstein, a tall man dressed in gray with a grizzled, but fine, youthful beard. I wasn't very sick. All of a sudden it has now begun to seem to me that I fell asleep then and have been asleep and dreaming ever since, and that all the years between have been my dream.

A little longer. A little longer.

Besides the usual uniform, there was also the so-called dress tunic. It was a tight-fitting short dark blue jacket with a row of nine buttons down the front and a stand-up collar with silver galloon. The dress tunics weren't required and only the more-or-less-wealthy boys had them. I never did.

That twilight was undoubtedly a harbinger of spring . . . Though early, springtime was already on its way. Gigantic cloudy ice floes were already drifting across the sky; bright blue ice holes were already gleaming there.

I walked down Richelieu, then turned onto Uspensky Street and descended the hill. I was a small figure, very small, a schoolboy in his first year, most likely. I was going to visit Saul Hershkovich. You might think by his name that he was the son of poor parents; no, he was from a bourgeois family.

Before me stood his apartment suite with its white doors and its broad white windows in which those same ice floes drifted. It was dusk, but the lights hadn't been turned on yet, and it was a marvelous time, especially in well-to-do apartments with their covered armchairs and steedlike grand pianos—yes, yes, brilliant black mounts!—and the golden gleam of their wallpaper.

Naturally, everyone greeted me with lamentations in view of my pallor.

At the time I was probably pitiful to look at: sickly, pale, and puny. But something attracted people to me. I was also poor, of course, but people were comfortable with me and I was invited to the homes of the rich.

Although the Orlovs lived in an expensive ground-floor apartment, it was still on the ground floor. In any event, you could walk across the cobblestones of the courtyard right up to any one of their windows, and pausing there, be reflected in your full height, provided the window was closed. Standing before those windows in the summer when they were open, I could see the interior of the room from slightly above, and to anybody inside, I was a rather impressive silhouette regarded from below.

The Orlovs were truly wealthy people, and it isn't at all clear to me why they lived on the ground floor. Of course, as I've indicated, that ground floor was hardly a residence for paupers. On the contrary, it was a bright, many-roomed apartment looking out on two sides—the courtyard and the street—and wouldn't have given those who lived in it any sense that they were merely on the ground floor.

The Orlovs very likely lived in that slightly inferior apartment because for some reason they wanted to be in that building and had temporarily agreed to live on the ground floor in expectation of something better.

Quite right, for as I now recall they did live on the second floor in a different apartment with a long, narrow balcony and a row of windows that extended the full length of the facade, windows I can now see merely by closing my eyes.

For the time being, however, the Orlovs were the ones on the ground floor, the people whose windows were level with the courtyard and whose wealthy life I could examine from slightly above.

I don't feel like remembering childhood anymore. Except perhaps for the Catholic church on Ekaterininsky Street, a not-very-large Gothic building with a rosace above the portal and loose steps under my sandals.

I thought that after graduating from the gymnasium I would buy a bicycle and make a tour of Europe. The First World War hadn't begun yet and everything was still very old-fashioned—soldiers in black dress tunics with red shoulder boards, the menagerie at Kulikovo Field with its single lion, the talking head in the mirror box at the fair. It was still a time of first love, when a girl stared at you from a balcony and you wondered if you weren't in some way deformed. It was still a time when the girl's father, a naval officer in his dress tunic, walked toward you with his saber clacking and acknowledged your greeting, from which you ran for all you were worth, yourself not knowing where, out of your wits with happiness. And they still sold kvass for a kopeck a glass from behind green counters, and you still came back from football games with the thump of the ball ringing in your ears.

I never bought that bicycle and I never took that trip through Europe. Verdun was burned, as was the cathedral of Reims where in her day the daughter of Yaroslav the Wise was married to the king of France.[4] The first tanks appeared, and airplanes began to drop bombs for the first time. However, hanging in the museums just as before were extraordinary paintings as beautiful as trees at sunset. Sometimes in my dreams I see that visit to

Europe that never took place. I dream most often of Kraków in the form of a wall climbing beside a road, an ancient wall from which trail plants that tap their branches against it and rustle their flowers.

I still feel like remembering.

I know a bit about life. Most of all I like it that there are beasts both large and small, and stars that stand out in relief as they gaze twinkling down at me from a clear sky, and trees as beautiful as paintings, and much, much more.

What an ample phenomenon a century is. How many generations, events, and cultural changes of face it manages to fit into itself.

Lev Tolstoy, who saw the dawn of the age of Nekrasov, Turgenev, and Dostoevsky, lived for eighty-two years and was still alive when the cinematograph and aviation first made their appearance. It's hard to imagine what he felt when he looked, say, at an aviator—he who had seen firsthand the rather frightening chestnut cloth of the overcoats of the Sevastopol sailors, now relegated to the museum.[5] Why, he was a contemporary of the Russo-Japanese war! That means he heard about searchlights and *mitrailleuses* and the Whitehead torpedo—he who had had to decide at Sevastopol whether to bow before cannonballs or not.

I remember the day Tolstoy died. It was the noon recess at the gymnasium, and the sunlight fell in pillars through the classroom windows on chalk dust still suspended in the air from the erasure of something on the blackboard. Suddenly, a voice was heard in the hallway:

"Tolstoy died!"

I ran outside and already it was everywhere:

"Tolstoy died! Tolstoy died!"

A lot has been fit into my life too. The day Tolstoy died, for example, or the young woman I saw reading *Anna Karenina* on a subway escalator yesterday, a young woman who was used to technology and who without looking or fear of falling stepped from the escalator onto solid ground, her hand sliding along the wandering rail.

I can say that a great technology appeared right before my eyes.

Just so: it still didn't exist when I was a boy . . . Windows then were completely unlike the ones we look through today. Instead of black power lines or electric streetlights you saw cobblestone streets or a passing horse-drawn cab or a government official walking by dressed in a visored uniform cap and carrying a folded umbrella under his arm. The roofs were etched in uncluttered silhouette against the sunset, and if anything seemed new and unprecedented to the eye, it was the zinc downspout. When it rained, a wide fan of water poured from it, and the stars of zinc, wet from the rain, were very beautiful. Zinc was truly a novelty, something much talked about, and people would stop to look at it, lifting their heads and directing their gazes upward along the pipe that with its bright silvery color stood out vividly against the stones of the wall.

"Zinc!" they would observe portentously.

You could feel the approach of something.

Then electric lights appeared.

That was a wonder.

When I want a clear sense of what has happened in technology, I consider the fact that I, somebody born a mere seventy-eight years after the death of Napoleon (so that between that event and my birth there stands but a single old man), yet live in a time when one of the creators of cybernetics could claim that in principle it's possible for a human being to be transmitted by telegraph wire!

I, for example, clearly recall the appearance of the first electric light bulbs.

They weren't the kind we see today, which reach their full incandescence in an instant, but bulbs that attained the required degree of luminosity only slowly and gradually. I think that's right . . . Possibly I'm confusing different memories and have in mind not a bulb for domestic use but something else I saw at the time. Probably, even domestic light bulbs of the very earliest era were of the so-called economical variety and could be turned on at once.

Whatever the case, I remember a crowd of neighbors from other apartments who had come to see our electric light.

It hung above the table in the dining room and didn't have any lampshade. Its bulb was screwed into a socket surrounded by a white disk that served as a reflector and light amplifier. I should point out that the whole device wasn't badly made—with an industrial elegance. By means of a no less elegantly made pulley and some tightly laced green cable, you could raise and lower the lamp by taking hold of the disk. Of course, the light from that lamp was naked and harsh, as in an entrance booth today.

But it was light of a new, unprecedented kind, the kind called by the then unfamiliar, astounding, barely understandable name "electric."

The sound of the cable running through the pulley is easy for me to restore to memory. So is the sight of the dozen or so faces gazing upward, their eyes fixed on the light source, on the light-emitting glass pear suspended from the ceiling.

I was strictly forbidden to play with the switch.

Just as now, it stood out black against the wallpaper. But children now are quite indifferent to light switches, and it's impossible to imagine any child who would want to play with one.

I remember standing with a crowd on Grechesky Street and waiting with everyone else for the appearance of the streetcar that had that day just gone into service for the first time. It would come around the corner of Kanatny Street, but from where we stood that corner wasn't visible, being hidden in the perspectival distance by the slight rise of Stroganovsky Bridge. We thus wouldn't be able to see the streetcar until it had reached the middle of the bridge.

Everyone was sure the streetcar would be lightning fast, so fast you wouldn't even have time to consider whether or not you could run across the street in front of it.

The streetcar came into view on the bridge, yellow and red with a glass-enclosed platform in front, moving quite fast, though far from the speed we had imagined. Greeted by our cheers, it passed by, the platform crowded with people, among whom were a high-ranking priest who sprinkled water in front and the mayor of Odessa, Tolmachyov, who wore glasses and had a ginger mustache. A gentleman in a derby stood behind the controls, and everyone spoke his name:

"Legoder!"

He was the director of the Belgian firm that had built that first streetcar line in Odessa.

I don't remember how, having only just seen a streetcar, I got used to the idea of riding on one . . . Certainly the period of adjustment didn't take long . . . Shortly after that first encounter, I was already riding on the streetcar without a thought, paying my five kopecks like everyone else, standing on the rear platform, and trying to grab hold of the branches rushing past.

In photographs, on the horizontal bar, and in conversation I saw reflected the feverish quavering of thought on the verge of discovering the secret of flight for machines heavier than air . . . But that secret would not reveal itself. The machines failed to rise into the air, thus provoking the derision of journalists. I sincerely sympathized with the people they mocked—the first aviation designers, lean, wiry men in caps with a button on the crown, turtleneck sweaters, and leather breeches with spanner wrenches of the type we called "French" sticking out of their pockets.

Suddenly the news spread that a machine constructed by brothers named Wright had got off the ground and flown a considerable distance. The brothers—one was called Wilbur and the other, Orville—were Americans. They conducted demonstration flights in Paris, and I remember a photograph in which their machine was shown skirting the Eiffel Tower. Not only could it fly, it could also circle; it was a machine whose direction could be controlled.

The aviation pavilion appealed to me most of all. Appealed to me? It bewitched me! It deprived me of the gift of speech! It would not let me go!

What was it, that pavilion? It was a building of colossal dimensions, but relatively insubstantial, since it was a many-storied void, a single hall . . .

I entered a huge barn, truly huge, in which swallows were freely darting . . . A huge barn full of golden summer shade where my eyes first had to adjust to the diminished light and where, abruptly and instantaneously, they saw several objects of strange appearance with wheels and wings. Those were the so-called aeroplanes, which had been transported from Europe for an exhibition in Odessa and then brought to that pavilion or barn some distance from the rest of the exhibition near its back entrance in a vacant lot full of unmown weeds and buttercups . . .

The aeroplanes were parked in such a way that when I entered the pavilion, each was turned with its nose toward me—its nose and engine-forehead bisected by a propeller.

It was announced that Ernesto Vitollo would jump by parachute—from a balloon, obviously, since at the time there was still no question of any other mode of flight.

I say it was announced, but how was that accomplished? By poster or by newspaper advertisement? I don't recall . . . There wasn't any radio, of course, and certainly no television. In short, it was passed by word of mouth: "Vitollo! Vitollo! What kind of jump? What's that? How will he jump? Vitollo!"

And then one bright blue afternoon, a balloon lit up the sky.

The parachute, by the way, remained a novelty for a long time, and even after I had become a writer, even during Soviet times and the period of the new technology, I remember going to an aerodrome with the express purpose of marveling at such a jump, and seeing the visiting German parachutist walk before the crowd to display the parachute on his back much as a magician's box might be shown to an audience at the circus in order to assure it that it will not be deceived . . .

Andronka and I were certain we could make a jump with a parachute of our own design. I can no longer say just what sort of construction we had in mind. It seemed a very easy matter to make something on the order of a large umbrella—a rigid circle with shrouds made of ordinary string drawn together in a single point, if not simply in a knot, which we would then hold on to as we made our jumps.

We stood on the third-floor landing of the iron stairway that rose in zigzags up the wall of our building to hang suspended above the courtyard. That courtyard, part asphalt, part cobblestone, part dirt, was right below us as we looked at down at it from a mere three stories up! All the same, we discussed with complete seriousness jumping into it by parachute, or rather merely by umbrella.

We failed to carry out that experiment not because we changed our minds or had second thoughts, but because of some other, most likely material reason. People's heads then were filled with thoughts of flight, and the dream of flying was dominant and overpowering. I had seen a parachute jump made by the touring skydiver Ernesto Vitollo, who traveled the world demonstrating those seemingly phenomenal leaps. He jumped from a balloon risen so high in the sky that it looked like a shining yellow speck. Of course, nobody on the ground could see the moment of his separation from the balloon (I stood in the middle of a crowd on Pushkin Street) but suddenly the whole city cried out, and we saw the incomparable manifestation out of nothing at all but the quiet over our heads of a small bright yellow shell that drifted slowly and obliquely toward the Stock Exchange . . . And so that first parachutist jumped right over the city, unafraid of all the possible dangers.

And then Max Linder.[6] It's hard for me to convey just how famous Max Linder was. Perfume, cigarettes, ties, women's overshoes, cuts of clothing, hairdos, and styles of behavior were all named after him.

"Max Linder!" you would hear on the street. "Max Linder!"

He was a small, elegant, restless young man, good-looking with black eyes and a thin mustache, whom we always saw nattily dressed. Max Linder's top hat. How much attention it attracted then.

He was of such small stature that when I climbed up onto the fence that surrounded the cafe, I saw his top hat from above. Exactly right, he was extremely small, tiny in fact, a little dandy in a top hat and black cloak with a cape, good-looking with a mustache.

We waited for him at the cafe, and then he arrived.

"Max Linder! Max Linder!"

I hung from the fence, grasping its iron filigree and holding in my cramped palms crumpled leaves as well, since the fence was entwined with ivy of some kind.

That took place in the evening in an era when floodlights still weren't used outdoors and electric lighting still wasn't very bright. Max Linder's mustache glowed just as it would have if the ends had been lit with a candle. His cheeks were rosy and his eyes glistened.

He was greeted by applause, and then he passed between railings of some kind and disappeared from me forever. Well, what of it? At least I got to see him once. He and his young wife committed suicide together. Chaplin called him his teacher. Max Linder, by the way, commented on Chaplin's great gifts as a composer. We are convinced of the rightness of that opinion.

"Max Linder!"

His name was known far and wide. It became a common noun. To be a "Max Linder" meant to be a dandy.

I tracked down that movie house, and I do mean track down and not set off for it along some customary route. I only knew that it was on Gradonachalnichesky Street. First came a Lutheran church you had to go around. I went around it, a bit intimidated by the gloom behind its statues. In the spring—and that spring too—flowers would appear in the church's front garden, flowers on narrow shrubs . . .

The city on the other side of the church was unknown to me. I was afraid to go there. Why? Was it class fear of poorer neighborhoods?

In any event, I did find that movie house. It was called the "Giant." By present standards, it was an ordinary movie theater, but for those days an exceptionally large one . . .

Today in a dream I saw my whole life in the abbreviated images of art.

Once when I was a small schoolboy, I went to an eye doctor, not, obviously, on my own initiative (certainly not) but in accordance with the will of the gymnasium authorities who had decided I needed glasses.

I remember with astounding clarity the building entrance filled with late afternoon sunshine, the twisting flight of stairs, the landing, the door. And I remember too that in those moments I was thinking about my life—thinking about it, in short, just as I am now. More than forty years have passed since then, but it feels like only half an hour. I thought in that entrance about how hard it is to be a human being. I was only about eleven, but already I was given to anxiety. I remember the doctor's telling me I needed to take care of my eyes. It's funny, over forty years ago I needed to protect my eyes! The eye examination itself has passed from memory, but I do recall going down Deribasovsky Street past Rosenblit's cinematograph and seeing before those same eyes a shining circle floating in the autumn air. That's me in the new glasses prescribed by the doctor. I even remember the way my voice sounded when I told my schoolmates about that circle. My goodness, I even remember the sound of my schoolmates' voices! It happened in the evening, in the fall, as I've already said, and because there was slush all around and a drizzle was falling, that spectral circle glittered all the more . . .

Grandma is already waking me for the third time.

"Yes, yes, in a moment," I reply. "Just a moment . . ."

All the same I have to get up. And I do. It's still night in the room, and the lamp burns as if it had never been turned off. It's dead of night in the hallway, lampless with phantoms still lurking.

I wash with icy winter water from the tap. It's still night in the kitchen too, but perhaps because the light in that room is weaker, I see in the window what appear to be intimations of the coming day, still dark blue like iron.

In the distance whistles are blowing, imparting a sadness so poignant it seems irreparable. Especially when you have to go to school.

It's easier after a glass of tea. Then a piece of bread with butter you get smeared on your fingers. How fast asleep Mama and Papa are behind their white door. It seems as if they aren't even there, it's so quiet. The protruding lips of the keyhole are the only things alive in that door. Perhaps I have neither a mama nor a papa and am alone? Neither a grandmother nor a sister but am alone? Who am I, then? Who am I? The person I gaze at in the mirror, still dark like water, doesn't answer. There's a face there in the mirror and something remarkable—a face with two . . . With two what? Are they eyes? Why are there two of them when only one person stares back? Is that me? What can you compare eyes to? They're quiet and they look. They're quiet, but it seems that they speak. What is it they're saying?

But Mama and Papa are there, and so are my grandmother and sister. And so is the day that already stands on every street and lane and even in the building entrances when I go out—a white, rather dirty November day crisscrossed with branches, yet somehow pleasant. Isn't it because there's a poster with a clown and the day is Saturday and thus will end with a visit to the circus?

My route was invariably the same. Once out the gate of our building on Karantinny, I went left to the intersection with Grechesky, turned right onto Grechesky, and then after crossing Stroganovsky Bridge went up Grechesky to Richelieu. There I turned right and went one more block on Richelieu, then turned left onto Deribasovsky.

Deribasovsky was the main part of my route. Both in size and in significance. It was Odessa's main street, better decked out than the rest and with the best shops.

I almost always hurried since I was afraid of being late, yet as far as I can remember I was late only once in eight years of going to school.

That route was surrounded with rituals and run through with superstitions and incantations. Certain sidewalk squares couldn't be omitted, for example, but had to be stepped in whatever the cost. Or the enormous old oak tree on Deribasovsky that had to be gone all the way around . . . Otherwise something unlucky might happen at the gymnasium, like getting a bad mark.

In Chernyavsky's leather goods shop there was a model of a horse. Or not a model, perhaps, but simply a stuffed animal. Yes, probably a stuffed animal, since individual hairs stuck out on it just as on a live horse.

It was a lean horse with a narrow neck, a kind I'd never seen before, a so-called hunter, most likely. It had a saddle with stirrups that hung down over its cardboardlike sides. I very much wanted to sit in that saddle and put my feet in those stirrups. It seems to me that even now I can see the eye of that hunter—a huge, brilliant black button . . .

I hadn't the faintest idea how poetry was written. I was a schoolboy, and we learned poems by heart: Pushkin, Lermontov, Pleshcheev, Krylov's fables, Dmitriev, the syllabic verse of Kantemir, the poems of Maikov.[7]

Maikov's "Who Is He?" was about Peter the Great and how he galloped around out-of-the-way places in the region where Petersburg was being built, and upon meeting a peasant, engaged him in conversation.

I remember,

There went a rider fighting through
To river Neva's radiant shores.[8]

We declaimed the memorized lines in front of the dais while facing the class.

"Recite the verses."

And wrinkling our brows and blinking with the effort to remember all the way to the end, we recited them.

We recited the fables with expression, in an almost old-womanish, didactic manner, perhaps even in the style of the Maly Theater, although being Odessa boys, we didn't know very much about that.[9]

When I was a schoolboy, the name Mayakovsky was already familiar to me, although not as the name of a poet but as a frightening word: it was the name of a very strict teacher.

He taught history.

Usually the Latin teachers are the school terrors. That's understandable. Latin is a subject requiring obligatory daily study from which your attention may not wander even for a moment . . . Failure to consider where to insert even the most insignificant little screw in that language-machine is enough for the whole thing to come tumbling down, burying the unfortunate schoolboy beneath. Hence the fear of Latinists. But history, if you will, is a lengthy, drawn-out, fluid sort of affair that can be managed without constant, concentrated attention. Nevertheless, the teacher, whose name was Ilya Lukich Mayakovsky, inspired in us an incomparable schoolboy fear, the kind capable of living on even after we have come to understand it, and of appearing, for example, in our dreams long after we have left our school days behind.

Though terrifying, the teacher was good-looking. With his dark blue uniform, sallow Mongol complexion, slanting Mongol cheekbones, black beard, and sleek rather than slender build, he looked something like Boris Godunov.

And now he enters the classroom. When forty boys simultaneously come to their feet, throwing back the tops of their desks to do so, the resulting sound is quite impressive, resembling a gust of wind. Into the room with its forty boys, Mayakovsky brings his black eyes, the dark blue patch of his uniform, and the peculiar hush that descends on a frightened class . . .

It was an utter surprise to hear during my first Latin lesson that Latin was the language spoken by the Romans.

"The language of our forebears, the Romans," said the gymnasium headmaster, who usually taught first-year Latin to the second-year class.

It seems odd to me now that the headmaster should have called the Romans our forebears, that is, of us Russian schoolboys . . . Of course, that isn't what he meant; he was speaking in general of the ancestors of our civilization. But that "the Romans spoke Latin" was unexpected and astonishing.

What? Those helmeted warriors with short swords and bucklers, those fantastic figures, some with beards and others with faces as if chiseled from stone—they spoke that difficult language?

I knew that the Catholic priest spoke Latin during the worship service. The priest was a figure from a world of mysteries, fears, threats, and punishments, and now suddenly his language was spoken by warriors who marched across the desert holding their bucklers before them and brandishing whole bunches of short swords like palm leaves? For me that was one of life's most astounding novelties.

I didn't realize then that the Church had adopted Latin from ancient Rome.

He had the fresh fragrance of eau de cologne, and his little beard was clean and bright. I swear he really did seem handsome to me . . . That blue uniform, that little head tipped elegantly to the side. I caught myself wanting to be like him when I grew up, to be like "Spats."

He taught Latin.

He had a head like that of Peter I on a small and moreover apoplectic trunk, although his cheeks were perhaps fuller than Peter's. He wore an especially blue, or rather light blue, uniform with strikingly pronounced flaps that fluttered as he walked down the hall through the honeyed sunlight.

His knowledge of literature was of course negligible. He called on us, asked questions, and gave out marks. I don't remember his teaching at all.

Our studies were approaching their conclusion—the seventh year. We already held sway in class, and the teachers paid court to many of us.

Now it seems to me that he looked not only like Peter I but also like a pudgy girl with a grave yet bewildered look on her face. If I close my eyes I can see him sitting there on the dais with his brilliant black hair brushed straight back, the little pink lumps of his hands, and the strata of doubt on his forehead.

Mathematics was taught by Nikolai Vasilievich Akimovich. In rank he was a state counselor, and a star therefore sat on the tab of each lapel of his dark blue double-breasted jacket.[10] Of those stars you could only say that they sat. Fluffy and of fine silver thread, they really did sit the way snowflakes do.

Akimovich was our friend—Mama and Papa's.

"The counselor!" my father's exclamation would suddenly be heard in the foyer.

That meant that Akimovich had arrived.

Most often it was connected with an evening's card game. They had dinner. It was awful to see my teacher peacefully at rest, so to speak, his gray beard in his fist. All of a sudden he would start looking at me. No, no, not to call me to account. On the contrary, he was only joking.

"Counselor," Papa said, "shall we have some beer?"

They sent me to get it. Akimovich was already tight. He tried to be witty about the fact that I was the one getting the beer. On the whole he was a kind man, neither dried up nor a tormentor—a good man. We were fond of him . . .

Where was beer sold? In the same grocery stores where they sold everything else, I think. Enni beer.

"No, no, anything but Enni!" Papa yelled after me. "Sanzenbacher!"

A short stretch of blossoming street led to the grocery store. The corner, the overhang of a large building, then steps you ran down. And then the little shop. And the grocer . . . No, it's his wife. She's standing on the other side of some barrels containing groats, flour, and rice. In each barrel is a very dry wooden scoop.

French was taught by Whitman, whose first name and patronymic were Panteleimon Karlovich. Not exactly common names for a Russian or for a Frenchman either. The general view was that he was Alsatian. He was a superb man who never got involved in conflicts with the students, a man without any hint of the formalism, red tape, and the like that in the other teachers gave rise to sadism.

We were all afraid of the headmaster. He really was terrifying. In appearance he was tall and emaciated, a gaunt man with a goatee who fairly flew through the gleaming hallways.

Sometimes he would enter a classroom without warning in a way that was always like the conclusion of a stormy blast of wind.

Whew!

That was forty boys coming to their feet. Forty heads faced the door. He stood in the doorway for a moment like a bird of prey, if a bird of prey could be tall and rear up on hind legs.

Tik-tik-tik-tik . . .

That was us sitting down.

He walked tall and erect but with a slight stoop, as if he were carrying the burden of knowing just how mean and base we pupils were. Oh, he was very theatrical. His every step was calculated to induce fear.

For example, why had he come?

Gymnastics was taught at the gymnasium by the wrestler Pytlyasinsky. He was an ex-world champion, an old war horse, or rather bull, although he wasn't a bull either, but a whale perched on its tail. No, he wasn't a whale either. He was simply an old wrestler dressed not in tights on a half-naked body as in the arena, but in a cheap three-piece suit, and the fact that he was a wrestler was evident from the inhuman breadth of his shoulders, his bulging calves, and his small head.

We were connoisseurs of the circus, and we anticipated Pytlyasinsky's arrival as something sensational.

"Pytlyasinsky!"

He appeared in front of our line, coming out of a small recess in the wall surrounding the courtyard. He entered the courtyard as he would have come into the arena, with his customary springy athletic gait. He was extraordinary, strange, alluring, with a simple face like that of a soldier or a Polish peasant but with a wrestler's cheekbones and little mustache, though sailors could have those cheekbones and mustaches too.

Those were the last years before the birth of sport in its contemporary form, before that international novelty that was subsequently fated to glitter so brightly before the world. Furthermore, gymnastics at the time wasn't especially widespread in the schools. It's even possible Sokol gymnastics appeared after the day the ex-champion of the world took his place in front of our line. I'm describing the period 1910–12 . . . Actually, I think the Prague Sokols were already twirling those wooden bottles with the colored stickers on their narrow necks . . .[11]

Be that as it may, the czarist regime still didn't know exactly what gymnastics was or what it was for. And that was why the school had decided to get as a teacher of gymnastics a former wrestler—to try it out. Pytlyasinsky didn't know how it was done either, and he came out to us with a baffled expression on his face. Yet here he turned a new page in my life, one so remarkable that in leafing through that book I stop on it time and again: Pytlyasinsky began teaching us how to jump.

Two tall rods fixed in crossbar stands and a long rope with a small, heavy bag attached to each end were brought out. There were factory-drilled holes the length of each rod, and the wrestler drove a wooden peg through a hole in one rod and then another peg through a hole in the other . . .

We understood.

"A rope!" spread through the line. "A rope!"

The rope rested on the pegs, stretched between the rods just as a tape marking the end of a race might have been extended between two poles. The two bags hung down to the ground on either side, pulling the rope so taut that it shimmered.

Rackets were given out in the so-called training room by an instructor named Ivan Stepanovich, who took them from a cabinet, catching several basketballs, large gym shoes, and boxing gloves that tumbled out at the same time.

He didn't like giving out the rackets, the most expensive items in his inventory. He was sure they would be damaged in the hands of the rough and careless schoolboy . . . And the gleaming gold of their strings really did impart to them the appearance of particular value, of belonging to a special world of beauty . . .

Two balls were handed out as well, very round and elastic—small white spheres with a terrific power of flight and impact hidden in them, balls that rebounded the instant they touched the racket's strings, causing the latter to sing.

Although Ivan Stepanovich was the sports instructor on the gymnasium playground, he was still a faculty member and wore the teacher's double-breasted jacket and uniform cap.

"Careful!" he warned, glancing at the rackets. "Just be careful!"

Outside the training room door summer waited with a full growth of grass, flowers, and trees. The shadow of a poplar flew at me like a dirigible . . .

The superintendent of the Odessa school district was Shcherbakov. He was a hunchback whom I saw only once when he came into our classroom dressed in the polygon of his dark blue uniform, holding his arms out wide as hunchbacks do, shorter than the other people who were with him but wider—a polygon-shaped figure with a small plowlike chest right under his chin.

He stayed for the lesson. The pupils answered questions and he listened. The whole time he was there I saw only his hands, first in front of his face where they looked like the two halves of a partly opened gate still rocking in the wind, then as they scattered in different directions like . . .

This passage shall remain unfinished. Go on sitting, hunchback, at the green table with the two giraffelike rows of your uniform buttons, the dusty tabs of your blue velvet collar, and the two stars of a state counselor amid the dust—two centipede stars.

Long live colorful language!

There were two Protopopov brothers, one of them ahead of us in class. They were in all likelihood Bulgarians. And there were three Lyakhnitsky brothers. At first, there was only one in our class—Volodya . . . The two older ones were ahead of us. But gradually all three were united as the two older boys fell further and further behind. Then all three Lyakhnitskys, who looked just like one another with their laughing monkey mouths, were sitting in the back of our classroom. Then the war. One Lyakhnitsky left school early and became an officer serving in an Odessa guard unit. Suddenly, we learned that he'd killed himself while on duty, shooting himself in the mouth. Then the White Guard movement.[12] One Protopopov was killed in the Don region on the side of the capitalists and landowners. Where Volodya Lyakhnitsky is now is unknown to me, it's hidden from me, although I can still see him in the form of a squiggling line on a sheet of paper . . . There it is! Look! Now a tiny man has already appeared on the paper, now a dog, and now a caricature of Seryozha Protopopov, who of course could draw better than I.

Of all the colors, the most beautiful is carmine. And its name is beautiful too. Why is it called "carmine"? Doesn't it come from shellfish? What could be nicer than holding in your hand a brush that has just been dipped in carmine? And now it begins to lie down on the heavy drawing paper, giving birth to a poppy petal—a little tongue that almost sways on the paper as in a breeze . . .

I'm interested in only one thing now: to learn to write abundantly and fluently. Let it be about the color carmine or about poppies, let it be about . . .

Let it be a story about a drawing class at the gymnasium, when seated in the assembly hall we drew a stuffed hawk from life. The drawing teacher was Ivan Arkhipovich Arkhipov, a flaxen blond dressed in an almost light blue tunic that fluttered as he walked among us, addressing approving words to each.

"What's this? Why, he just lays it on! Take a look!" he exclaimed, stopping next to Kolya Danchev.

He was especially fond of Kolya Danchev.

Kolya Danchev was a Bulgarian. There were a lot of them in Odessa, a whole colony. Besides the Danchevs, there were the Rasheevs, the Bolgarovs, the Gulevs, and the Uvalievs. Danchev wasn't rich, but he was still a landowner, so we teased him about his wealthy connections. He had a large nose often afflicted by colds, and he was strong, although a bit unsteady on his feet, as strong boys sometimes are . . .

I drew and painted all night with watercolors, working on a picture intended to decorate a little program that was supposed to be presented to one of the high-ranking guests at a school concert the next day. I think I drew a folklore warrior hacking a bear with his sword. Samokish-Sudkovsky? Vasnetsov?[13] Obviously, I drew and painted fairly well if that little program was meant to be given to a distinguished guest the following day . . . I don't remember the drawing and painting as such, but I do remember how tired I was and how my eyelids stuck together . . . I remember sitting at the dining-room table, alone in the sleeping apartment, the windows at my back looking out onto the courtyard and the night. I remember the warrior's face and beard under his helmet and my fear of making a wrong stroke with the slender brush holding brilliant green or carmine. Behind me were the windows, and a little farther on Stroganovsky Bridge stretched out over the grassy streets of the port, and still farther on steamships from Italy and England with Negroes asleep in their cabins. And somewhere in a room I never saw slept Polya Ausheva, a short schoolgirl with a hard, white face, a hard, white little nose, and eyes that peer out at me now from behind the wallpaper.

Polya Ausheva! A few years later she became an actress, a second-rate actress in a regional theater, as people would say now. Nonetheless, I waited for the hour when on my way up Grechesky I would pass by her window on the other side of the street and see her sitting there as she always did at that time, always responding to my nod.

Mileev drew, imitating Vrubel.[14] Actually, he didn't draw, he painted with watercolors. Small sheets of heavy drawing paper and on them representations of something like the kingdom of Berendei as it might have been depicted in an opera or burned into the top of a wooden box.[15] The resemblance to Vrubel was probably evident from the fact that in the paint thickly covering the little sheets the lilac had been mixed with ceruse. Ceruse, as everybody knows, is alien to watercolors, and its presence thus seemed extravagant and radical. But that was Vrubel. Obviously, the names of the artists contemporary to us meant very little to those sitting in that class, and the art teacher had brought Vrubel to our attention by singling out Mileev as one of his disciples. There was something annoying in that alliance between teacher and pupil, especially to me. I felt that the priestly disdain exhibited by Mileev in all his relations with us lacked any basis. On the contrary, I sensed that he had no talent at all, and that nothing is easier than to pass yourself off as a genius by imitating a nonconformist.

Mileev seriously believed he was a genius. I remember to this day looking at his pictures, which resembled, as I now realize, sketches for operatic scenes. He was the tenth, indeed the hundredth, echo of that Vrubel who himself didn't seem especially remarkable—the Vrubel of *The Daydream Princess.*[16]

I saw Mileev once again long after we had left the gymnasium behind. He was swollen and sickly yet haughty—a classic type of the man of unrecognized talents. I naturally asked him what he was doing, how he kept himself busy, and he replied in a manner that in substance and tone was mainly calculated to counter what he supposed to be my attack, although it had been nothing of the kind.

There were, by the way, two truly gifted artists in our class who displayed their ability not in watercolors, where it's possible, after all, to be inaccurate and still make an impression, but in pen and ink. They were illustrators, caricaturists, who, I now believe, were in brilliant control of that medium, a difficult one requiring genuine craft. And they were only seventeen! One was Seryozha Protopopov and the other was Volodya Lyakhnitsky. The charming thing about them was that each would say of the other, "He draws so well, whereas my stuff's just rubbish." Seryozha Protopopov was ugly with the captivating ugliness that suggests genius: he lisped and laughed with a cramped little mouth that made him pucker up his young face like an old woman . . . Volodya Lyakhnitsky was a monkeylike boy who also liked to laugh, but with a highly capacious grin—from ear to ear—a boy who was fond of practical jokes, yet who time and again revealed a great and generous heart.

"Look! Look how Seryozhka draws!" he would exclaim, waving a picture on which the schoolroom ink was still wet.

I marveled at them both, and now when I think of those people of talent I've known, I'm prepared to come to the conclusion that those two—that pair of strange, youthful, carefree, loudly laughing boys—were masters, and that it is they who hover and soar like cherubim with trumpets at the corners of the charter of my life, the life of an artist.

Seryozha Todorovich was one of the handsomest boys in class, although he was perhaps a bit plump for his age . . . And it's true we did sometimes make fun of his chubbiness, slapping him on the behind. But he was handsome all the same: that profile with its filigreed nose and those prominent blue eyes . . .

He and I sat at the same desk. He was a weak student who copied his written work from me, for which he got bad marks. But he laughed and never lost his jolly disposition. He wasn't even particularly upset by his chronic gonorrhea. Dressed in a light blue uniform with an expensive patent leather belt, elegantly plump, and living in a good apartment since his father was a government lawyer, he generally prospered and was happy.

He was gently stupid is how I'd put it—gently stupid.

Skshivan was a sickly boy, very sickly, which sometimes manifested itself in front of everyone when suddenly during a lesson he would have an attack of nausea ending in vomiting. He was a Pole and his first name was Faddei, or Tadeusz in Polish, and his lips were of a characteristically Polish design, as if continuously compressed for smacking—a pale boy with slightly sallow cheekbones and streaky blond hair.

The headmaster, who was a complete boor and who moreover paraded his boorishness, treated Skshivan with a kind of emphatic courtesy. I have no idea why, since Skshivan belonged neither to a rich family nor to a bureaucratic one . . . Perhaps some intimate reason played a role here, some woman remote from the gymnasium who was close to the headmaster . . .

One of those who sat at the first desk in the middle row—ahead of me in the channel, so to speak—was Sperande. He was a small boy built on a miniature scale and very fast, so provocatively fast, in fact, that everyone wanted to catch him. He was constantly pursued in the hallway and in the courtyard; boys of every age ran after him, and, occasionally, even some of the teachers. So Sperande remains in my memory in the act of fleeing somebody . . . And on all sides they cried:

"Spirka! Spirka! Faster! Spirka!"

And with a squeal, Spirka ran in several directions at once, flew off between two acacias into the sky-blue expanse, jumped across a wooden step, and even—and this was forbidden—ran out into the street, where he was straightaway pursued and where both the chaser and the chased abruptly came to a halt. Out of breath, they slowly returned to the courtyard . . .

I suppose he was a little Greek, that Sperande-Spirka. Of course, the color of his mane was yellow and his small nose was pointed, so perhaps he wasn't Greek after all. Thus does he run through my memory, that Spirka, who was probably killed long ago fighting with the White Guards in the Don campaign, or, the other way around, with the soldiers of the Latvian Division.[17] It's possible too that he lives somewhere in Athens and serves on the Greek police force or owns a little shop. And it's even possible that now and again he dreams, as I do, of the gymnasium and of that little corner full of fresh smells rushing in, where, grabbing our coats, we schoolboys crowded together, swearing at each other and kissing each other, knowing that in a moment we would run out into the street and fly away on acacia wings.

Where did Lukashevker go? Why, home for lunch. It was exactly at noon, or a little after, when the sun made its turn beneath the celestial dome. Lukashevker carried his stout body in front of me, inasmuch as he had just said good-bye. He carried his fat body clothed in its gymnasium uniform among the flower beds and glass spheres of that splendid manorial front garden, carried it toward the cool, rich black front door that stood on the other side of a flower bed with sculptures of lilies and gladioli.

I felt somewhat better than I do now as I entered his apartment with Grishka Silberberg, who had invited me home as his guest . . .

Probably I felt good because I was still very young, was still a boy, a healthy boy who did his lessons well and who sensed that many interesting things lay ahead of him. The elder Silberberg was a wealthy man; Grishka had his own room, for example. We were greeted in that room by disorder—a yellow, wooden disorder, attractive rather than oppressive, I would say. I think there was even a rocking horse perched on two wooden bows that had been left over from childhood.

A complete nonentity, even in the gymnasium scheme of things. True, he was a handsome lad, with golden hair and black eyes. His last name was Shiyan.

"Pavka Shiyan!"

Thus he pops phonetically from the least interesting folds of consciousness—a mere phonogram, a transcription not even of his own voice but of other voices calling him:

"Pavka!"

And suddenly an image appears as well . . . A sunny day, the descent down Grechesky from Pushkin Street to Polsky, past the gate and past the Melisaratos' pastry shop—a sunny little section of street beneath the trees, and we were walking on that section, or rather, in it—a few of us, a few young people, although I couldn't name them all.

That was a very, very long time ago. A different social order, a different world. There were the war and the czar and chasubles; there were icons borne in carriages—large dark images in proximity to the trouser stripes and military tunic of the chief of police; there were the blue cupolas of churches; and there were sailors with little mustaches and barrel chests . . .

Two of those sailors came down the hill toward us past the Melisaratos' pastry shop.

"Bastard!" Pavka Shiyan said to one of them. "Bastard!"

Pavka Shiyan had just become an officer two or three days before.

The golden head, the golden epaulets, the golden double-breasted jacket . . .

"Bastard!"

"I beg your pardon," said the one with the soft little mustache, a handsome man, neat, with a healthy flush. "I beg your pardon, sir."

The two of them stood at attention, two adults . . .

We waited for him to appear, and when we saw he was already nearby, we occupied our places with even greater calculation so that as he continued on his way he would meet each of us in turn—first one, then the next, then the third, and each of us boys stood at attention and saluted him.

The general returned our salutes with extraordinary seriousness and courtesy. His overcoat, whether from a gust of wind or from some movement on his part, suddenly revealed its red lining, and it was that moment that pleased us most of all. The general had a slightly graying mustache that curved down over his lip and made him look like Alexander I. His last name was Ignatiev, so that he was perhaps a relative of the author of *Fifty Years in the Service*.[18] Of course, if he had been, he would have been a count, and he wasn't.

I remember some so clearly it seems we've only just parted.

Grishka Berberov and I were walking across sunlight-flooded Stroganovsky Bridge. I don't know where we were going. Maybe we were coming back from somewhere . . . There was never any shadow on the bridge. The only shadows belonged to pedestrians, very black, round-headed shadows . . .

Below through the bars of the railing lay the port. But later about the port. Later about the port. Now about Berberov. He was the son of a barber, a pale, slender, freckled Jew who knew many secrets, a wicked boy with a man's prominent gaze. He had a sunken chest with an adult nose suspended above it. His last name was African . . . Grishka carried a lot of weight among the schoolboys: he was repeating his class. But the main thing was that he knew secrets, that he knew secrets . . .

We stopped above the port and looked down. There in the sparkling depths were cobblestones, and among them grass.

"Let's go, let's go," said the unpoetic Berberov. "Let's go."

"Where?"

Maybe he would acquaint me with some of his secrets.

Just after I had entered the gymnasium and was, although in uniform, still a small boy walking through the halls marveling at the grown-up students, the news suddenly spread that one of them—Olshevsky—had committed suicide, shooting himself with a revolver. How was that to be understood? The act did, in any case, fill us with profound awe, and we elementary students crept up to the door of the classroom to which the suicide had belonged and called out, "Olshevsky!" frightening, so we thought, his schoolmates within . . . Little fools! How did we ever come to imagine that poor youth as a ghost? I don't remember why he shot himself. We wouldn't have understood anyway if we had learned, say, that the reason was syphilis. That was a common occurrence then. Sometime, I shall tell how, when we were older, one of my classmates, the son of a Greek baker, after learning he had caught the disease, fell down on his knees before us all, cynics for the most part, and prayed, begging God for a miracle—to be healed . . . I saw that ulcer, that terrible hard chancre, through whose crater so many lives cast themselves into oblivion. I shall tell of that and also of the great Glavche, the leading Russian venereologist of his day, who did not recognize the ulcer as syphilitic, giving one to understand that some physicians were making fortunes even there—on that fear that now and again cost a life.

I was eleven years old and sitting in a circus building for the Greco-Roman wrestling championships. Since it was summertime and the circuses were closed for the season, that particular one had been turned into a kind of combination circus and movie theater; that is, an enormous screen had been hung above the arena and the seats rearranged so that the spectators could look at the screen. The wrestling obviously took place on some sort of platform in front of the screen, although I'm unable to restore it to memory.

But that isn't the point. The point is that in order to see better I kept raising myself up, or rather kept standing up, no doubt making a nuisance of myself. And one of those times when I got up, I—a young schoolboy, capable, intelligent, and in general an individual undemanding of the world—was restrained from behind by someone's heavy hands.

"If you permit yourself to get up again," I heard, "I shall remove you from the circus."

I was shaken by a sensation of enormous anger accumulated against me in a person I still couldn't see. And then I saw him. It was the police superintendent Radchenko, a well-known figure in Odessa. In his own way, he was even handsome in his gray military overcoat and black mustache. There the recollection ends. I remember only a feeling of insult that was clearly the same one felt by the student terrorists, although on a different scale.

No sooner had we come to terms with the fact that one of our number had fallen into its terrible clutches than it became known that he had been defeated. Having just got up on a winter morning, having barely removed our wraps in the cloakroom, it was quite distressing to learn that Volodya Dolgov had died.

Yes, that's right, from scarlet fever. What could have been more terrifying than that word? Even the sound "scarla" made me shudder. It's different in other languages. In German, for example, it's *Scharlach*. There's none of that "scarla," which seemed a kind of animate figure, a kind of evil spirit that crept into bedrooms after the souls of children.

I'm writing of a time when there still wasn't any penicillin. Scarlet fever was the scourge of childhood, of the first classes at the gymnasium. There was also croup, something that was perhaps even more frightening, something that made us shudder even more, but it was linked to the countryside and a sojourn somewhere behind dark windows into which, sitting next to the light, you didn't very much want to look.

I don't remember Volodya Dolgov's appearance. His death is an event from the early years of my life, an event in the life of first-year pupils, of boys who were little more than eleven . . . Nevertheless, it was an unforgettable event. Whether I want it to or not, it rises to the surface of my memory in all its solemn significance.

He was one of the taller boys. That I recall—he was tall. I remember him in the form of a tall, light blue patch—that was him standing nearby while I talked to somebody. A light blue patch because we wore gray-blue school uniforms. Good Lord, how can you remember if it was only the first year? Hardly had we a chance to make friends or even look each other over when suddenly there was a death. What was that—death?

Again, Dobrodeev, you surface in the dark expanse of closed eyelids. And besides you, I see in that expanse the bones of Stroganovsky Bridge . . . There you are running out of your cafe, clean-shaven, lively, your head bare—looking more like a priest than the proprietor of an eating establishment where waves of teapots rushed, settling down here and there, waves of teapots with grass and fish and birds painted on them.

Do you remember me, Dobrodeev? I was a boy then, and somehow you noticed me or at least had a laugh with me over something now forgotten . . . The teapots flew, and the grass didn't pour from them nor did the fish slip out. I had already started to write the language that Pushkin wrote.

All is well, Dobrodeev. Soon I shall be a skull, but they won't have my funeral at the Catholic church on Ekaterininsky, where you, though Orthodox, peered in, hoping to catch in the darkness a glimpse of the kerchief of Marianna, whom you loved.

The Commerce Association was located in one of the more fashionable parts of town in a superb private house—a graceful gray two-storied building with a flagstaff over its front door, which opened onto a corner. I remember the imposingly dark, rich edifice of that building on an overcast morning when on my way to the gymnasium I caught sight of it in the distance from the next block.

It was a club for card play, but really a clip joint, however masked in decorum, impressiveness, and even philanthropy . . . I, for example, went to school at the expense of the Commerce Association as its stipendiary.

The Odessa rich. I never saw a single one of them. I only heard their names: Brodsky, Hepner, Khari, Ashkinazy, Ptashnikov, Anatra . . . There were others whom I can't remember.

They were bankers, grain exporters, dark and criminal . . .

Economics never interested me. My whole economic existence was expressed in the fact that I bought bread at the bakery, shoes at the shoe store, and tickets at the theater box office. It never occurred to me that the state of affairs whereby I received money for something or paid it out for something else depended on circumstances that could be changed and that for some reason ought to be changed. To me, that state of affairs seemed fixed and not even capable of discussion—to have been established once and for all a long time ago as fortunate, proper, and ideal. And, really, what could have been more deserving of the imagination's approval than, say, a grocery store? It was lit by the yellow light of a kerosene lamp, which cast on the cobblestone sidewalk yellow rectangles that were sometimes skewed in anticipation of French painting. The grocery store was always situated in the corner of a large building with caryatids, and to enter you had to run down several steps, which put you in a cheerful mood. You could buy postage stamps there, or decals, a pound of groats, cucumbers, and a rocket.

There were some delicious little things that looked, I would say, like small cucumbers made of dough. Yes, that's right: little crimped pastry cucumbers . . . But what can the dough be compared to? It wasn't, you see, the kind that pirozhki are made of: soft, white, wadded, yet springy . . . No, that dough was, first of all, granular, and second, it was oily; in fact, it exuded oil, and the oil was sweet.

They were called *chibriki*.

Usually they were sold by shady dark-faced people from among the Bulgarians or Turks, sinister people whose eyes peered out at you from their swarthy faces . . . The *chibrik* was sprinkled with powdered sugar.

Isaewicz's pastry shop was located next to the exit from the open courtyard of the Catholic church on Richelieu Street. Some part of the sweetness present in communion or in funeral rites with their hyacinths, lace gatherings, and flies on the face of the deceased was also present in the very essence of that shop.

Narrow little pastries in the Polish manner with thick planks of dough stuck together with sweet filling were sold there. They cost three kopecks, but only for students; everyone else had to pay four. After school, boys and girls came there from every direction and the small, dusky shop was filled with people. Behind the counter against a background of two narrow, barely noticeable windows towered the shop's owners, husband and wife.

They knew we smoked. It would have been impossible not to know, since clouds of blue smoke frankly tumbled from the lavatory door. A distressing impression of that lavatory has remained with me. I learned to smoke there, even though I didn't want to, even though what I really wanted was to be a quiet, obedient little fellow . . .

When Seva Orlov had to have an operation for appendicitis, he was taken to the so-called Hospital of the Evangelist—to that visually seductive little white building that stood in an iris and rose garden at the beginning of French Boulevard and that you always stopped in front of whenever you passed it, attracted first by the fragrance of its flowers, then by the lovely reflection of the sky in one of its windows (windows not in the least aware of their own beauty), and then by the thought that it was the best hospital in the city, and that no sooner should you find yourself within that beautiful, clean building surrounded by flowers than you would be healed of even the most terrible disease.

Seva Orlov was a sickly youth, small and slight of build, and even in those young years unable to manage without his glasses. As Orlov's illegitimate son, he always seemed to us to be on the edge of family quarrels and banishment from his home. Clearly we exaggerated. Seva enjoyed full rights in his family. Nevertheless, the fact that he had been put in the finest hospital in the city struck us as an especially generous act on the part of Orlov.

It was required of gymnasium students that they diligently fulfill the responsibilities of church membership.

I was a Catholic, but I too was expected to observe that discipline. I therefore had to go to mass every Sunday.

Here's one of those Sundays.

I passed through the wall surrounding the church courtyard and walked across the wide bluish flagstones, which rang beneath my feet. Then some steps. I climbed them and found myself within the darkness and chill of the church's stone, or perhaps iron, portico . . .

Mendicants stood there, their heads bowed, echoes reigned there, and there I removed my cap.

The church sang to me in greeting. The organ, the voices of boys, the tinkling of bells. Giant, sweeping pulsations of sound. In the distance by the altar, I saw a whole crowd, part of which moved and part of which was motionless: they were people and statues. The people were dressed in black and white; the statues were suffused with a yellow the color of butter. The sunlight lay mightily upon them, falling from above. Or it didn't lie; it stood among them like a ship in full rigging.

The people and the organ sang. The little bells did too.

I entered the church and saw for the first time what each time I forgot . . .

As I entered the church I saw standing along the wall at the second-story level statues of angels—children almost, in any case beings no older than I, dressed in light tunics through which their bodies showed. To the extent I moved toward the altar, a foreshortening occurred, as a result of which the angels one after another turned more and more away from me, the last one, seemingly, burying its face in the wall and weeping, grieving for me but not having the right to forgive.

A tall handsome priest naturally dressed all in black—soutane and stole and dangling tassels . . . He was dark-haired, rather long-faced, of ruddy complexion, and it goes without saying clean-shaven. Sometimes his sparkling black eyes would turn kindly and smiling and then he would look each of us in the eye with the understanding gaze of an older comrade, a young man. And indeed there was something for us to be glancing at each other about in those spring days when the lilac lay upon the windowsills, when a noisy-winged angel appeared out of the pages of a lesson book, and when somewhere somebody's heel tapped and somewhere else somebody sang.

I remember the Spaniard Calsada, Kolka Calsada, sitting to my left by the window where he was transformed into a silhouette. Directly in front of him was the lectern, behind which sat the priest, Father Erismani. The Spaniard said something, the priest answered, and the two of them laughed. In the book I was holding were pictures by Doré, prodigious compositions, it seemed to me: Absalom caught fast to a tree by his hair, Joshua beneath a dark cloud through which a lyre of sunlight fell obliquely, a suicide in the act of impaling himself on a sword whose handle he had stuck in the ground.[19] Those pictures hummed and sang, but the priest continued to smile at the Spaniard, who took in his hand first a violet, then a blue, then a white lilac from the bushes that almost knocked against the windowsill with the edges of their tiny bells.

It is essential to finish.

We'll start with something short, so finishing will be easier.

When was the first time I shaved? I don't recall the day itself, but I do remember that before I started shaving, I used to trim my mustache with scissors, or not my mustache but whatever it was that grew on my upper lip. I trimmed it, trying to be as thorough as possible, putting the scissors as close to the place in question as I could. I can still recall the cold metal next to my nose.

My family thought it was very funny. Especially my sister with her young woman's archness. She was the only one in my family who considered my appearance tolerable. My parents didn't approve of the way I looked. I should say that the idea of masculine and feminine beauty had changed considerably since my parents were young. In the first place, a man's unattractiveness isn't something that particularly lends itself to discussion nowadays; in the second, women view masculine beauty differently. The tragedy of the ugly Ivanhoe wouldn't be possible today. In the era of my parents' youth, there had existed an aesthetic of handsome men. My sister, already a member of the new generation, felt that beauty lay in something else.

To me, the handsomest men were the Decembrists, the Russian aristocrats who were infatuated with Napoleon yet who fought against him at Borodino.[20]

Of the distinguished names of my childhood, I recall that of Jan Kubelík. He was a violinist, a Czech, who had come to Russia on tour.[21] I neither saw him nor heard him play, for my parents never went to concerts, or if they had gone, would never have taken me, a child. That name caught my fancy, however, for it was often repeated around our table at home. It was sensational, since Kubelík was no ordinary violinist but, as my parents said, the finest in the world. I liked it that his name was "Kubelík." I didn't perceive the name as Czech, and so it sounded strange and interesting.

The sensation increased when the rumor spread in Odessa that some student had shot himself after hearing one of Kubelík's concerts, and that the violinist had had a wreath sent to the youth's grave.

Kubelík—I hear in the distant past—Kubelík, and I see a violin and a wreath.

Osip Mandelstam, describing one of Kubelík's concerts in his *Noise of Time*, says the maestro was Lilliputian.[22]

That's true, for he was, you see, a Kubelík; that is, even though I never saw him, I knew beyond any doubt that he was small and made of dough.[23]

Another famous name of the day was that of the wrestler, Ivan Zaikin. There are no wrestlers anymore of the circus type so common in those times. Today wrestling is a sport, but then it was merely a spectacle, something done in the circus. There weren't, by the way, any stadiums then either. Football, for example, was played in what were almost vacant lots, sometimes with a hump and wildflowers in the middle—obviously not trimmed as they are today to resemble a carpet of grass.

The wrestlers came out in tights—large white figures who looked like women. Ivan Zaikin was one of the strongest wrestlers in the world and was introduced as the "Volga Warrior." I remember once when he was defeated. He wept, smearing the tears all over his face and shouting that he had been beaten unfairly, that he would stand up for Russia (clearly he'd been defeated by a foreign wrestler), and so on in a patriotic vein. Very likely it had all been arranged beforehand, as was always the case with circus championships at that time. At least I sensed some pretense about it. As I see him now, Ivan Zaikin is striding around the arena, wiping away his tears and placing his palms on the two halves of his buttocks.

"Brothers, I shall not betray Russia! I shall not betray her!"

I was given five kopecks for lunch. That wasn't a lot, but not so little that I couldn't buy, say, a roll, an apple, and a glass of tea. Or a meat patty, although the latter would have exhausted the entire sum. The patty, it's true, was plump and good between its two circles of bread, both well saturated with juice.

Obviously, however, five kopecks wasn't much. And it wasn't much because I was always hungry by the first break . . . And so, let's say, an apple was purchased. Then on the second break, a roll was consumed. By lunch break, when you were actually supposed to eat, all the money was gone. But that was when lunch was brought for the rich Agarkov. When we ran into the dining room, a covered dish containing his lunch was already sitting on the table. Sometimes, there were even two of them. They were flat—two silver turtles and all the more turtlelike for the tips of the spoons and forks that stuck out from under their lids. Upon seeing those dishes, your appetite was naturally whetted . . . But I'd managed at the outside, as they say, to save only a kopeck for a glass of tea. It will remain in my memory for the rest of my life, that faceted glass yellow with the fresh tea you got for one kopeck but without a saucer, so that you had to hold the glass by its top with your fingers till the steam scalded your palm. Bless you, O glass of gymnasium tea! Never leave my memory, never abandon it!

Most often, however, I didn't spend my five kopecks on lunch. I saved it so that by the end of the week I would have thirty kopecks. To that thirty I made every effort to add another twenty, and on Saturday I went to the circus, purchasing a student ticket for fifty kopecks. How I got the twenty kopecks I lacked is another story. I'll merely observe that I had a grandmother with a lot of silver change who loved me. Once on my name day she even gave me a gold five-ruble piece, whose little sun peeping from the brown folds of its purse I shall never forget, just as I shall never forget my grandmother lying in her coffin as in a small boat.

The circus was always seen through falling snow. Well, why not? It was always winter when the circus was open. I walked through the falling snow, marveling at the snowflakes. And in truth they did resemble the contrivances of some technology. And it struck me too that as they floated between the streetlight and the circus wall, the snowflakes cast a shadow in the form of a little cloud. On the circus wall hung posters depicting yellow lions and a red lion tamer, a depiction that seemed to move, since it contained rings and a cracking whip and lions with their hind legs thrust out into the air.

On the evening I want to tell about, a boy-wonder was supposed to appear at the circus. What the boy-wonder would do the posters didn't say. They merely announced he would appear and that was all. I myself was a boy, and the existence of some boy-wonder rather upset my equanimity. Why, damn it, I was a boy-wonder myself! And, really, I did constantly hear about how intelligent and able I was.

The story I'm obliged to write and have been intending to write for several years now should begin, perhaps, with a description of the snow that fell that particular evening. It was snow of a special filigreed kind, the kind where the snowflakes are shaped like miniature artifacts that, however useless, are nonetheless made with absolute precision—concentric octagons, multifaceted crosses with rays shooting from their corners, stars with cross beams on each ray . . . Despite the fact that they were phenomenally light, those little bodies weren't destroyed when they got caught on you as you walked. On the contrary, they clung to your eyelashes, hooked there, say, by the edge of an octagon, and you had to blink for a long time to shake the shaggy and cumbersome things loose. And what's more, though falling, say, onto your sleeve, they still retained a certain shape.

An illuminated wall, a poster . . . I read the words on it that in ten minutes, as soon as the lights above the arena had reached their full intensity, would be transformed into clowns and mandolins and little dogs, into tambourines and horses and slender bodies hurtling between trapezes. But what the words "Volodya Zubritsky" would turn into, I couldn't imagine.

"Volodya Zubritsky," the poster said, "Boy-Wonder."

A large blackboard was brought into the arena, a bit smaller than the one at the gymnasium, but a good rectangle on a stand with a chalk-dust-covered rag hanging from its bottom edge. Given such a prop, it was hard to imagine what the next act might consist of. I had managed a glance at somebody else's program, however, where I read that the boy-wonder would now appear.

The boy-wonder set out across the sandy floor of the arena, his white satin shoes slightly sinking into it. Next to him, but a little behind, walked a student in a black double-breasted jacket, pince-nez, mustache, and goatee.

The boy-wonder was merely a rather plump boy, a blond with bangs who was dressed not only in white satin shoes but also in a sailor suit with short pants and a blouse whose sleeves had pink anchors on them and whose collar, instead of being dark blue like a sailor's, was also pink and made of satin.

As a boy and for many years afterward as an adult, the show I liked best of all was the circus.

Yes, and it wasn't merely as a show that I regarded the circus; my attitude toward it was more complex. Dreams of glory were mixed up in it. I imagined that one day I myself would be a famous circus performer, an acrobat, in fact. And an awakening sensuality found its secret embodiments in circus images as well . . . Whoever was clad in tights or clothed in gold-spangled velvet, whoever appeared with a fixed crimson smile on her face, assured me of the presence in the world of a great mystery that I would soon grasp and for the sake of which I was alive.

It's worth recalling how proud we are in youth. That pride is based on an awareness of our beauty and strength, ugly and weak though we may be. Yes, of beauty and strength, for youth is essentially beautiful and strong. Perhaps because of the intuition that someone will cleave to us and only to us, that someone will be devoted to us and love us.

That pride is probably one of the chief experiences of youth . . . I remember being very proud myself, dressed in the gray uniform overcoat of a gymnasium student with its black astrakhan collar, and possessed of a face that glowed and of eyebrows whose softness even I sensed, the truly sable eyebrows of a boy.

So there I sat at the circus on a Saturday evening, my ticket bought with money saved during the week from five-kopeck pieces provided for lunch. Oh, that didn't lessen my pride any. My goodness, I was strong and handsome—I was young!—and the fact that I had no money, well, what demigod does?

I studied well and was in the adult sense an intelligent boy, but in those childhood or rather adolescent years I didn't sense any inkling in myself that I would become a writer. What I wanted to be was a circus performer, in particular an acrobat. To be able to do somersaults was the object of my dreams. I tried to learn how to do them at school, but nothing came of it, since the appropriate equipment was lacking, equipment unnecessary for a course in gymnastics that didn't include acrobatics. I didn't realize, of course, that special equipment was required, attributing the fantastic leaps I'd seen to secret abilities known only to a few. I envied those few. I had seen them in the circus—boys and girls in white shoes, a throng of children who ran out of the circus's crimson wings into the arena and almost with a laugh did right before my eyes what I could never have done even in my wildest dreams.

Incidentally, I sometimes tell acquaintances that I knew how to do somersaults as a child. They believe me, and I who am not fond of making things up even report the details.

Perhaps the dream of being able to do somersaults was the first stirring in me of the artist, the first sign that my attention would be directed toward the world of imagination, toward the creation of things new and out of the ordinary, toward brightness and beauty.

I obtained that ticket by means of direct spiritual and physical effort: I waited in line, believing there would be enough seats, then suddenly losing faith . . . I acquired it honorably, that thin piece of paper stamped in violet.

Here it is in my hands. A thin, almost translucent piece of yellowish paper with violet ink . . . But it conferred the right to pass into that plush paradise, that paradise of marble and gold, of steps and little corridors, of arches and frosted lamps and echoes and laughter, of shining eyes and perfume and the clicking of heels—oh, what couldn't you find there!

The circus made a tremendous impression on me as a child. Sometimes I even want to say that it's the circus's yellow arena that lies at the base of my life. Just so—the base of my life, since glancing into the past, into its depths, I see most clearly that yellow ring with its scattered little figures of animals and people dressed in crimson velvet and in sequins and feathers, and I hear most distinctly the crack of a whip like a pistol shot (and it pleases me to know that the whip was called a *chambrière*) and the shout of the clown, "Hello, Max!" and the reply, "Hello, August!"

The whirling clown, a vortex of gold, white, and crimson with his mask a motionless stone at the center—I have at any moment only to think of him and he flies into memory. In those days, clowns spoke as if in English. They wore white stockings and brilliant gold shoes. They gave each other slaps, producing a sound that filled the auditorium but whose mechanism was difficult to grasp, however much you tried.

They were a trio: two men and a young woman. Or no, not two men, but two boys, and not a young woman, but a girl. There they are, doing somersaults in front of me! There they are, right there! Don't you see them? Nobody does. Only I see them, and I see them in the nonexistent place called memory that swirls before my eyes.

Executing a somersault, the girl was transformed into a vision of stunning power, even though nothing particular happened to her in that moment except that she did a somersault and her hair floated in the air. I was merely a boy at the time, and it didn't occur to me that rather more substantial things are needed for love than floating hair.

I fell in love with the girl acrobat. If her hair hadn't fluttered as she jumped, perhaps I wouldn't have. If her hair hadn't floated and her white suede shoes hadn't stood out first against the sand, then in the air, then in the completed circle of her jump . . . Nobody knew I was in love with the girl acrobat, yet whenever she ran into the ring I felt shame. How was she dressed? I don't recall. I remember only her white suede shoes, tight-fitting like the ones little children wear and buttoned up the side with large white buttons, and her flying hair. It's possible that I myself didn't know I was in love with her. I felt only shame, shame for her that she could evoke such a pleasant, such an unfamiliar but pleasant feeling in me.

Once it was snowing and the circus was open, and I set off in that magical direction. There was a cafe in the circus building where the performers gathered. Out of the cafe came three young people, among whom I recognized the acrobats who worked with the girl. One of the three spat—a short, ugly, rather pitiful and unhealthy-looking person with a wide mouth and a cloth cap. He spat the way self-confident young people who are held down by their comrades sometimes do: a long, noisy jet of saliva from between his lips. "Why are there three of them?" I wondered. "The other one's probably a friend of theirs"—of the two, that is, whom I was glad to see since they worked with her. And then suddenly I recognized her in the third one. That unpleasant third boy, that long and noisy spitter, was her! He'd been dressed as a girl, and the fluttering hair had therefore been a wig. Nonetheless, I've remained in love with that girl acrobat to this day, and even now when in my memory I see that fluttering hair, I'm seized with a kind of shame.

The Efimov Brothers circus was an excellent one. We were well acquainted with all its acts: the Siberian marksmen, the floor acrobats known as the Saltons, a trio of aerial gymnasts, the Tanti clowns and the Rosetti clowns . . . There were two horseback riders as well: Mademoiselle Clara and Maria the Serbian. Mademoiselle Clara was a so-called trick rider; that is, she performed her act for the most part from a broad satin saddle: she stood on it, she sat on it, she jumped over long ribbons held in her path by the circus attendants, then she returned to the saddle again.

The phrase "circus attendants" was spoken with scorn in those days. But none was felt for the people dressed in green and gold uniforms who stood in two columns near the exit for the manège. On the contrary, they were loved and respected. You see, the attendants were the performers themselves. I recall what a pleasure it was to recognize among those fine fellows the young Tanti and the young Salton . . .

Maria the Serbian was a trick rider, too. She suddenly appeared one evening without any preliminary announcement in the posters that a new act would be shown . . . She galloped out on a lean, sharp-nosed horse, and barely had we even a chance to take in her first circuit than she fell. She fell on the red plush of the circus ring and tumbled head over heels toward the pit in a scattering of clothing, her body exposed for a thrilling instant. The audience gasped, but she had already darted out of her death trap, and running back into the arena she did in quick succession several of what in circus and ballet lingo are called "compliments" . . . She meant to leap back into the satin saddle, but the attendants were still attempting to catch her horse as it ran around the arena trying to avoid capture, and it was clear she wouldn't be able to go on with her act. The fault wasn't hers but the horse's. And so, scattering another box of compliments, Maria the Serbian ran into the wings.

We listened with pleasure to the wild-animal roaring that reached us while we were watching the stable numbers. There were no two people who upon hearing that sound wouldn't look at each other. It erupted into the arena suddenly: either a yawn or a kind of prodigious "Hello there!" You might even say that when the wild beasts entered the arena after the second intermission, the circus was filled with a sound like wind or an echo.

The cage was set up during the second intermission. It was brought in pieces which were then noisily assembled. It consisted of spears whose points had been turned away from the spectators. Children know that measure makes it even harder for the animals to jump out.

The second intermission thus filled the arena with an activity we very much wanted to watch, although that was just what we couldn't do. Present there were the braided jackets of the circus attendants, the long spears of the cage, little wooden chairs with flowers painted on them—extremely naive little flowers when you considered what was to come—and the tamer himself, still dressed in a gray robe. And then the bell rang—a whole river of sound pouring over us—and when we got back to our seats the arena was ready . . . It was yellower now than at any time before, since we knew that in a moment the lions would come running in.

I once saw a circus act that at the time was called the "Motofozo." Probably if Arnold were reminded of it today, he could describe it exactly . . .[24]

The Motofozo was a human doll. Not an especially outlandish one—neither frightening nor comic, just a young person in top hat and tails, a young dandy with a pink and blue doll's face and blue eyelashes drawn almost down to his cheeks. And, of course, with a doll's motionless yet gleaming eyes. He, that dandy, was carried into the arena. He was a doll. Everybody could see that. But so much was he a doll that when the attendants, for a moment forgetting what he was, stopped holding him up and walked away, he toppled over, and moreover toppled over onto his back, which made the audience cry out in alarm. Shaking their heads in vexation, the attendants propped him up again.

There followed a whole series of similar episodes, each precisely calculated to create the impression that he was a real doll, and with that the act came to an end . . . With that it came to an end . . . Oh yes, on the orders of childhood, it came to an end with their carrying the doll around the front-row seats, stopping first in front of a boy, then in front of another, then in front of a girl who drew back from shyness, so that we could almost have kissed him on the cheek, that older boy in a white vest. His eyelashes didn't move and neither did his nostrils, but the charming spirit of his smile, of that mask of laughter, communed with us in a chummy way, as if it had appeared for but an instant on his otherwise expressionless face.

Where are you, my fairy-tale older brother?

Suddenly, at the sound of galloping, he snatched off his top hat and held it high over his head, and from joy that he had come to life, he tossed it and a glove and something else (his cloak?) into the air and ran out of the arena. He was at once accompanied by children's clapping hands, and not merely hands but feet, since several kids fell over onto their backs with delight.

He always had money, so he could allow himself a thing or two. Thus he got tickets to the circus for himself and me.

"Do you want to go?"

Of course I did.

"Only ask your mama."

He was teasing me. Let him. It didn't bother me, since I had no reason to worry about whether or not they would let me go; of course they would. Nor did I see anything disgraceful about the fact that I was younger than he was. He was a university student, while I was in my second year at the gymnasium. The difference was vast, of course, but in that case why did he even bother to seek my company?

Perhaps he just wasn't a very confident person, and my companionship presented no threat in the sense that I wouldn't insult him.

We called him "Uncle Manzheli." His real name was something quite different, but we called him that because of his resemblance to the horse trainer Manzheli whom we saw at the circus on Saturdays.

That's really all about Uncle Manzheli. No, I need at least a couple more lines. He was a Greek, a relative of the Melisaratos, with a slicked-down black mustache and brilliantine on his fingers and perhaps his neck . . .

That's all about Uncle Manzheli.

I can say that I saw the dawn of football. We gymnasium students walked down French Boulevard and turned off onto a side street where a gigantic bottle of champagne had been erected as an advertisement . . . Let not the reader suppose that our route passed through urban beauties, as indeed he might, given the boulevard's name and that advertising bottle of champagne. On the contrary, French Boulevard was on the outskirts of Odessa, and that gigantic bottle stood behind a gray fence among the burdocks and tall weeds and advertised not so much the sale of champagne as the proximity of the company's warehouse.

Or perhaps the champagne merchant had brought it from France and then had no idea where to put it . . . And so it was placed on a side street, or even in an alley, a dusty, narrow alley between two fences, but an attractive, even poetic one, it seemed to me, since it was close to the sea, and since along its side at its highest point you could see a carved balcony and a pendent rose.

Dust, the sun declining toward the west, Sunday . . . In the middle of the street a crowd, a throng. A large wooden gate, about to open inward, is starting to give way under the pressure of those wishing to pass into the . . . the stadium? No, that word still wasn't used then. Simply the match.

A half-tumbled-down wall stood in the middle of a field, and I walked along it among the weeds and thistles . . . That wall was about thirty meters long, so that I managed to stay within its shadow where the chalicelike blossoms of the thistles had turned a vivid pink. Near the top of the wall were openings where, before the building's demolition, there had once been windows. In a few instances, the openings were very large, merging with the sky, and sometimes on the contrary they were overgrown with something that swayed in the wind . . . But rarely did I look up, since I was wrapped in ribbons of conversation about football and players.

We were on our way to the Sporting Club Field for the next match.

"Who are the backs?" I heard next to me.

"Borka Mizersky and . . ."

Somebody besides Borka Mizersky, although I didn't manage to catch who, since the speakers had already outpaced me. But I myself knew who the other one was: Tikhonyuk.

In the years of the dawn of football, the two defensive players (and there were only two then) were called by the English name—"backs." That name was kept for a long time, even in Soviet football. The "backs"; then came the semidefenders, three in a line—the "halfbacks"; and then the attacking players—the "forwards." The goal defender was called by his English name too—the "goalkeeper." Of course, I'm not telling anything new to people who know football.

Football was just beginning. It was considered a childish pastime. Adults didn't go to football matches. Only rarely would you see a gentleman with an umbrella, and then he was someone already well known in the city as an eccentric.

There weren't any stands, but what would stands be doing there? The field itself wasn't equipped; it could have been uneven and have had clumps of wildflowers growing in it.

Along the sidelines stood benches without backs, simply ordinary flat wooden benches. The majority of the spectators stood; those who had got onto the field sat on the benches. And what spectators they were! Children and youths, I repeat.

Nevertheless, the teams came out in their club colors, and they played according to game schedules, and sometimes they even put up posters.

My own adults didn't really have any idea what football was about, the football I went to every Saturday and Sunday.

"They play ball . . . With their feet? How can that be, with their feet?"

To the adult spectators, the game seemed unaesthetic, almost hooliganism—something dreamed up by the less-able students or by boys in the street.

"It's a mistake to let Yura go to football matches."

"Where is this taking place?"

"At the Sporting Club field," I would answer.

"Where?"

"At the Sporting Club field."

"What's that? I don't understand," my father would say. "What field?"

"The Sporting Club field," I replied with all the obduracy of a new culture.

These notes of mine at least have the benefit of teaching me mastery of the sentence. And in fact they are training me to write, something I once was very far from being able to do. To sit down at a desk and take a pen in my hand would have been very difficult, oh, almost impossible—like passing from a wakeful state into the world of dreams without ever falling asleep.

I don't want to complain about anything.

I only want to recall Grisha Bogemsky posing in his Sporting Club uniform for the photographer Perepelitsyn before the beginning of a match. If you were watching from the tennis-court side, he stood closer to the training room where the road bordered the fence and was completely covered with grass—was uniformly green, even in the shade and under the fence. Grisha Bogemsky, I repeat, was wearing the white uniform of the Sporting Club. Is that right? The Sporting Club? He had a plain white uniform on. If he'd been wearing a Sporting Club uniform, the club's dark blue symbol would have been visible on his chest—that small blue and white shield. First, the shield. Second, he would hardly have been allowed to wear his club uniform for a school match. He himself wouldn't have wanted to. Therefore, simply a white uniform, a white, very thin cotton knit shirt and white trunks. What football players now call a football jersey was then just called a shirt, although it was the same thing—a jersey stretched over the torso. But that shirt now seems, in Bogemsky's case, simply to have been made of plaster . . . On his legs he wore long black socks rolled down over his calves like donuts, leaving his knees bare, while on his feet he wore boots, old badly battered boots that had been tied like barrels with leather thongs across his insteps. The most astonishing thing—and this always astonishes me whenever I see pictures of Bogemsky or think about him—was that he wasn't dark or hard-looking, but on the contrary rather pudgy, with a rosy complexion and rings of dirty blond hair on his forehead and deep-set, barely visible eyes. Sometimes the two circles of a pince-nez even gleamed in front of those eyes. And just think, that person with the unathletic appearance was a remarkable athlete. Even apart from the fact that he was a hundred-meter sprint champion and champion high jumper and pole vaulter, he achieved legendary feats on the football field. And not only in Odessa, but in St. Petersburg, Sweden, and Norway! In the first place, he was fast; in the second, he could kick; and in the third, he could guide the ball. Afterward, I learned that the technique of guiding the ball is called "dribbling." Oh, that was one of the most thrilling sights of my childhood, which cheered along with everybody else, leaping to its feet and applauding. Bogemsky could dribble better than anyone. But it wasn't just that he was better than the rest; it was that this was the emergence of a true champion.

And it's strange, while Petya Perepelitsyn was aiming the little box of his camera at him, Bogemsky stood there just like some coach . . . No, that's wrong. Take a real look at him, dunce! Can you really not see the exceptional grace of his manner, his lightness, his "Just a second!" and off he runs with the whole field after him—the whole field, the public, flags, clouds, and life?

I haven't seen play like that since. I'm not talking about quality or effectiveness but style. Bogemsky was, paradoxically, not a running forward, but a floating one. And really, if you look at the playing field as you would a picture and not at the movement itself, then you'll see the running football players as figures with basically erect torsos: during the rapid movement of their legs, during that almost wheel-like movement, their torsos remain upright. But Bogemsky ran leaning forward. Perhaps that style was later repeated only by Grigory Fedotov, who in his day so struck his first spectators.

I was saving money for a pair of boots. You had to pay five rubles down, at which time you received the boots. Then you had to pay three rubles more.

The store was located on the corner of Sadovy and Deribasovsky. Its proprietor was a small well-built Jew, a little pillar of a man whom you couldn't help liking, first because he allowed credit, and second because he sold football boots.

I enter the store with my five rubles in hand. The little pillar stands rooted behind the counter. He remembers that I've been in before. Yes, certainly he remembers. Yes, of course he has an installment plan. That's right, if you pay five rubles down, you get the boots.

"Here's five rubles, please."

I extend my hand holding a five-ruble note, a czarist five-ruble note, blue, rather wide, and satiny from use. How could I have saved so much! No sooner do I present the five-ruble note than from the world on the other side of the counter there flashes a semicircle of dazzling whiteness. Football boots! He had actually got the boots!

Do you know what boots are?

No, of course you don't.

We rode only as far as Gymnasium No. 3, then walked the rest of the way. A bench next to a pharmacy with red crosses in its windows . . . One could also admire the enormous bottles filled with pink and yellow tinted water . . . They represented medicines . . . By the pharmacy's entrance was a little iron device stuck into the ground so that visitors wouldn't track mud onto the steps and into the store but would first scrape it from their soles. The steps were stone: two or three stone steps worn almost to the thinness of a pancake.

On past the pharmacy. Farther.

A public garden lay across our path. We didn't look at it; it was very much on the periphery. Only our elbows saw it. It was on Lidersovsky Boulevard. Is that right? Memory, do you still exist? Lidersovsky Boulevard.

I'm tired. Lord, take pity on me. There were five or six of us boys and we were going to play football.

I never learned to swim or skate, but I was a decent football player and good at track and field, especially in the jumping events and the hundred-meter dash. I also pole vaulted, which was frightening and fantastic, a world with different physical laws.

Why success in one sport and failure in another? Faintheartedness, when you come down to it. To swim you have to venture onto the surface of depths capable of swallowing you up; to skate you take a chance of falling down and bumping or cracking your head.

But football, isn't that a dangerous battle?

All that was unimportant. What was important was that the sport smelled of grass. Bless you, bitter smell! Bless you, sweet color! Bless you, stems and yellow crowns! Bless you, world!

The playing field had probably already started to turn a fresh green. Yes, undoubtedly the new grass had already started to come up.

Our boots stood out a remarkably vivid white against the green. You could see them moving quickly in the middle of the field, then on its edge, then at its corners. White, rapidly moving boots.

For us those were already the days of spring. They had the bitter fragrance of grass. Oh, wait! Wait! I can almost smell that fragrance now! I can almost smell it now!

Besides the other contests of the Odessa school-district Olympic games, a final match was held for first place among the gymnasium football teams, a match in which I took part as one of eleven teammates representing Richelieu Gymnasium.

I played right wing. I scored a goal, one of six knocked in by us against Gymnasium No. 4, also entered in the final.

After the match I was tossed into the air by students from various schools who had run out onto the field. Clearly my play had pleased the spectators. I was dressed in white, in white trunks and a white jersey. My boots were white too, and my socks were black and green and rolled down over my calves like donuts.

However, the district school inspector Mardanov, a regally handsome Armenian in wax and black oakum, noticed that this young football player—me, that is—was a bit pale. Mightn't it be dangerous for him to be playing football?

Several days later the doctor listened to my heart in the training room by the football field. He said I had a nervous heart and couldn't play football anymore. All of a sudden I had the feeling I was gravely ill. I became aware of the beating of my own heart and for no reason at all wanted to sit down.

That Mardanov played a fateful role in my life; because of him I sensed for the first time the existence of impossibility and restriction.

It's hard to imagine all this happened to me. How much lay before me, even that scene when . . . What scenes didn't lie before me!

It was already dusk when we started back. The flowers all seemed to have turned white and become very still, those little white twilight crosses.

Our feet in their football boots trod over them. We simply didn't see them. It is only now, suddenly looking back, that I see an entire cloak of flowers—a knight's white cloak fallen on the grass.

Sometimes we returned from the playing field not by way of French Boulevard but through the Botanical Garden. That meant a shortcut for us, but it also meant a route fraught with danger. The Botanical Garden, or "Botanica" as we boys called it, had nothing in common with botanical science. Maybe there had been a time when flowers or trees had grown there, planted in the name of science and knowledge, but obviously none of us gymnasium students remembered it. None of the adults did either. A wood? No, it was too sparse for a wood, and in its middle stood the wooden remains of a puppet booth. A park? No, it was too bare for a park, too sandy, too dusty. A vacant lot with trees growing wild? Probably that was it. In any case, it was overgrown, and passing through it was frightening. To us gymnasium students, it was especially frightening; they hunted schoolboys there. Who did? Other boys—residents of the nearby streets or simply outcasts who hid there.

One of the peculiarities of youth is of course the conviction that you are immortal, and not in any unreal or abstract sense but literally: you will never die. And this in spite of youth's characteristic melancholy, in spite of its thoughts of suicide . . .

I'll certainly never die, I told myself as a youth. When I've grown up, when the years have passed, something will have been invented to keep people from dying. That "when the years have passed" I imagined in the form of a distant, golden city, a city of the future like the ones depicted on the covers of science-fiction novels, a place where people had long ago become immortal. It's interesting that I imagined eternal life as the result of a discovery or invention. Great machines emitting lightning bolts of current the breadth of a tree . . .

It's odd no writer has mentioned this certainty of the young that they are immortal.

By February, certainly by the end of February, it was in those days already spring in Odessa. In any event, violets were already on sale. In any event, clambering down the rocks anywhere on the shore at Bolshoy Fontan, you would suddenly see from behind those rocks not the gray chaos of the winter sea, but the sea itself—as blue and fresh as an eye.[25]

Violets were sold in bouquets—five or six flowers that hung from your hand on little stems. The violets were a rich purple color, like the velvet of royal pages . . . The violets felt warm to the touch, since your fingers were cold from just having been dipped in water to take out the bouquet . . . That's how spring began when I was young.

I was standing in a crowd on a cobblestone street listening with everyone else to singing coming through a window.

It was the voice of an opera singer whom we couldn't see. Where was he? Nobody in the crowd could tell. There was only a horn directing its blue and gold bell-shaped mouth at us. Yes, a horn, although I would say that in front of me there was something on the order of an immense bluebell; just so, the horn looked like a monstrously enlarged bluebell torn off at the stem and set in place at an angle.

The singing came from it.

"Caruso!" announced a government official who had just joined the crowd, a man with a folded black umbrella under his arm, an umbrella that was somehow reminiscent of a bird's leg. "It's Canio's aria. That's Caruso."[26]

Where was he then, if it was Caruso?

The horn wasn't motionless. No, it never stopped moving, although the nature of its movement was difficult to define or name. It moved while remaining in place; it moved back and forth.

The taller people could see something called a disk.

"That's right," the official said, "it's inscribed on the disk. The performer's voice is inscribed on the disk, and now we hear it."

The gramophone's owners appeared in the window, several adults and children. They recognized the official in the crowd and beckoned to him, calling him to come in. He answered he'd be right there and minced toward the steps. The street was short and covered with cobblestones through which grass was growing. The official climbed the building's iron stairway, through which more grass was growing and next to which there was a zinc drainpipe covered with zinc stars . . .

I became familiar with classical music for the first time as an adult. And I grew to understand and like it even later. What was music before that? I had always known and been fond of Chopin, but for me music was primarily popular concert waltzes, operetta music, marches, tangos, dances like the cracovienne, and everything else that was played in parks and on phonograph records.

Military brass bands performed in the parks, and for me as a child it was even more fun to watch them play than to listen to them: the way the band moved, for example, or the way the frail young leader conducted. They played in so-called rotundas or shells, which were wooden hemispheres open on one side, like half a drum. There, on the floorboards under the legs of the music stands, fallen leaves accumulated, as well as gravel and every other kind of litter carried there from the park walkways by ragamuffins, so that the band shells were images of neglect, of the end of something . . . Of what? In those years, at least, merely of summer vacation.

I arrived to give his regular lesson to a young pupil at the dacha where he lived with his parents.

They lived on Kuyalnitsky Estuary.[27]

The day was hot, a hot yellow day in melon rinds, in the intoxicating fragrance of fried fish, in the cries of cooks and peddlers, in the squealing of kitchen knives . . . And just think, amid that indifference to everything intellectual, amid that atmosphere of sensual well-being, which had begun with a discussion of how best to prepare corn and ended with a favorite cat rolled over on its back, I, a young gymnasium student, had to give a lesson in geometry and the subordinate clause, and not only that, but to a boy himself in the clutches of that same sensuality . . .

How pleasurable in the time of first love to come out onto the clearing in front of a dacha and suddenly see the girl you loved wearing not the dress you were used to seeing her in, but a different one, evidently just newly made. Probably it was dark blue and trimmed around the collar and hem and on the cuffs with red ribbon. Her sudden appearance in that new dress strengthened my love for her almost to the point of palpitation, indeed, almost of moaning. It was even frightening to approach her, and she, just as delighted with herself, remained standing near a black tree, her curls distinctly visible in the distance. Separating us was a space of hummocked autumnal earth on which the leaves would suddenly for no reason at all start turning somersaults.

Sometimes you think how brief life is. But it isn't—I've lived for a long time. How distant, for example, is that day when, going out onto Nikolaevsky Boulevard, I walked along its edge suspended above the panorama of the port and, peering at the gray sea, searched for signs of what had taken place the night before. A Turkish battleship had burst into the port and, opening fire, had sunk one of our gunboats and damaged a French merchant vessel. 1915? That's how long ago it was—the First World War! To my contemporaries today, and even to those not so young, indeed, to all mature people of our epoch, what I'm recalling now as an eyewitness seems in all likelihood as remote in the past as, say, the tales of my older contemporaries about the taking of Shipka once seemed to me.[28]

The shell that struck the French vessel pierced the cabin of the stewardess. Besides her, it was rumored that the cook had also been killed. To us schoolboys, that news merely provided an occasion for ribald conversation. A few days later on another gray morning, I saw the burial of the stewardess and the cook. A short but compact procession made its way up Polish Hill.

I remember sailors with pompoms on their berets and their magnificent captain in a dark blue two-tiered pelerine and a helmet with a brilliant visor. A priest in a lace surplice also walked with them.

I watched from the bridge. The two narrow coffins seemed to me to be lying upon the procession, two narrow silver coffins that looked like beetles with long folded wings.

I had stopped to watch the procession while on my way to school. I ought to have hurried, but still I gazed after the dark blue back of the captain and the two coffins of the unknown French stewardess and cook. It was a gray morning, and ahead lay a school day full of anxiety, ahead lay life, a life full of such days . . .

The pupil Schneiderman said that whoever signed up for the military subscription loan was contributing to bloodshed. Slender, redheaded, droll Schneiderman who liked my poems . . .

Kolya Lukin denounced Schneiderman. No, he himself didn't consider it denunciation. It was his duty—Kolya Lukin was from a monarchist family and himself an admirer of the czar. Schneiderman, I remember, was expelled from school almost the next day. Even though only half a year remained until graduation. Thus, Schneiderman was threatened with having eight years left entirely out of account. Now when I recall that image from the past, I hear that youth saying to me once again, just as he did then,

"Remember, verses must have content. You write well, but real poetry is about the struggle."

Yes, of course he was a revolutionary, that youth. We didn't know that. But they did, who just before graduation had expelled him from the gymnasium where he had studied for eight years.

And there Schneiderman's track disappears. I don't remember his passing through the doors of the classroom for the last time, nor saying goodby to him. Then he turned up again. He was a commissar, a communist assigned to the Don region. That's why he told me to write verses with content. That's why he was opposed to the bloodshed.

Further on his own track turned bloody. He was executed by a Cossack hetman as a Jew and a communist.

As for the headmaster who had expelled Schneiderman, it was rumored that after the revolution he became a shepherd. A Latinist, he retreated beneath the protective canopy of an acacia. It was said that he read the Roman classics while tending his flocks. He too was executed. They found him all the same, and he took his punishment. What happened to Lukin? That I don't know. I think he entered a military academy ahead of schedule, as did many that year. Probably he laid down his life for the czar—for that portrait hanging in the headmaster's office at the gymnasium: a little angel standing on the grass in a Caucasian lambskin cap, and next to him a young ram, also in lambskin of the whitest white.

I have seen a lot in my life. For example, once in the steppe near Odessa, I managed to catch a sight rarely glimpsed in earthly observation: a will-o'-the-wisp. As everybody knows, that sight has been sought by dreamers the world over—at least the ones celebrated in novels. The sight is rare because a combination of circumstances is required for it to appear: a given atmospheric condition, a given quality of weather, and a given angle of view . . .

I was on so-called "terms" at the rather large estate of a German colonist. Terms was the same as tutoring except that the tutor lived on the premises, since it was summer.

I was on my way from the Lutz estate to the town of Domanyovka. The road split the steppe from my feet all the way to the horizon. Beside the road were wildflowers of the most varied sizes, shapes, and colors—little pink, blue, and yellow bells, a kind of miniature lilac sausage stretched upward, whole handfuls of little blue crowns, and chamomile with tiny pillows on which the invisible sick of another world might have slept. All of it was burningly redolent of almost nothing at all—the air? The distance? The sky?

Dragonflies hovered and darted in the air, as if flying backward. Properly speaking, the quivering of their glassy dark blue wings was the air of the steppe. Occasionally an improbably large and active dragonfly would bump against me. Its tail cracked and squeaked against my shoulder, a crooked tail resembling a pea pod. I managed a look at its eyes, which provoked an almost irresistible desire to tear at them—water-drop eyes that perhaps saw me too. The dragonfly darted back and forth beside me, and it seemed as it hovered there that its tiny feet were clutching the air to keep it from flying away.

I was going to Domanyovka to buy caramels.

Since it happened on the way to Nikolaevsky Boulevard set above the sea, all of us who took part in that encounter were enveloped in its clean, empty blue expanse. At first there were only two of us walking in the direction of the sea—Kataev and I. Inasmuch as we were in fact on our way somewhere, we didn't pay much attention to the surrounding expanse . . . And then a third person joined us. And it became clear just how enclosed we were by that empty blueness.

"Let me introduce you, Yura," Kataev said, and then added, by way of characterizing me to the one I was meeting, "This is the poet I was telling you about."

Kataev didn't dare speak the name of the person to whom he was introducing me; that I would have to figure out for myself.

The stranger extended his hand to me. I thought he was an old man, a spiteful old man. His hand, I thought, was hard and spiteful. He was wearing a cap of a kind I'd never seen before—of gray calico. Yes, and he also had a walking stick. He stood with his back to the sea, to the light, and therefore, although he was in the midst of blueness, he was still a silhouette; and since he was a silhouette, his small tuft of a beard was visible to me only in profile, and like the handle of his stick, it too was hard, turned up, and spiteful . . .

That old man lived a great many years more—a whole lifetime. He wrote many excellent pages and received from the hands of the Swedish king a prize for what he had written. And not long ago that old man died. He was Ivan Bunin.[29]

Shengeli once told me that he'd like to live in a lighthouse.[30] Well, that's not such a bad fantasy. What's it like in a lighthouse? What are the accommodations like? Is it a room, several rooms, or a small barracks? I can't imagine. I've never been inside a lighthouse; I've only seen them shining. But that hardly expresses it. My whole youth was spent under the turning of one of those gigantic lights, first ruby, then emerald. It flashed in the distance, in relative terms not very far away—about two kilometers—but in the uncluttered expanse of the sea, that meant nothing. It shone at sea in the darkness of a summer night, as if appearing from around a corner, as if looking right at you. My God, how many figures might be found to describe something as wonderful as a lighthouse—such an ancient thing, really, and for such a long time the guest of poetry, history, and philosophy . . .

I think lighthouses use neon lights now.

Shengeli in fact managed every kind of maritime, seacoast meditation, so to speak, and he did so because his childhood memories nourished them. He had lived in Kerch on the Black Sea. He told me he was of Gypsy descent. A very talented person.

In the distance an orange-topaz
Majestic river sways,
In its mirror showing
Swirling, melting clouds.[31]

This isn't a particularly good passage (it reveals its debt to Severyanin,[32] whom one should never imitate) and anyway I've probably got something wrong. Shengeli has some charming sea poems—about a captain's cottage in Kerch, and so on. Precise diction, precise word placement, superb epithets, and above all poetry. He has unfortunate peculiarities he holds to. The admiration of Bryusov, for example.[33] But that's his business.

I remember you, Georgy Arkadievich, standing above the footlights on a corner of the Sibiryakovs' stage in Odessa, dressed in a black frock coat, your hair black and curly. You were impassioned, it seemed to me, but not loud: a small but splendid figure, Georgy Arkadievich, handsome in a strange and distinctive way, your black eyes gleaming with a heavy honey brightness as you read your poems. I remember only one line:

And in the thickets of confessionals . . .

No, surely that isn't right. What could it mean, "in the thickets of confessionals"?[34]

It was in Odessa on a clear spring evening when I was eighteen and Severyanin was performing—the magus himself, poem and stanza.

It's true I was very young then, and it's true it was spring in Odessa . . . Those two circumstances obviously assisted to no small degree in augmenting the charm of what I was witnessing. The onset of life, the Odessa spring with its lilacs and tulips, and then suddenly against that background, you happen on a "poetry concert" by Igor Severyanin, the unusual Severyanin, a poet you had long been enamored of, who had written about the carriage from the city that one sees so rarely at the shore.[35]

It's very likely that at the time I still retained some connection to the Sibiryakovs for whom I had worked as a tutor. Only by such a link can I now explain how I happened to be sitting in a box seat at that poetry concert. A box seat in the Sibiryakovs' theater. A clear evening, although I don't remember it, but undoubtedly clear, since, in the first place, it was spring, and in the second, whenever I recall that evening, it always seems that it took place in the afternoon . . .

Yes, a clear May evening in Odessa . . .

I was walking against the stream, so that several times I had to jump out of the way of those running toward me.

It was a sky-blue Odessa day with something golden in it. Trees? Cupolas?

The stream of people was moving toward me along the sidewalk and the pavement, and the main thing in that stream was a car in which a man was standing at his full height, a rather tall, shabby figure with a red ribbon pulled diagonally across his chest with great white letters on it that had started to peel like a kitchen wall. I still couldn't see what was written there, I still couldn't see, I still couldn't see, and then I saw: "Socialist Minister!"

It was the arrival of Kerensky in Odessa.[36]

People were running after him, beside him, and ahead of him. He stood with one hand thrust in the breast of his service jacket. The hand was gloved. That's right, I remember he was wearing a glove. They said it was because something had happened to him while shaking hands.

"Hurrah! Hurrah!"

He stood motionless in the car with his ribbon and his glove. His face was raw and a bit doglike, with sausage cheeks hanging down on either side of his lips.

I jotted down in a hunting magazine,
"The fourteenth of July was nothing."

But on July 14, the Bastille fell. It's from a sonnet by Maximilian Voloshin.[37] I made his acquaintance in Odessa. The Germans were there at the time. No, my memory deceives me; it was the French who were there. They had replaced the Germans after the latter had been defeated in the war and become preoccupied with their own revolution. Somewhat later Grigoriev would arrive in Odessa.[38] Maximilian Voloshin was fleeing to the Crimea.

He treated us young poets with condescension. (Several of us deserved recognition as masters.) He recited for our literary circle some poems whose general features I recall to this day.

In Uglich you lay, clutching a fistful
Of nuts in your childish, bloody hand,
And your mother, who had in a passage
Lingered, cried out over you in terror.

I think that's right. It's about Dmitry.[39]

Voloshin had a well-nourished build and a large head covered with russet hair that suggested either a turban or something to sit on; in a word, his head evoked Turkish associations. He did wear a pince-nez, however. He recited his verses superbly. He was something from the capital.

The occupation forces were moving out of Odessa . . . They were, I suppose, not even French, but Greeks with mules they fed on peas. They were small, swarthy soldiers who wore grassy green and yellow khaki uniforms and forage caps, which incidentally still weren't worn in our army. Fall? Spring? Summer? Winter? I don't know. It's all in the fog-enshrouded past. The figure of the symbolist poet stands out quite clearly, however. With his shaggy russet beard and no less shaggy hair. Where did his sympathies lie? What did he want for his native land? He wouldn't answer those questions then. He gave his answer later, when, dying in Soviet Crimea, he ordered that instead of a stone, a seat be placed over his grave, a small bench where a young man and woman might make declarations of love.

An odd procession was moving in my direction along Ekaterininsky Street. The first thing I saw was a donkey, its large head. It was in harness and pulling a wagon on whose box sat a Zouave and next to him a Greek in a grass-colored uniform. The wagon was covered with bowed rods over which something had been stretched that was now torn in several places, thus allowing the sunlight to enter.

Looming about the wagon were several other soldiers in various worn-out garments, but I paid no attention to them. It was difficult to concentrate on anything else after seeing that the light penetrating the tattered wagon fell on a corpse. A coffin lay in the wagon, its foot in the direction of movement, that is, toward the driver's back, and in the coffin was a dead soldier, his face seemingly ablaze from the beams of sunlight falling upon it. It wasn't clear for whose crown he had fought . . . I don't know where the procession was heading, and I don't know what had brought together the at least half dozen nationalities that surrounded the one in the coffin . . .

Units under the command of Hetman Grigoriev entered the city. Although still called a hetman thanks to his having earlier led what was merely a Cossack band, he was now a Red Army commander and under the discipline of and subordinate to orders from the center. He said of himself that he had knocked Poincaré's seat out from under him, since the retreat of French troops from Odessa under pressure from his own troops could have been seen as the end of intervention, the recognition of which had led to a change of ministers in France.[40]

I didn't see Grigoriev himself. I saw his troops, and an impression has remained with me of the huge red bows or rags fastened to their gray Caucasian caps, of the yellow coffins in which the fallen soldiers of those detachments were carried down Deribasovsky, of the trucks in which military bands stood and played, their helicons gleaming, and of something else I didn't fully understand—perhaps it was the light of compassion that sometimes shone in their faces.

Our family was financially ruined. My father was out of work, since the work he had done before the revolution no longer existed, and he didn't play cards either, since the clubs had long since operated only fitfully, first closing down, then opening up again. . . .

I didn't know that I'd been exposed during the disease's incubation period, and I didn't understand what was happening to me. Why had I suddenly begun to have such chills? Why, suddenly overwhelmed with fatigue, did I immediately look for somewhere to sit down, lest I fall down? I came home and everything seemed fine. They were drinking tea and eating sausage and bread and butter, the samovar was boiling, and the familiar knitted cozy covered the teapot . . . Why then was I so terribly depressed? My goodness, I didn't even know what I was depressed about. I took a piece of sausage and put it on some bread.

"Thank you, Mama!"

I set the glass of tea down on its saucer before me and all of a sudden sensed that everything had taken on a rosy hue, that everything had begun to swirl before me, and that only one thing remained that I was in any condition to do—lie down.

And lie down I did, smiling from an entirely illusory sense of well-being. Just think, I smiled at the doctor who said that if I'd gone around like that another day, I would have died of a perforated intestine. I smiled at the doctor who told me I had typhus.

"A cloud," the doctor said. "Typhus is a cloud. In Greek *typhos* means 'cloud.' You are in a cloud."

Why was he talking to me like that? He was a very fashionable Odessa doctor, a very good, expensive, and famous one. It seemed a carcass was sitting over me with its hands thrust into my body—into my liver and stomach. A round-faced carcass that I, a poet, readily likened to Azef.[41] A hulk with an oily face shiny from good health and gluttony and as if unshaven, as if it had not had time to shave.

"*Typhos*. A cloud. You are in a cloud."

He was talking to me like that because he hated me for being a poet.

There's already almost nothing left to write about. I could, of course, write novels with casts of characters of the sort written by Lev Tolstoy or Goncharov (who, by the way, also fell into a period when he was unable to write) but it would be depressing to do so.

A time to smolder.

I saw my sister die, the actual moment of death. Her face sank into the pillow and instantly turned darker, as if somebody had put his hand on it. She moaned the night before she died, and it seemed to us that she was singing. Still earlier she asked us if her coffin had been brought. And before that there had been a consultation in which the doctors had spoken in an undertone and from which it was possible to gather that they were concerned about perforation of her intestine.

The instant my sister died, my mother ran from the room and, stamping her foot on the floor, cried out,

"She's dying! She's dying!"

As if someone were to blame for it, as if it were possible to stop it . . .

Then she lay in a brilliant yellow coffin that gleamed like parquet, her feet extended toward me, her head in the direction of the window, and her arms folded across her breast like a small wax article lit up by the sun, indeed as if smoking from the sunlight caught in the little vessel of her interlaced fingers positioned not by herself, but by other, interfering hands.

The priest chanted in Latin, emphasizing the word *miserere*, which I, a Latinist, was hearing for the first time under such circumstances.

Then the coffin was carried to the door, onto the landing, down the stairs, and away. I wasn't at the cemetery, since I still couldn't go outside because of the typhus that had killed my sister. Eduard Bagritsky came to visit, as I recall.[42] It was a chilly day with pink windows . . . We read poetry.

It was called *kolevo*. On a small plate had been heaped something like brown porridge sprinkled with powdered sugar. It was a tradition at funerals.

"*Kolevo*," you heard first on one side, then on the other.

It was very important to have *kolevo*, to have it in the right place, and to serve it at the right time. The little plate appeared somewhere in the middle of a crowd the same somber color as the church above it and the ground below.

The experienced eye saw candied orange peel among the little brown grains. In short, it was what in the central regions is called *kutya*.

I managed to taste *kolevo* only once. I remember from that moment a noble flavor that was sweet but not cloying. A little spoon hovered in the air, I opened my mouth, the spoon struck, and the sweet grains trickled onto my tongue. *Kolevo* was given to everyone. Some old lady who had worked very hard on the funeral was obviously counting on the leftovers.

I didn't allow myself to think about my own death. It seemed impossible that the defenses of my family—of Mama and Grandma, indeed of the very evening around the table—would prove powerless against its intrusion. The first death I saw close at hand was that of a bandit who had fallen in the street from gunshot wounds. His was a slow, impressive, sensational death—or rather, dying. He lay on his back with his arms spread wide like one of Gogol's Cossacks, not far from the jewelry store he had attempted to rob.[43] He was dressed in blue. His chest rose up like a mountain. I didn't see him die. The sun shone brightly, and the crowd pressed on. The one life given to him in a million years, in a hundred million years, in a million million years, had come to an end. I remember that raised-up mountain of a chest, that whole world, that whole independent, gigantic universe, greater than ours perhaps, greater than all the millions of years, greater perhaps just because it was individual and independent.

Who am I, then? Who? That's a question that needs to be solved or answered. What is my view of the world? As a youth I was a savage. When it was necessary after my sister died to celebrate a requiem mass at the church within the prescribed period following a death, I went to the church to see the priest and conduct the appropriate negotiations. The priest's attitude toward the poor, it seemed to me, lacked the proper sympathy. I loudly expressed my indignation, probably even pounding the table with my fist. The priest, though horrified at first, answered me in a rather hooligan-like manner. Thus we parted, and on my way out I threatened him with nothing more or less than execution.

But the little bells were still rung at the requiem mass, and the priest still pronounced the benediction of sorrow and humility in a sad and broken voice . . .

Actually, I was a believer then. When it was thought that my grandmother was going to die from pneumonia, I fell down on my knees and begged God not to let it happen. It was spring, early spring, and Easter was drawing near. It was already getting dark late, and the not-very-bright streetlights of that era had already been turned on in the still bluish afternoon.

Alexander Mikhailovich Deribas was a respected man in Odessa, an expert on the city and its history who had lived there a long time and who in addition to that was the director of the public library. He was a tall old man with a long white beard and lips he shaped in conversation in a way that revealed his origin: he was French.

Once we young poets invited him to take part in an evening dedicated to Baudelaire. Eduard Bagritsky recited a translation of "L'Albatros" with his customary fire, and then somebody announced that Alexander Mikhailovich Deribas would now read one of the poems in French.

We noisily greeted the old man as he came up to the dais. He shaped his lips in the French manner and began to read the long alexandrines.

Sometimes the port was filled with gray military vessels. A large battleship, and surrounding it a bustle of smaller craft all the way down to motor launches . . . When a squadron put into Odessa in those days, the sailors strolled around the city captivating the hearts of its young women. There were always lots of ordinary sailors in Odessa, but these were the naval variety, with shoulder boards on their white jumpers.

In those days they wore mustaches in both the army and the navy. Sailors, especially, sported that adornment—small, brilliant as if lacquered, and, in the majority of cases (since the fleet had been assembled in the Ukraine), black mustaches. The sailors had dark, ruddy faces, their chests bulged handsomely, and their mustaches were silken . . . Sometimes, the generalization suggested itself that it was in fact the sailors who were the physical strength of the revolution in its first years.

I knew an intellectual sailor who while talking to me about communism used Maeterlinck's bluebird of happiness as a metaphor—Anatoly Zheleznyakov, the same man who had been given the responsibility (its technical execution, so to speak) of breaking up the meeting of the Constituent Assembly. As is well known, he suddenly approached Chernov, who was presiding, and said,

"It's time for you to adjourn now. The watch is tired."

The watch consisted of sailors.[44]

He was a very handsome man, Zheleznyakov, fair-haired, refined, and, I would say, of lofty bearing. He was killed in the Don region during a battle with Denikin, killed just after he had thrust himself from the embrasure of an armored train and simultaneously fired his two revolvers.[45] He hung from the embrasure, his head down, his arms extending over the side of the train and the revolvers dropping from his hands. This was told to me by an eyewitness.

At first I just looked at those windows beyond which bread could be seen on the tables, looked at them in the distance from across the street. And then I decided to go into that student cafeteria. Three or four steps, the entry way brightly lit by the light falling from the cafeteria itself, a towel twisted from frequent use hanging on a nail.

Most of all I wanted to try the sliced bread sticking out of the bowls. I sat down in front of one of those bowls. The names of the dishes and their prices were written in pencil on the menu card. I decided to have some barley soup and meat patties.

He appeared in our doorway dressed in a pea jacket, the skirts of which flapped and then flapped again . . . And then they flapped again, as he put his rifle down on its butt next to his foot, not knowing how to put it down or where else to put it, not knowing what else to do with a rifle in such a situation, the kind where you go into a home looking for spare provisions.

"Do you have any surplus?" he asked sternly, although he was a Ukrainian and the breath that came from his mouth along with the sounds was a peaceable one.

He grasped at once that there was nothing to spare. It was a different surplus than the one he needed. He had thought a rich apartment would be opened to him, but it wasn't rich. Before him was only a poor heap of furniture.

Stadnichenko used to visit me at the battery. Oh, what a handsome lad he was! In those days dark bushy eyebrows were much admired, and that's the kind he had. With dark bushy eyebrows, a broad, strong, yet not too prominent chest, ruby lips, and the ardent gaze of a youth . . .

Besides that, I loved him as a comrade . . . In our years at the gymnasium he and I had shared the same desk for a long time. Although I was serving in an artillery battery, we still weren't very far beyond those years. Again and again we told each other about meetings with former teachers and classmates.

"I saw Fudya!" chortled Stadnichenko. "He was wearing sandals!"

"Sandals!" I guffawed. "Fudya in sandals!"

Fudya had been the assistant headmaster at the gymnasium, an imbecile bureaucrat whose tortuous speech the whole school could imitate.

I served in the battery with sailors, those splendid sailors of revolutionary cast who talked about Lenin, those true sailors of the revolution whom

Alexei Tolstoy described in his *Road to Calvary* . . .[46] I still remember the names of a few of them, as well as their faces and voices. There was one whose last name was Shkolnik, a Ukrainian with a thin mustache instead of the stiff variety worn in the czarist army, a handsome lad in a pea jacket and sailor's cap with ribbons, vain like all sailors, sometimes even to the point of tears, and hot-tempered besides. I remember Nedvetsky, called Yury—Yury Nedvetsky. I think he was a Pole. He had, in any case, a kind of Polish elegance.

I had my midday meal at Dasha's, the Stogovs' maid. For eight rubles, as I recall, she gave me a first and second course—two dishes of tasty, rich food with garlic and red pepper.

I didn't eat in Dasha's kitchen, but next door in the dining room of my friends the Melisaratos after they themselves had finished eating. I don't know how or why it happened that I, with a house and parents of my own, had suddenly gone off by myself in such an odd way . . . I could, after all, have given the eight rubles to my own family. And how, moreover, did the Melisaratos reconcile themselves to the fact that I was eating somebody else's cooking in their dining room? And by myself. It's all in a fog.

Actually, it's not in a fog. On the contrary, that three in the afternoon exists very distinctly for me, that afternoon when I climbed the steps of the rather elegant iron stairway and, lifting my head to window level from one of those steps, yelled, or rather merely said,

"Dasha!"

"Come in," a woman's voice replied.

Then a plate with green contents entered the room, and then another with two slices of fragrant bread. I was at the Melisaratos'. They had just eaten and the crumbs still hadn't been cleared away. Possibly there was also something whitish with mustard on it still on the table, something stained with mustard like fresh excrement that didn't have a very appetizing appearance. The Melisaratos were Greeks, southerners, and not overly tidy.

With what gusto I ate! How delicious everything was! It too was Greek, southern. A cooked bell pepper lay powerfully in the borscht like the body of a bull, lay in the borscht presenting its flank like the bull that abducted Europa.[47]

"Is it good?" Dasha asked, appearing for a moment.

"Oh yes, very," I answered, given even in those years to politeness.

It was, I remember, a moonlit night. In that era, by the way, it was somehow more noticeable that a night was moonlit. Or rather, in comparison with that era, there is in our own no difference at all between a moonlit night and an ordinary one. Somewhere in a sky reddish with the reflection of neon lights, you will suddenly and unexpectedly see the disk of the moon, not shining, but flat and white and at any rate unbewitching. That really is the whole effect of a moonlit night in our time. I swear it's been many years since I've seen the black shadow of a moonlit wall, many years since I've seen the silhouette of a cat in the moonlight. It's even odd to think that there were such effects. It's as if we were once children together whom the world not only frightened but also delighted. Moonlight on the threshold of a front door! Moonlight in a garden! And the city, its roofs, chimneys, trees, and distant balconies all in moonlight! They'll tell me, go to the country, visit a small town. No, it isn't there either. In the country you'll find the same red glow, the shriek of radios, and a small, round, very remote moon that has almost lost its value for us. Now it influences only the ebb and flow of tides. Just try and tell the young the way ivy looked on a white wall in moonlight, or how you could see the gleam of moonlight on the back of a June bug creeping along a path, or how still the world became in moonlight—with that stillness of which Gogol spoke, when it seems that everything's asleep with its eyes open.[48]

And so it was on a moonlit night that I was walking the streets of Odessa with another young person. He was taller than I, with a larger nose and thicker lips, quite a bit louder, and stars blazed in his eyes. He recited poetry by heart, even striking his chest so I would listen.

As is well known, Eduard Bagritsky started out in Odessa. I was younger than he, not so much in years as in the fact that his poetry had been published many times, while mine had been published only once or twice . . .[49] He had taken a liking to me, however, and we became friends. Now, by the way, I pause with special feeling on the circumstance that he had taken a liking to me. Evidently he saw something in the beginner.

"Oh, Yurka's a fine fellow!" he would say to the others.

Why "fine"? There was nothing fine about me. I wrote under the influence of Igor Severyanin—mannered, idiotically pretentious . . . Yes, but all the same Bagritsky saw something.

I was walking around the city with Bagritsky. He, of course, held sway in everything: when one poem or another was being judged, when it was being decided where to go, when there was talk of a reconciliation or a falling out with somebody.

Once we came to a halt in front of a group of poets coming toward us, almost the entire group of Odessa poets, also out for a walk.[50] Odessa is a southern city and very pleasant to walk in. The city was southern, we were young, it was spring, and we were out for a walk. And so almost the entire group of Odessa poets came up to Bagritsky (and in fact to him, since I wasn't in the reckoning). Imagine an empty square with the little yellow tongues of tulips visible here and there, and in that empty space, or rather against its background with the fluttering flames of the tulips a certain distance beyond, five or so young men and women. They stood erect—slender and attractive—the women's faces partly concealed in the shadow of their cloches and their eyes gleaming in that shadow . . . Imagine that scene, and keep in mind as well that those young people wrote splendid poetry. Wouldn't it be something to remember the rest of your life? Wouldn't it, indeed!

"We have to be at the university tomorrow," Bagritsky said.

"Yes, that's right! They invited us," everyone remembered. "Yes, the university."

One might suppose that something like a literary reception was being held there . . . No, the students had merely invited us to come by in the afternoon to recite in one of the lecture halls and talk to them.

And so we arrived at the university lecture hall. It was one of the smaller ones, and it was filled to the brim—above you could see students silhouetted against the sky-blue balcony windows. A tall, dark, one-eyed professor of Turkic appearance was in charge—a well-known Odessa philologist. I don't remember the details—who did well and who didn't—but I do remember the professor's face as being, if not contemptuous, then at least disdainful. Accustomed to talking to his students about Milton, Homer, Dante, and Byron, he was now compelled to give his attention to nothing more than some young people from Odessa, simply to young people from Odessa who had, don't you see, taken up writing poetry. Sometimes it seemed that he wasn't even listening to the poems themselves, but was merely enduring the fact that here were "some young people from Odessa who had somehow got mixed up with poetry . . ."

I certainly don't wish that professor to be a negative character in my memoir. He doesn't deserve it. He was the most ordinary sort of professor; what was out of the ordinary was that in front of him stood a whole group of fine poets. Just try to judge such a phenomenon calmly, just try not to set yourself against it! And somewhere too it galled that bourgeois professor that the young poets shining so brilliantly before him were on the side of the revolution—were with the sailors and the cavalrymen in their pointed headgear and the Cheka.[51] But whatever the case, he did set himself against us, trying—and this you could not help but see—to protect his students from our influence.

"Byron," we heard from his lips again and again. "Byron, when he . . ."

And there followed something against us about Byron.

"The incomparable Dante . . ."

Then something against us about Dante.

"The sonnets of Petrarch . . ."

"The sonnets of Petrarch?" Bagritsky repeated. "Shall I write a complete sonnet for you right now?"

Bagritsky, to be sure, had no wish to enter into a competition with Petrarch . . . He was merely irritated by the professor's above-mentioned disdain and by the snobbish way he pronounced "Petrarch," drawling the "a."

"That's right," said the poet, nodding his tousled head, "I shall write a sonnet right here on the blackboard in front of everyone without making any corrections."

"Well, all right," said the professor, "you are like the cockerel who . . ."

"What's a cockerel got to do with it!" Bagritsky exploded. "Why, he's patting me on the head!"

That was impolite in regard to the well-known professor, but in that era of a great revaluation of values, who cared what was polite and what wasn't?

"Without corrections! A sonnet in five minutes without corrections!"

"Ha, ha, in five minutes, even?" the professor chuckled.

"In five minutes! Now I'll tell them what a sonnet is."

And facing the students with a piece of chalk already in his hand, Bagritsky conducted the explanation. And we too shall explain what a sonnet is to our own students. It is a poem written in observance of a special, rather difficult form consisting of two quatrains and two tercets—fourteen lines in all. The rhyme scheme of the first quatrain must be repeated in the second. And although that scheme is not repeated in the tercets, they must have a definite scheme of their own. What's important, however, is not the rhyme but the content; the sonnet's ideas must be set out in a particular way: in the first quatrain, the thesis, in the second, the antithesis, and in the two tercets, the conclusion—the proposition the poet wants to demonstrate.

"Clear?" asked Bagritsky.

"Clear!" answered the audience.

"Now give me a theme."

"A stone," someone said.

"All right, a stone!"

And the athlete strode into the arena.

"Perhaps some kind of potboiler will result," the professor began, "but . . ."

He immediately fell silent, for the first line had already appeared on the blackboard. A sling figured in it. The professor understood that if a poet who has been given "stone" as the theme of his sonnet begins with a sling, then he grasps what a sonnet is, and if he is able to control the idea, then so much more will he be able to control the form. The audience, the professor in front with his arms folded firmly across his chest, and we who were sitting in a group off to the side of the blackboard watched that prodigy of intellect flash. The chalk crumbling, Bagritsky walked along the letters appearing on the blackboard, completed a line, returned, walked back along another line, then returned again . . . The audience read the first word out loud, then the second, then the third, and then the whole line in its entirety, which was received like a gift with applause and cheering. The athlete quickly turned and smiled in acknowledgment.

"Quiet!" called the professor, raising his hand. "Quiet!"

The sonnet, written in the proper form, was finished in less than five minutes. On the blackboard behind the crumbling white letters loomed the images of a hero with a sling, a battle, and a gravestone.

Several days later, it happened that the professor came to doubt the authenticity, so to speak, of Bagritsky's experiment.

"It was prepared beforehand," he said. "Somebody in the audience called out a theme you had already chosen beforehand, and you . . ."

"All right," I can hear Bagritsky's soft voice, "let me write on another theme right now. What shall it be? Then it was a stone, now let it be water."

"Well, isn't that clever! The exact opposite! You thought of that beforehand, too. Water, a stone! Clever! You've written a sonnet on the theme of 'water'!"

Bagritsky waved his hand and we walked away.

"Bagritsky!" we heard after we had taken five or ten steps.

"Bagritsky!"

It was the professor calling.

"Bagritsky!"

And still louder.

"Bagritsky, at least turn around!"

Bagritsky walked on without looking back.

"At least turn around, my friend! At least turn around!"

Bagritsky glanced back and waved at the professor.

"Forgive me!" the professor called out. "I believe you! I believe you! It's hard to believe, but I do! It's hard to believe, hard! The unsurpassed Dante . . ."

Not waiting to hear the rest, Bagritsky turned and continued on his way.

Farther and farther. Further and further.

Moscow

I MANAGED TO SEE Sukharev Tower, which stood on the square whose main feature now is Sklifosovsky Hospital.[1]

I've just read that the tower was about sixty-four meters high and of Gothic design. I don't recall any impression of its height, only that it was big. I don't recall any impression of its being Gothic either. It was beautiful, fantastical, and pink, and Puss 'n Boots might have walked along its pathways visible from the square.

Private trade—foodstuffs and wares—was carried on from hand and hawker's stand at the tower's base and farther along the square in that year of my arrival in Moscow at the beginning of NEP.[2] I remember raisin bread, large loaves that looked like Suzdal churches.

I don't remember how the tower disappeared. Suddenly a broad, boring expanse was cleared. You couldn't even find a shard of glass through which it might have been possible to gaze into the past with Peter the Great and Leibniz as his guest.[3]

I saw the Red Gate, of which all that remains is the metro station named after it, the one with its entrance on Lermontov Square, so difficult to cross.

It was a small, flesh-colored triumphal arch with white plaster figures in baroque style, I think. I remember it on a wintry day, a reddish-brown arch amid the whiteness of the heavy snow on the pavement and rooftops.[4]

Who passed under that arch? The troops of Elizaveta Petrovna? That I didn't see, although the periods are very compressed. Just think, I was born seventy-eight years after the death of Napoleon. And within forty or so years of my birth, with nothing less than a fairy tale not very far behind me, a great technology emerged that has so transformed the world it's possible to describe it as a new planet.

One of my life's dearest memories is my work at the *Whistle*.[5] Everything came together there: my own youth, the youth of my Soviet homeland, and, if one may put it this way, the youth of our press, our journalism . . .

I began at the *Whistle* not as a journalist, incidentally. I served in what was called the "information section," and my job consisted of stuffing envelopes with letters written by the section head to the various addresses of the worker correspondents. I wrote in the addresses . . . Before that I'd already had something of a poet's calling, but since I'd embarked on it in Odessa, and I'd come from Odessa, the provinces, to Moscow, the capital, I had to start everything all over again. That's why I took the job of sealing envelopes.

Once—I don't remember anymore what the reasons were—the section head, Ivan Semyonovich Ovchinnikov, suggested that I write a verse satire based on a letter from one of the worker correspondents. And I wrote the satire . . . There was something in it about the Moscow River, about a certain captain, about a riverboat and its captain who stopped his boat not where he was supposed to according to the schedule but where his sweetheart lived. As it seems to me now, the satire wasn't badly done.[6]

"How shall I sign it?" I asked my section comrades. "Eh? What do you think? I need a pen name that's interesting but that still has an industrial tinge . . . Help me out."

"Sign it 'Chisel,'" said Grigorievich, one of my colleagues, fat and amiable.

"Well, why not?" I agreed. "That's not bad. I'll sign it 'Chisel.'"

When I think now how it happened that one day a young man unknown to anybody walked into the *Whistle* and soon afterward the pen name "Chisel" became familiar to almost every railroad worker, I can find but one answer. The young man clearly knew how to write verse satires with amusing rhymes, refrains, and jokes. But it wasn't only that.

It was above all that his verse satires reflected the life, daily routine, and labor of the railroad workers. And the worker correspondents played an enormous role in this. For it was they who obtained the material for him about the bureaucrats, grafters, shirkers, and other "operators" who were impeding the establishment of the transport system—its consolidation, growth, and development. The verse satires were composed in collaboration with the worker correspondents. To the correspondent's complaint, correct idea, observation, or wish, a verse form was added, and in a newspaper column topical things appeared that found a lively response in the reader.

Today I want to remember with a heartfelt word the worker correspondents of those years, frequently nameless but all passionate and courageous people who assisted in the building of the transportation system of those times.

Chisel was in essence a collective phenomenon, the creation of the railroad workers themselves. He was linked to his readers and helpers not only by the letters he received. Often he went out on the road with couplers, trackwalkers, and switchmen. And that was the connection with life so necessary and valuable to every journalist and writer.

The friends and others he talked to smelled of smoke and machine oil. They carried great lanterns in their hands, and from those lanterns latticed shadows fell upon the snow. He was enveloped by the steam of switching engines and deafened by the clang of metal. Bearded fellows in sheepskin coats vied to take him home. And he was happy. Even now in conversation he sometimes flaunts his knowledge of railroad terms; even now he tells of his journeys on freight trains, when he stood on the engine platform, a blizzard blowing in his face, and he was warm because the brakeman, addressing him, always said,

"Listen, friend!"

Circumstances were such that Chisel parted with the *Whistle.* Now he knows the railway life only through newspapers, photographs, and newsreels. It has become majestic, marvelous, that life. A new, perfected technology, a new form of existence. And new people. Now and then such a freight train sweeps by on television that you clasp your hands in delight. Now and then such a bridge rises up that it seems its scale will make your head spin. Bright homes, schools, cafeterias. And the magnificent faces of the people in the windows of locomotives, beside lathes and drafting tables, and in the radiance of festive gatherings and the soot of working days. And you are cheered by the thought that you too were with them all at the beginning of their splendid journey, that you too walked with those who were laying the road to the present . . .

One fall evening soon after my arrival in Moscow when Kataev and I were out walking in the city and on our way up Rozhdestvensky Boulevard, we saw coming toward us—that is, coming down past Rozhdestvensky Monastery—a tall, long-striding man wearing a short coat and fur cap and carrying a walking stick.

"Mayakovsky," Kataev whispered. "Look, it's Mayakovsky!"

I agreed at once that it was Mayakovsky. He strode past us, that person, all in the dull yellow haze of the fog—strode past a streetlight, where it seemed he had not two but dozens of legs, as it always does in the fog.

I wasn't really sure that it had been Mayakovsky, and neither was Kataev, but as time went by we became more and more convinced that of course it had been him. We told our acquaintances how we had run into Mayakovsky on Rozhdestvensky Boulevard, how he was walking through a fog, and how the fog made his legs flash like bicycle spokes . . . That's how much we craved association with that figure, that's the sort of general interest there was in him.

I still want to recall just when that name first caught my attention . . . No, not when the futurists came to Odessa. I still wasn't a poet then; I still lived for sport, for the football that was then getting under way in our country. Oh, that was remote from literature—those games on a green playing field with pennants marking the four corners—remote and even hostile. We were athletes, runners; we vaulted and played with poles—what had literature to do with that? True, I had translated the introduction to Ovid's *Metamorphoses* and got a five in Latin for it . . . But I was still deaf to the miracle taking place beside me: the birth of Mayakovsky's metaphors. I still hadn't heard that the heart is like a little church, or that you could try to leap out of yourself by bracing against your own ribs.[7]

Obviously it isn't enough for a great poet to be merely a poet. Pushkin, we shall recall, was disconsolate because the Decembrists, although they knew his verse by heart, still hadn't taken him into their plans. The author of *The Divine Comedy* populated Hell with his political enemies. Lord Byron helped the Greek insurgents in their struggle against the Turks.

And so it was with Mayakovsky; it didn't suit him either to be merely a poet. He took the path of agitation, the kindred path of the political tribune. Let's remember: in the beginning he was a youth dressed in a non-Russian velvet blouse, an artist with a predilection for radical art who wrote verses that were clearly influenced by French painting, that were simply full of allusions to its masters:

An automobile colored its lips
Next to Carrière's pale woman . . .[8]

And let's recall as well that he was at the same time a youth who thought about revolution, who had served time in prison, and who was photographed full face and in profile for the files of the police.

A screen adaptation of *Fathers and Sons* had been proposed. Meyerhold was supposed to direct.[9] I asked him whom he wanted for the role of Bazarov. He replied,

"Mayakovsky."

I saw some early silent movies in which Mayakovsky had roles.[10] Or not movies, really, since only fragments had been preserved that were difficult to make out: pale and guttering like running water, almost without images. And in those fragments the face of the young Mayakovsky—melancholy, passionate, evoking endless pity, the face of a strong and suffering person. Mayakovsky's acting was somehow reminiscent of Chaplin's. There was an affinity: the same realization that man is doomed to sadness and misfortune, and the same weapon against them—poetry.

The first time I saw Mayakovsky was in a Kharkov theater at a recital of the recently completed *150,000,000*.[11] Valentin Kataev and I sat in a box seat and waited with intense curiosity for the emergence on stage of the person who had just been announced by the chair. The stage was empty but for a small table at which the executive committee sat—probably people from the party's municipal council, its editorial offices, and the Komsomol leadership. A vast empty stage, and in its depths, bare walls with balconies of some kind . . .

Not only were Kataev and I—two young poets—excited. We didn't look around, so we couldn't tell what the rest of the audience was feeling, but those sitting at the table—experienced and even, one sensed, skeptical people—were eagerly peering into the secret of the wings.

I was sure someone of theatrical appearance would come out—red-haired, almost a buffoon . . . We could easily have had such an idea about Mayakovsky; we were, after all, well acquainted with the yellow blouse and the literary scandals of the past.

An entirely different sort of person stepped from the wings.

Certainly we were impressed by his great height and by the eyes of exceptional power and beauty that gazed from under his brow . . . Generally speaking, however, he was someone of ordinary Soviet demeanor, a slightly weary person dressed in a sheepskin jacket with a lambskin collar and a lambskin cap pushed slightly back on his head. It at once became clear that although a famous poet, he had come not to win laurels for himself but to work.

Later on I would see Mayakovsky perform at the Polytechnic Museum in Moscow, and the image of a man at work would be confirmed: before going on stage, he would take off his jacket and roll up his sleeves.

It is essential the reader understand the nature of Mayakovsky's celebrity. We have famous writers today, famous actors, famous people in a variety of fields. But Mayakovsky's fame was legendary. What do I mean by that? That someone is constantly remembered, that people strive with each other to have their say about him . . . And not only about what he has done, but about the man himself.

"I saw Mayakovsky yesterday, and he . . ."

"You know, Mayakovsky . . ."

"Mayakovsky, they say . . ."

That's what legendary fame is. Esenin had it.[12] And, judging by the testimony of his contemporaries, so did Shalyapin, and very likely to equal degree.[13] And without question the whole country, indeed the whole world, kept its eyes fixed on Maxim Gorky . . .

That legendariness is inherent in the person himself. Perhaps it derives from his looks. More likely it comes from his having done something impressive in the past. Thus Gorky was a tramp, thus Shalyapin came from the people, thus Mayakovsky was a futurist. Gorky discouraged that fame ("What do you think I am, a ballerina?") . . . Indeed, none of those I've mentioned especially troubled himself about it; it came of its own accord. Mayakovsky, by the way, never postured or behaved in an affected way. I remember his saying facetiously but still with irritation after noticing somebody staring at him in awe,

"He's looking at me and whispering something."

The appearance of his figure on any threshold was sensational, bringing joy and evoking passionate interest, like the parting of a curtain in some wonderful theater. That figure was as tall as the lintel, wore a cap, and carried a walking stick.

I was young when I first made Mayakovsky's acquaintance, but I could still forget any lover's tryst if I knew I might spend that hour with him.

Being in his company was extraordinarily flattering to one's self-esteem.

Probably he was aware of that, but his influence on people—or rather the powerful impression he made on them—he managed with great subtlety, care, and delicacy, always relying on self-deprecating humor to spare the other person's feelings. Like all outstanding people, he was a kind man.

Whenever there was occasion to do so, he spoke of his mother with pleasure.

I remember a group standing at an intersection. It was a hot day and the sunlight gleamed in the car's surface. The car was Mayakovsky's own, a small-engine Chevrolet.

"Where to, Vladimir Vladimirovich?" I asked.

"My mama's," he readily answered.

He had bought that car in America, I think. In those days it was unusual to have your own vehicle, and that Mayakovsky had one was a topic of conversation in our circles. The acquisition of a car bespoke his fondness for the contemporary, for the industrial, for technology and journalism, something that was also expressed in the fact that fountain pens stuck out of his pockets, that he walked around on ultracontemporary thick soles, and that he had written "Brooklyn Bridge."[14]

Here we are, he and I, walking down Pimenovsky Lane past a fence with a garden on the other side. I'm walking along the fence, and he's following the outside edge of the sidewalk, as tall people usually prefer to do in order to feel less constrained.

Whatever company or situation we find ourselves in, I sense an inexhaustible interest in him, a constant astonishment and deference. He has a walking stick in his hand. He doesn't so much strike the ground with it as swing it in the air. In order to see his face, my gaze has to clamber a rather long time up his vest, along the buttons of his shirt, then over the knot of his tie . . . True, it could also fly up at once.

"Vladimir Vladimirovich," I ask, "what are you writing now?"

"A comedy with a murder."

I take this to mean that he's writing a comedy in which, among other things, a murder takes place . . . It turns out it's also the comedy's title.[15]

I nearly exclaim,

"Bravo!"

"Guests are invited in it according to the principle of 'who won't be here,'" he says.

"How's that?"

"Come on over, the Ivanovs won't be here . . . Come on over, Mikhail Petrovich won't be here. Lyubochka won't be here either . . . Come on over . . ."

Mayakovsky drank little, mainly the type of wine now known as "Soviet Champagne" but in those years called "Abrau-Dyurso."

Once when I shouted to a waiter, "Some champagne!" Mayakovsky said, "Oh no, what's the matter with you? Just say, 'Abrau'!"

Although he drank little, I nevertheless heard him say that he liked to be a bit tight, a bit intoxicated. But he wasn't in any way a drinker. I remember bowls of punch. Punch truly enjoyed his affection, although with orange peels and apples as in a compote it's a sweet concoction, more a refreshing drink than an alcoholic beverage. It's of course possible that he drank in the Petersburg period, but that's outside my competence, so to speak.

Sometimes he would turn up on the verandah of the Herzen House restaurant in the summertime when its patrons were sitting at little tables next to the railing with its flower boxes, sitting among the leaves, the green tendrils, and the tiny sticks used to prop the flowers up, sitting, indeed, among the red and yellow flowers themselves—geraniums, most likely . . .

Everyone had already seen his figure by the gate at the far end of the garden. Whenever he turned up, everyone would start whispering and exchanging glances and, as always happens at the beginning of a show, settling back in their chairs. A few acquaintances greeted him. He slowed his pace, looking for an empty table. Everyone looked at his sport jacket—blue, at his trousers—gray, at his walking stick—in his hand, at his face—long, and at his eyes—unendurable.

Once he sat down at a table not far from mine and, reading from the *Evening Moscow,* suddenly tossed off in my direction,

"Olesha's writing a novel called *Nietzsche.*"

He'd just read a note in the paper's literary chronicle section. I knew there was nothing there about a novel called *Nietzsche;* rather, it was about one called *The Beggar* . . .[16]

"*The Beggar,* Vladimir Vladimirovich," I corrected him, taking enormous pleasure in the fact that he was associating with me. "The novel's called *The Beggar.*"

"It's the same thing," he answered brilliantly. And in fact, hasn't somebody writing a novel about a beggar—and you have to take the period and my tendencies as a writer into consideration—hasn't such a person read a lot of Nietzsche?

It didn't happen just yesterday, as people say of such events; it's happening at this very moment. I see that table off to my left the distance of a rowboat; I see the syphon of seltzer water, the page of newsprint, the walking stick hidden in a corner of the tablecloth, and Mayakovsky's eyes, the kind of which it's said in Homer that they are like a bullock's.

I made several attempts to list Mayakovsky's metaphors. But no sooner had I begun than I gave up, each time convinced that such a listing would be tantamount to transcribing almost every one of his lines.

Which one is the best? Isn't it the idea that by bracing against your ribs you can leap out of your own heart?

I came upon that metaphor for the first time while reading *A Cloud in Pants* at a very young age. I still didn't have any real grasp of what poems were. Obviously there'd been meetings with the galloping statue, the czar who feasted in Petersburg town, and the star that spoke to another star.[17] The joyful apprehension of it, however, had been hindered by the fact that the experience hadn't taken place freely of its own accord but had been accompanied by a sense of obligation, since those verses were "taught" in school and familiarity with them was as much a lesson, say, as mathematics or the law. Their beauty was thus extinguished. But here, all of a sudden, was an encounter with poetry on the loose, so to speak, with poetry on its own . . . So that's what poetry is. "I will leap out!" the poet cries. "I will leap out! I will leap out!"

He wants to leap out of his own heart. He braces against his ribs and tries to leap out of himself.

It's strange, but in that instant I had visions of an urban sort—velodromes, the arcs of of bridges—and maybe my gaze really did fall upon something grandiosely urban then . . . In any case, that person clambering out of himself on the spiral of his own rib cage entered my consciousness as something enormous, something capable of blocking out the sunset . . . Thus, when I later met the real Mayakovsky, he always seemed to me more than a mere human being: either a city or the blaze of the sunset above it.

I would say a whole theater of metaphors is revealed in his books. From the sweet rolls about which "the scrolls of violins are twisted" to the bridge in which he glimpsed the vertebrae of a culture.[18]

I once offered to sell Mayakovsky a rhyme.

"Of course," he said, in a serious, businesslike manner. "What is it?"

"'Medicamént' and 'copper cént.'"

"A ruble."

"But why so little?" I asked, taken aback.

"Because 'medícament' is pronounced with the stress on the second syllable."

"Then why do you want it at all?"

"Just in case."

I was infatuated with Mayakovsky. Whenever he turned up I was overcome with confusion; whatever the reason I trembled whenever his attention fell on me . . . As regards my own, it was invariably on him. I missed no gesture, no glance, and obviously no word. I've already written that even though I was young when I was associating with him, I would still forgo a lover's tryst if I learned that I might see him at a friend's house instead. No, I would decide, it's better to see Mayakovsky . . .

I was younger than he was—significantly, about ten years—and only starting out then. True, I was starting out well, and he liked that. Was he aware of my rapturous regard for him? Whatever the case, from time to time, at one gathering of literary people or another, a tacit understanding was established between us, and it was then ineffably pleasant to sense that some rejoinder not actually directed at me was nonetheless essentially intended for my consideration and awaited my agreement or judgment . . .

He was very strict with me, just as he was with everyone, and he spoke his mind about those things of mine he didn't like, never sugaring the pill:

"I read your story. I've never read anything so boring!"

But he could praise too. How happy I was when he did! I remember once sitting in an actors' tavern, drinking wine and eating crayfish, and he was praising something of mine, and I was on the summit of happiness. Couples were dancing round us, and the young women were looking over their shoulders right at Mayakovsky, at the luminary, and I was proud to be sitting with him—the two of us together, just the two of us—I was proud and exultant . . . We were eating crayfish. When you remove their shells, you keep pricking your fingers on them, and Mayakovsky said to the maître d',

"You should at least have given them a manicure or something."

He was very affectionate and comradely with those who shared his literary tastes and views. Though ferocious in attacking his enemies, he was really quite considerate with like-minded people—sympathetic to them, attentive like a physician. The unexpectedness of that transformation—from fierce gladiator on the tribune to thoughtful friend of those close to him in spirit—extraordinarily adorned his image. I too shared his tastes and views. I remember once when we were playing cards . . . There were many players, and it was loud and smoky. I had lost, and I remarked to the person sitting next to me that I had also lost the money intended for a friend undergoing treatment in the Crimea. Mayakovsky too had lost and was agitated and upset . . . Could I have thought that he'd heard the words spoken to my neighbor?

The next morning the phone rang.

"This is Mayakovsky speaking. Did you send your friend the money? If you didn't, I can lend it to you."

Ill-wishers thought him crude, but he was a kind man and, as I have already said, even considerate.

It's astonishing that the poet who began as a futurist writing chiefly for the few, began after the October Revolution to strain passionately toward the masses, the reading multitudes. He was almost constantly off somewhere, performing at factories and universities or before military units in various cities throughout the country. He couldn't live without that contact with the public; it was a source of joy and inspiration, and it kept him young.

"I'll recite something new for them, something new," I remember his saying as he paced in the wings off stage at the Polytechnic Museum in Moscow. The student-filled auditorium buzzed with anticipation. "Students! For them, you have to recite something new! I'm nervous!"

Rolling up his sleeves—many have remembered this, but it's impossible not to—rolling up the sleeves of his "freshly laundered shirt"[19] after removing his jacket as if preparing to set down to work, he strode toward the stage entrance.

On stage he was magnificent. Leaving aside the remarkable poems and their remarkable recitation, his very relation with the audience was thrilling. The brilliant wit of his retorts to the sallies of one or another listener, the surprising observations eliciting stormy applause, the forceful views on poetry producing a hush in the auditorium—all that was unique, inimitable, and impressive to the highest degree, and it compelled one's astonishment at the talent of the man, at his intellect and vitality.

Mayakovsky was tall, or rather, large, since unlike most tall people he wasn't asthenic but of powerful build. He had a large but for his size proportionate head, a strong nose, also big and frequently whistling with a cold (Mayakovsky said that as a southerner he was always catching cold in Moscow), and a prominent chin.

His eyes were incomparable—large, black, and with a gaze that seemed, when you looked at him, to be the only thing in the world at that moment. It seemed that around you nothing else existed in that moment but his gaze.

Whenever I remember Mayakovsky, I immediately see those eyes peering through the wallpaper or foliage. They're looking at me, and it seems that the world has become still and mysterious. What kind of gaze was it? It was the gaze of genius.

He was the king of metaphor. Once he and the poet Iosif Utkin, who has passed away too, were playing billiards.[20] After a shot, something happened to the balls, causing them to crash together and bounce . . .

"The steeds of fortune," I said.

"The blind steeds of fortune," Mayakovsky corrected me, leaning on his cue.

There is among the thousands of metaphors he created one I find astonishing. Speaking of the power of words, he said that to the power that "box seats applaud," he preferred the one that makes "coffins break loose to stride upon their four oaken feet."[21] Only a Dante could have said that.

I remember the heartrending sense of loss I experienced when I was told Mayakovsky had passed away but an hour before.

"What? My God, forever? Forever?"

A short time later I saw his body. He lay covered with a sheet on a couch against the wall, the shadow of death on his face. That evening I stood on the truck that took him in his coffin to the Writers' Club, a coffin whose paint was still tacky. It was an April evening, cold, with a tiny moon in the sky, and I shall never forget it.

Mayakovsky wasn't a party member, as is well known. But he was a communist with all his heart. When he recited poems directed against the enemies of the country's new life—enemies of whatever kind, from Chamberlain to bureaucrats and bribe takers—it seemed that a sword flashed in his hands.[22]

I once dreamed Mayakovsky and I were talking face to face. There was nobody else in the room and we were sitting very close together . . . I saw his face in front of mine, and I was saying that besides the truly great poems he had written, this book here (I was holding a book in my hands), this book, I was saying, this book here . . . I don't remember what else I said, but there was delight in my words. I told him I could write a book about him . . . He enjoyed that. I spoke with special meaning, since all the while I sensed subconsciously that he was dead. His face was kind and sad, and it even seemed to me that there were tears in his eyes.

When the evening after his death we had gathered on Gendrikov Lane in what is now a museum but what was then merely the Briks' apartment,[23] we suddenly heard loud noises coming from Mayakovsky's room—very loud noises, unceremoniously loud, as if somebody were chopping wood. It was the opening of Mayakovsky's cranium to allow the removal of his brain. We listened in horror-struck silence. Then a man in a white gown and boots came out of the room—either an attendant or a medical assistant, but a stranger to us—and in his hands he held a basin covered with a white cloth raised in the middle almost like a pyramid, indeed, just as if that soldier in boots had been carrying a paschal cream-cheese pudding. In the basin was Mayakovsky's brain.

There are two monuments to Mayakovsky in Moscow, one a statue he would very likely have regarded severely, and the other the subway station bearing his name, which he, who was so fond of everything industrial, would surely have viewed with delight.

It's a very beautiful station, with walls made of steel arches whose steel has mostly been left in its natural state, so to speak, even though it's been painted here and there with minium. The combination of the two colors reminds you of machinery—it's very industrial.

Once it occurred to me that the arches were the armholes of some gigantic vest. The next instant I knew how the station would be conceived.

"Mayakovsky's steel blouse," my imagination told me.

That isn't bad. He who had once worn the yellow blouse of the futurist now stands before us in the steel blouse of a giant.

Hamlet is a strong, weary person, a sort of Mayakovsky. I first saw *Hamlet* in Odessa. He was played by Slonov.[24] I was a gymnasium student then in one of the earlier classes. I understood nothing and liked nothing except at the end of the play when one of the bodies rolled crosswise down a stairway.

"What do you read, my lord?"

"Words, words, words."[25]

That would be a good title for this book:

Yu. OLESHA
Words, Words, Words
Yu. OLESHA
I think, therefore I am.

One day I shall part with you solemnly, choosing a special occasion, but for now, a parting in memory. I bought a roast chicken at a store and, carrying it by the leg, tore off individual pieces of meat, ripped off the wings, extracted the plow of its breastbone . . . In a word, it's clear: I consumed the chicken on my way home. Then, afraid a whole chicken was too much for one person, I tossed it, already in finished form, onto the pavement to my right. Since it was evening and the street was hardly a main one and thus quite dark, nobody saw me. The chicken splashed white and was gone. I continued on my way home, that is, to the printing office of the *Whistle* on Stankevich Street.

Here's a farewell in rough draft, dear life.

By the way, I can already recall beyond the frame, as the expression has it, the little wooden room at the printing office where I lived. However, it shouldn't be recalled beyond the frame.

Next door on the other side of the plywood wall of my room lived Ilf in another room just like it.[26]

They were narrow though cheerful and brightly lit little closets. Perhaps more than anything else, it was as if Ilf and I were living in matchboxes.

Ilf and I also shared an apartment. Once Kataev showed up accompanied by several other people, including Esenin. Although he was wearing a dinner jacket and patent-leather pumps, Esenin had a disheveled appearance; apparently he had been in a fight. There was a young man with him whom he kept taunting, even taking off a patent-leather shoe and striking him in the face with it.

"You disgust me with your Catholicism!" he kept repeating. "You disgust me!"

Then he recited "The Black Man." While doing so, he unsteadily grabbed hold of the bookcase (since he was drunk) and it fell down.

I hadn't heard "The Black Man" till then.

My friend, my friend, I'm very, very ill,
I don't even know what's causing the pain.
Either a fierce wind is whistling
Over an empty and desolate plain,
Or else, like rain a grove in September,
Alcohol is pelting my brain.[27]

It was splendid. And he was singular: drunk, mean, golden-haired, and well-dressed, although disheveled and bruised after a fight.

When I came to Moscow to live—to begin my life there, in fact—Esenin's fame was in full flower. In the literary circles in which I too moved, he was talked about constantly: his poetry, his beauty, how he had been dressed the night before, whom he'd been seen with, his scandals, even his fame.

I heard no hostile notes in those conversations; on the contrary, one had the sense that Esenin was liked.

That was soon after the end of his affair with Isadora Duncan. He had gone to America with her and had just returned, and now they were saying the affair was over. By the way, after he got back from America, Esenin published his impressions of New York in *Izvestiya,* calling the piece "The Iron Mirgorod."[28] I remember my pleasure in that fine title even now, and I remember just as well the newspaper with his feature article, or rather, I remember the morning I stood reading the paper and, turning a page, seeing the headline.

"'The Iron Mirgorod,'" I read out loud, obviously inviting someone else to join in my delight in that title.

I was still young, very young.

Today is the solstice. It's very hot, and one could repeat everything that was recorded last year on approximately the same date in June.

Some gaze as if from a fog; others are even worse—as if immersed in dough. Anatoly Marienhof gazed up at me in a restaurant yesterday as just such a pie decoration. Good Lord, the handsome dandy Marienhof?[29]

"How's Nikritina getting along?"

"She's waiting for your play."

Words! Nikritina was an elegant or rather sinuous woman with a small, dark head, an actress who among other plays had acted in one of mine.[30] Marienhof, the imagist poet and author of memoirs about Esenin, has of late been writing plays that have fatally become the object of strong political censure even before reaching the stage. Thus, only their titles have remained, usually memorable and beautiful: "The Conspiracy of Fools," "The White Lily," "The Crown Prince." The picturesqueness of the imagists is still strong in him. Yet how much higher, how incomparably greater than the imagists was their comrade Esenin.

I might also have run into Esenin in a restaurant corridor like that. He too might have looked at me through a fog or from a pie crust. No, obviously it could only have happened as it did. He passed away while still young and golden, the strands of his hair streaming in the wind. I saw him only a few times in my life.

I saw the celebrated chess player Capablanca. He was then, after his match with Alekhine, the ex–world champion.[31]

Ilf and I entered the premises of a club on Bolshaya Lubyanka where we knew Capablanca was supposed to appear in a program of simultaneous play. The program was already well under way when we arrived. Between two rows of small tables at which the challengers sat and on which were placed black and yellow boards with chess pieces in a few instances already gathered in whole crowds, a dark-haired young man walked, stopping in turn before each table to make his move. Though tall, he was portly, and he had a pale, yet swarthy face—rather ugly and a bit effeminate, with proboscis-like, haughtily sensual protruding lips. It was clear at once that he was a southerner and moreover the resident of a tropical south altogether alien to us, with bananas and stars low in the sky.

He kept his small hands in the pockets of his jacket, which, since it was buttoned, crept up over his belly. Coming up to a table, he would linger for a moment, then deftly pick up a piece and move it. Sometimes while passing to the next table, he would glance back at the previous one . . . A multitude of eyes gazed up at him. He was careless and offhand, even lackadaisical, with only his proboscis-lips moving in a sort of quiver as he puckered and extended them.

He wore a black suit, and the tie lying on his white shirt was black as well. There was something old-fashioned and individual in his figure that called more for an illustration than a photograph, something of genius.

In Kharkov? Yes, yes, it was in Kharkov. Somebody said to me,

"Why, that's Mandelstam."

Two figures, male and female, were moving toward us along a deserted section of street. Although it wasn't a winter day, the male figure was wearing a fur coat and moreover one that rendered him unnaturally broad, since it was patently the wrong size. On the path between the massif of his fur coat and the lofty peak of his matching fur cap gleamed the tiny pebble of his face . . . Mandelstam was clean-shaven, toothless, old-looking, yet of regal appearance. His head was thrown back, and his hands were perpetually beginning or ending some impractical, outlandish gesture.

Europe of the Caesars! Since Metternich
Directed a goose quill at Bonaparte,
For the first time in a century your
Mysterious map changes before my eyes![32]

I'd like to write a whole study of Mandelstam, a portrait of him. Is a study a portrait? Certainly.

Mandelstam was for us Odessans above all a Petersburg poet.

Anna Akhmatova's real name is Gorenko. She was born near Odessa in the village of Nerubaiskoe (in the Odessa area, as people say now).[33] It pleases me to know that she and I are from the same parts. Altman painted her.[34] Hook-nosed, slender. Mandelstam wrote about her: of her voice that it "unchains the depths of the soul," of herself that for him she resembled Rachel—where now, he says, in front of him sits Akhmatova, "a pseudo-classical Phaedra, there once sat Rachel!"[35] I consider her one of the most talented poets of the twentieth-century Russian constellation. When I was a schoolboy she was already famous. After I became well known as a writer myself, I was still unable to make her acquaintance. I thought a lot of myself then, although I had the excuse that everyone "recognized" me. Finally in Leningrad at the Hotel Europe, when toward evening I had entered the restaurant and sat down at a table, the writer P. came over to me and said,

"Come on, I'll introduce you to Akhmatova."

I went up to her. I had, perhaps, a desire to provoke her. In any event, she would, damn it, have to realize whom she was dealing with. I sat down at her table. I have no idea whether my turning up made any impression on her. Just as I did then with almost everyone, I started showing off. Suddenly she began to speak. Among other things she said she was translating *Macbeth*. There are, she said, some lines in it where a character observes that his country is more like a stepmother than a mother and that people die there even before the flowers in their bonnets have had a chance to wilt.[36] She said she liked that. Or rather, she didn't say it, she showed it in her face. It's possible that knowing of my fame she had the same notion I did: to give me to understand who she was. For her part, it came off extremely well. I still felt like a little boy, a schoolboy.

I notice that there are many people more intelligent than I, people who aren't especially creative, or who aren't creative at all but who have a gift for reflection. Thus, the psychiatrist Berkovich (the brother of the Berkovich who was famous for arguing with Mayakovsky in the latter's public debates and who, incidentally, even got the better of him, to Mayakovsky's good-natured satisfaction); thus, that psychiatrist spoke intelligently today about Lev Tolstoy's determinism in *Anna Karenina*.

I saw Stanislavsky several times in my life.[37] The first was when the Moscow Art Theater was celebrating what was probably its thirtieth anniversary. I had written a play, *The Three Fat Men,* that had been accepted by the Art Theater, and I was thus present at the celebration as an author—for both the gala performance and the banquet afterward.[38] While the welcoming addresses were being read to the audience before the performance, Stanislavsky and Nemirovich stood very close together, indeed, virtually arm in arm, and each tried to keep from upstaging the other. They shifted their feet slightly in place, and their efforts not to upstage each other were quite noticeable, thereby sometimes creating if not a ridiculous impression then at least a comical one . . .

Later at the banquet, Stanislavsky, grinning, gray-haired, dressed in a black suit, and bending low to keep from bumping into the multicolored balloons that were hanging or rather hovering in the air in great numbers, suddenly came over to me with a goblet in his hand. There he was in front of me. I barely managed to get to my feet. Sitting next to me, I recall, were Erdman and Bulgakov . . .[39]

Holding his goblet for clinking, he said flattering things about my play, and I made some sort of reply. We were all a bit tight. The balloons hung like lianas. Raising her downy lip, the young Elanskaya smiled languidly with an air of long suffering . . .[40]

Behind the invention of the Stanislavsky system (and perhaps as a reason for it) one senses the author-actor's aggrieved insight that the performance is never as good as the drama itself. Great actors, Stanislavsky realized, have known how to defeat that superiority of the drama, but could one be content with such private, isolated instances? And so he undertook the execution of a striking plan: to give every actor the possibility of achieving the level of the great.

When the play's in rehearsal, I see in general how well written *The List of Assets* is.[41] And here one might even go a bit further and add what a remarkable work it is. It was written, you see, by somebody only thirty-two years old and, moreover, in the land of the Soviets amid entirely new relationships then still hard to grasp.

My Margeret, whom Meyerhold permitted to run about the stage carrying nothing more or less than a whip, is no less vivid a character than the Icelandic dramatist's Feilan.[42]

In one version of the play I spoke of the heart as being a muscle. The Icelander has the same definition. Thus, on different points of the globe sit artists who see the same way.

In Central Asia they especially esteemed my line where it's said that a young woman stood the "distance of a whisper from a young man." The "distance of a whisper" isn't bad.[43]

Once Valentin Kataev and I were sitting in box seats at the old, still unrenovated Vakhtangov Theater watching my play *The Conspiracy of Feelings.*[44]

There was a small antechamber behind the box, and when we stepped into that little room during intermission, we found a large, dark, rumpled man sitting by himself in a corner against the wallpaper. A moment later the actor Ruslanov came in (the son of Sergeenko, who had lived in Tolstoy's time and been his biographer) and presented us to the stranger, who turned out to be Vladimir Grigorievich Chertkov.[45]

Naturally, the presence of Tolstoy's famous friend at a performance of my play rather unnerved me.

"Did you like it?" I asked.

He answered (so here was the famous candor!),

"Excuse me, I'm deaf."

But he said it so that it would be clear; he had no wish to needle or mock me or show disdain. He was simply acknowledging a fact. And so from the groves and lawns of Yasnaya Polyana departed so far into the past there flew in that instant the sound of some implement unfamiliar to me.[46]

Kataev with his bent for sarcasm continually made jokes on that theme: "So, the great are deaf to your work. They are deaf to it . . ."

It's my conviction I've written a book—*Envy*—that will last for centuries. I've kept the manuscript written in longhand. Elegance emanates from its pages. See how I talk about myself!

I've been reading *A Lone Sail Gleams.* It's good. Kataev writes better than I do. He's written a lot. I've written only fragments, a mere collection of metaphors. He has one about hyacinths. The pale yet strong arrow of the hyacinth. Not bad.

In a time of black drudgery, my legs slid apart, the icy sleet flew low, and I ran against the wind, ran because against that wind another wind drove me on.

How much work remains to be done, how much toil.

(A subject.)

A voice teacher (Tsvetkov) passionately dreams of reading one of Shakespeare's tragedies to the whole school. In his opinion, none of the young people is acquainted with Shakespeare. (One girl said she had seen *Intrigue and Love* in Moscow. Tsvetkov: "There, you see? That's by Schiller!")[47]

The point isn't whether they know Shakespeare or not; it's Tsvetkov's passionate desire that that world of images should pour from his lips and no one else's.

Once while talking with the schoolchildren, he says that if he should ever actually read them a Shakespeare tragedy, it wouldn't hurt to organize that "encounter of youth and Shakespeare" with a special festiveness. (If the play's in verse, he says,

Twelve drummers drumming let us then call forth!

Write the play in blank verse, attempting to do it so that the verse isn't noticeable—it should be felt only occasionally, at points of heightened emotion.)

The idea of a festive occasion (twelve young pioneers with drums) makes the children laugh and appeals to them (Tsvetkov had in fact tossed it out as a joke), and when the evening cherished by Tsvetkov in his dreams at last has begun—he has already started, has already read the first lines—suddenly, to general laughter and applause, a drum roll breaks forth, and twelve young pioneers with drums enter with Tonya at the head. She's dressed in a theater costume (she got it from the local playhouse) that had seemed Shakespearean to her (a broad hat with a plume, a short military tunic, a belt over her shoulder with a sword hanging from it, and boots with low tops). The young pioneers form a rank, and Tonya reports to Tsvetkov.

The reading is spoiled.

The old man's mortification.

Tonya (she had been his favorite voice student in the lower grades) is upset at having distressed the old man. Mortification really is fatal (both internally and physically), and it's possible Tsvetkov will leave the little town on foot . . . Here there might be a scene in which Tonya, catching up with the departing Tsvetkov at a railway stop, asks him to forgive her, after which they have a conversation about youth and culture.

Tonya (she's unpretentious, merry, affectionate) promises the old man that she herself will give a talk on Shakespeare. He's delighted: "Yes, yes, you'll give a talk, and then I'll read a tragedy."

With that the first act comes to an end, and the audience is left in expectation of events having to do with the schoolgirl Tonya's talk on Shakespeare.

Then the war and the arrival of Hitler's troops in the little town. And what happens to Tonya. What happens is something heroic that reveals how like a character from Shakespeare she is, how like a Shakespearean heroine. This is her "talk on Shakespeare."

The basic idea of the play: anyone can acquaint himself with Shakespeare; the important thing is to be heroic yourself.

Here the following is possible. The fascists have bivouacked in the school, now half-destroyed. An old and flabby sergeant major of the storm troopers is fond of flowers (he had cultivated them at home). He asks Tonya, who turns up in the school yard in the course of the act's development,

"What blooms here in the spring?"

"What difference does that make to you?" she asks. "After all, you won't be here then, will you?"

Offended in his finest feelings ("That isn't good; I was merely asking about flowers in a peaceable way") the sergeant major orders Tonya to be hanged, and she is.

And then little by little a legend takes form among the German soldiers about the Soviet girl who had spoken such proud and beautiful words to the terrible sergeant major's face (his ferocious fame has spread to many garrisons) . . . The legend is at once full of respect for the girl and of popular sympathy with her. (Contrast the ranks with their fascist commanders.)

The unit stationed in the region is commanded by a half-insane officer (his theme is the worldwide rule of the German race). It becomes known to him that the image of the proud schoolgirl has deeply affected his soldiers, that a legend has sprung up . . . This infuriates him, and bursting into a tavern where, as it happens, frightened, half-drunk soldiers are recounting the legend, he orders the machine gunners accompanying him to open fire on them. And all who are in the tavern perish—hanging from the railings, falling over the tables, tumbling down the stairs.

The commander (he's of high rank) is visited by a friend from Berlin, a well-known fascist playwright (named Hans Kafka) who has been sent to the front by Hitler to write an "epic about the fall of Russia." Conversing with the commander about Russian history and culture and about Russian legends, he mentions the story of the ancient city of Kitezh.[48]

The commander, almost reaching for his pistol, shrieks in a fury,

"You made that up yourself! You're lying! Lying! They can create nothing beautiful! You're lying!"

(For the play.)

At that time a German soldier asks Tsvetkov (who has turned up in the town on assignment from a partisan detachment) where he learned German so well. The old man says that he was probably helped by long acquaintance, continuing almost his whole life, with a certain German general.

The soldier involuntarily comes to attention.

Having said these words—extremely impressive-sounding, especially for a German soldier ("He knows a general!")—the old man takes a candle from the piano (the scene occurs at night in the half-demolished school) and withdraws into the darkened depths of the room.

"Here's the general!" he says.

His hand, holding the candle with its dancing flame, is raised aloft. In the flickering light the soldier sees a bust of Beethoven, the shadows lodged in its hair.

Henceforth I ought to try to keep these notes in such a way that something finished will come from them. What are they if that finish is lacking? Does an unfinished note have any interest? What is it? What's it for? Is it merely the glint of some deposit or vein? And will anyone else proceed further along that lilac zigzag, that amethyst?

According to legend, little gnomes, whom the Poles call *krasnoludki* and about whom Heine has written so well, had the task of finding and cutting gemstones.[49] They carried out that work in the mountains of Bohemia. Dressed in red, blue, and green caps, they wore long blond beards without mustaches and had the ruddy, slightly venous faces of revelers and gluttons. Sometimes they would set out in incomprehensible processions . . .

Heine says that judging by such testimony as has been preserved, the gnomes associated with people quite gladly and even performed a number of different kinds of magic beneficial to them. The break between humans and *krasnoludki* happened not as a result of something the latter had done; rather, it was people with their rudeness and egoism who were to blame. Once, for example, the gnomes had come to watch a village celebration. They sat themselves in a row on a long tree branch and were happily watching the festivities. One of the villagers, some crude chap, sawed off the branch, and all the *krasnoludki* fell down with it, to the village's guffawing. Thus, the gnomes gradually grew cool toward human beings, whom they had once loved and served with their magic.

Probably it was the end of fall. Most likely, that's when it was—the end of fall. At first I thought, wasn't it the end of winter? No, it wasn't, for even though that mixture of snow and patchy black earth and those bare trees are part of the late winter landscape, in that season you will also suddenly see above the gray masses of storm cloud an azure gleam, a small section of unobstructed sky . . . But there was none of that here; here, everything was depressingly gray and wet. Fall.

Three blind musicians come toward me. One has a flute wrapped in a green cover, the second, a violin gleaming brightly in the sun, the third, an accordion tipped over onto its side . . . No, now I see that it's not an accordion. It's the musician's unbuttoned vest, a dashing red vest decorated with silver buttons.

I had wanted when Igor died to ask the sculptor Merkurov to make a headstone in the form of a marble slab with an image on it of a boy in a skiff.[50]

I never carried out that plan, since all my higher-order ties to other people had by then begun to deteriorate as a result of my mode of life. And that included my ties to Merkurov.

Merkurov was a huge man with a black, very black beard, a beard as black as night, a beard almost brimful of stars. Very likely a full beard was the custom among sculptors then as an expression of love and respect for Rodin. (It's said Rodin was a bearded dwarf, a gnome.) I used to know Merkurov's wife, Stella, quite well. They're both departed now. I'll write some more about Merkurov, who took Lev Tolstoy's death mask and told me about it.

Forgive me, Igor!

I was present when Merkurov took Andrei Bely's death mask.[51] There were several of us in a reception hall at the Writers' Club, as the Littérateurs' House used to be known, and we were crowded round a coffin in which the poet lay—lay disfigured, it seemed to me, and even humiliated by the plaster that covered his face, turning it into a white, rather high mound.

Since Merkurov was working with plaster, he was dressed in a gown and his hands were stained white.

He chatted with us and it was clear he was waiting for something. From time to time he would look at his watch, pushing back his taped sleeve. Then suddenly he went over to the white mound and tapped it with his fingers, causing it to resonate.

"It's ready," he said. "Fyodor!"

His assistant, Fyodor, who was also wearing a white gown, came over and took off the mound, which required no effort. It came off easily, as if he were removing the cover of a box. I don't remember what we saw—if I should start to describe it, it wouldn't be a recollection but something invented. We merely saw the face of the dead Andrei Bely.

"Here's the mask," Merkurov said.

It was still on the inside of the plaster, still in its negative form, so to speak, and we understood nothing of what the sculptor understood as he peered into the concavity of that piece of plaster much as one might gaze into a basin.

"You also took Lev Tolstoy's mask, didn't you?" someone asked.

"I did."

"Well, what was it like?" the questioner blurted out.

"His beard got stuck."

It's certainly not my intention to discredit the sculptor by citing this apparently cynical reply. He was at that moment being anything but cynical. He was merely responding in a professional manner.

A whole wall of Merkurov's studio was hung with copies of the masks he had taken from famous people. I saw that wall neither awake nor in my sleep.

So important is it not to move someone who has had a heart attack that his clothing is immediately cut away from him rather than taken off. It may well be that everyone should from time to time have recourse to such absolute rest, such absolute immobility.

The organism itself indicates what one ought to do. But we're so at the mercy of circumstances that it would be awkward for us to undertake any treatment that was different from those commonly accepted: "No, no, don't bother me, I'm going to lie absolutely still for three days."

Incidentally, as regards the organism itself indicating what one ought to do, Zoshchenko in fact holds the opposite view. He says that even though the organism might give some indication, there's much for him that remains unclear. Out of a desire to help you, the organism may instead prove your undoing. Thus, if you don't very much feel like going into a building into which you go anyway, your organism may contrive your death on the stairway from a stroke. Zoshchenko calls this theory of his the "brain-fool."[52]

Zoshchenko is a very generous person, one of those philanthropic souls who assist others in secret—who, as Lev Tolstoy once put it, do good without an address (without an address in the sense that they don't leave their addresses behind). True, the catastrophe that befell him hardly permitted Zoshchenko to remain the philanthropist he had been.[53] He's a melancholy person, someone given more often than not to repeating Nietzsche's line about "pitiful life and its pitiful pleasures" . . . Besides that, he values ritual, is exacting, and sees and is fond of the little things. And he has a capacity for work. He took an affectionate interest in me when we used to meet in Leningrad. He was easy with me, just as I was with him. By the way, he knows how to cobble and sew. My trousers had once got torn, and he magnificently repaired the damage. In that connection, I remember saying to Fadeev, who had recently arrived in Leningrad and who had turned up in Zoshchenko's and my company,

"You think the important event in our literature at the present moment is the fact that you've come to Leningrad? You are mistaken. Of greater importance is the fact that the writer Zoshchenko has mended the trousers of the writer Olesha."[54]

Two young women entered, one larger, the other smaller, and both dolled up as if going to a party. From the threshold they began seeking someone with their eyes. I sensed it was me. And so it was.

"Is Olyosha here?" asked the larger one, naturally mispronouncing my name.

"Is Olyosha here?"

"Yes, that's me."

They moved toward me in a springy gait in plucked eyebrows and curled hair, although both of them were wearing white hospital gowns, and one was carrying a box containing tubes of different calibrations—a porcupine box, all in glass bristles . . .

I remember saying to them in greeting,

"The blood service."

They had in fact come to draw my blood for analysis. Both sat down, one with her legs over the left side of the bed, the other, over the right. The larger of the two took a syringe from the box.

"Stick out your finger. No, that one."

The prick is quite painful. Then your blood runs into the tube, and you're amazed at how bright it is. Then a wad of cotton, then a slide, then your blood in the form of a spot, then the young woman blowing into the tube.

You make jokes. Both women are silent. You joke well. "Blood service," for example, is pretty good. But they remain silent. They see a horrible creature with suppurating eyes and scaly hands. You were a condemned man; they know that. Gracefully rising to their feet, they move off to the next bed, and you sigh and almost break into tears.

I don't think I saw the hunchback until the first evening after my operation. First there was a loud knocking noise with more or less regular intervals, a knocking noise clearly coming from somewhere outside the room I was lying in, somewhere in the corridor, although I didn't know that. Very loud yet elegant: a dry, clicking noise. The noise tormented me just as everything else did, just as my own existence tormented me. Then the noise unexpectedly stopped, and I realized what it was. Somebody I hadn't seen enter the room was now talking nearby about a game of dominoes. So that's what it was. But how could they allow them to click so loudly in a hospital?

In a voice no less loud and just as elegant and dry-sounding, the man talked about his game of dominoes. He accompanied his story with jokes that were neither funny nor original, simply figures of speech that had once been considered amusing but that now caused torment in all your being.

And then I managed a glimpse of the speaker. He was a hunchback dressed in a dark hospital gown. So that's why his speech was elegant and dry. He was a hunchback—that's characteristic of them.

He was young with a large, slender, plow-shaped nose of the kind many hunchbacks have. His hair was brushed back, and his arms described large motions that suggested, as he turned his hands (large like hunchbacks have), the idea of opening sluice gates. He was, I thought, clean, dry, and elegant. All this, of course, in the evening light, the evening shadows, but how could I have lain any differently? In the hospital that posture with the legs thrust forward acquired a special kind of visual meaning. I saw everything from beyond the other side of my legs, of my feet, of my feet sticking up a short distance away, merely the distance of an arm if I had sat up, although I could neither sit up nor extend my arm.

The dying Mussorgsky was taken to a hospital where only a certain class of military personnel could be treated. They didn't want to admit him, but somebody interceded and the composer was given the name of someone else's orderly. And so he died under another's name.

The fact that Mozart was buried in a pauper's grave sets your teeth on edge. But any intelligence that one or another genius in the realm of art has died in poverty no longer amazes us; on the contrary, it seems in the order of things. Rembrandt, Beethoven, Edgar Poe, Verlaine, Van Gogh, and many, many others. It's strange, but the genius at once seems to enter into discord with the property side of life. Why? Most likely the artist's obsession doesn't leave his mind or soul even for an instant: he has no free spiritual fibers, so to speak, to place in service of the quotidian.

Who was that old man wrapped up like an old woman who wandered aimlessly, who was probably already reconciled to poverty, and who even found comfort there? It was the painter of Danaë and the shower of gold.[55] Who was that one-armed eccentric sitting on a bench under a wooden overhang waiting for two shrewish women, his wife and daughter, to feed him? It was Cervantes. Who was that gentleman in a cravat and heavy top hat standing before a pawnbroker and inexhaustibly pulling from the breast of his frock coat a magically endless Turkish shawl? It was Pushkin.

Delacroix writes in his journal of Diderot's poverty.[56] The philosopher believed he was destined to live in a hovel. Catherine's intervention helped him when already an old man to begin living in comfort in a fine apartment with decent furniture and the like.[57]

I remembered that journal entry of Delacroix's while walking down Pyatnitsky today calculating whether or not I had enough money for two hundred grams of sugar and therefore the right to buy a newspaper. It was no different three years ago when I lived in the same neighborhood: I'd sometimes go outside to borrow a three-ruble note for breakfast from some other writer. If three years have passed and it's still the same, then I too might think it's no accident but my destiny.

What characterizes me worst of all here is the comparison with Diderot. Actually, I've no doubt at all that there still lives in me someone powerful, a kind of athlete—or rather the wreck of one, a torso without arms or legs—who painfully moves within my body, thereby tormenting both himself and me. Sometimes I manage to catch what he's saying, I repeat it, and others consider me intelligent . . . Pasternak listens to me and, I notice, with pleasure. Pasternak, the author of reams of splendid poetry, prose, and translations from Shakespeare and Goethe; Pasternak, who astonished Akhmatova with his comparison of smoke to Laocoön[58]—he listens to me, the author of no more than a few hundred pages of prose, and he flushes and his eyes sparkle. It's that genius, that broken statue stirring within me, within its accidental envelope, forming along with that envelope the result of some strange and terrible magic, some detail of a myth of which I can grasp only one thing: my own death.

Chopin somehow especially moves us, undoubtedly evoking what is called sweet melancholy. Undoubtedly he returns our thoughts to vistas of youth—returns us old folks, that is. The young he very likely disposes to thoughts of unrequited love.

To think he was only thirty-nine when he died, and yet how many melodies he created. They hover within our hearing like the living creatures of another life.

Most people know him as the composer of the "Marche funèbre." Or rather, most people know the "Marche funèbre," whose composer nobody thinks about. What orchestras haven't played it? I saw the dingy, battered trumpets from which it poured forth at the funerals of those who gave their lives for the revolution—poured forth over flimsy coffin-boats in which yellow-faced sailors lay.

You're walking in a crowd across the patchy black and white snow of early spring, and it passes over you on great wings, enveloping you, that march, that gigantic sob which burst a hundred years or more ago from the narrow breast of a young man.

Sometimes through the actual circumstances of my life, through its furnishings—the objects and walls of my home—shine images of another life, also mine, but not altogether apprehensible to me, not always, so to speak, in view. A room suddenly shows through, azure from the twilight and oil-painted walls. A clean room with toys in the middle, small beds along the sides, and a frieze depicting toys on one of the oil-painted walls. A nursery? Whose then? I never had children of my own. Suddenly I sense for an instant that they are my daughter's children. I never had a daughter.

Yes, but I've come to my daughter's home. I'm a father and grandfather. I'm visiting my daughter and grandchildren on a Sunday, and I'm expected for dinner. Perhaps I've come for dinner. Most likely, I haven't come for any reason at all . . . But to make up for it I've brought a cake. Good Lord, how I remember that quadrangle of cake so awkward to carry!

Let not the reader think that this book, however much it may appear to be made up of separate pieces on disparate themes, is only drawn out lengthwise. No, it is rounded. If you like, it even has a subject, a very interesting one. Someone has lived and survived till old age. That's the subject. And it's an interesting, even fantastic one. In surviving till old age there really is something fantastic. I'm not joking in the least. After all, I might not have survived, isn't that right? But I did survive, and the fantastic thing is that it's as if I'm being shown to myself. Since nothing has happened to the sensation "I'm alive," which is the same as it was in infancy, with that sensation I now perceive myself, an old man, no less youthfully and freshly than before, and that old man is extraordinarily novel to me—for, I repeat, I might not have lived to see him. In any event, for many, many years I didn't think that I would. And then suddenly at the young me, young both inside and out, an old man gazes from the mirror. It's fantasy! It's a theater! When I move away from the mirror and lie back down on the couch, I don't think of myself as the one I've just seen. No, I lie there as the same "I" who lay down when I was a boy. The other remains in the mirror. Now there are two of us—I and the other one. When I was young I also changed, but imperceptibly, remaining most of my life virtually one and the same. But now this abrupt change into something entirely different.

"Hello, who are you?"

"I'm you."

"No, you're not."

Sometimes I even laugh. And the one in the mirror laughs. I laugh till I cry. And the one in the mirror cries too.

That's the fantastic subject.

There's a kind of theater in old age. Unquestionably something is being shown to me. I might indeed never have reached old age. I'll be told that I might just as well not have survived till the end of any year. True, but in youth and maturity one year hardly differs from the next or from whole dozens of years . . . But old age is something entirely and abruptly new. And I'm seeing it. Hence the feeling that something is being shown to you, that you're in a theater.

Yesterday a Jewish newspaper vendor simply drove me away from his kiosk.

I was meddling in a transaction of his that seemed improper to me. He was detaining a young woman who wanted to buy a book by Gorky.

"Eight rubles," the girl said.

"It's a few kopecks more," he said, thrusting his ruddy face into the pages. "A few kopecks . . ."

"Kopecks!" I started yelling. "Aren't you ashamed! The young woman wants to buy a book, and you're going on about kopecks!"

He simply started to drive me away.

"Who the hell are you? Get out of here! Get going!"

Well, of course. I was just an old man in ragged clothing.

The young woman gleamed between us; Gorky smiled.

"You've got one foot in the grave, old man," I said. "How could you . . ."

"I told you to get out of here!"

He turned so livid I thought he was going to die. Perhaps I seemed a drunken old man to him, a Christian, somebody hanging about in that, from his Jewish point of view, forbidden hour.

"Get out of here!" I heard as I was leaving. "Get out of here!"

Of course it's a theater. Did I, a boy playing soccer, did I, a famous writer (at whom, incidentally, the entire audience was looking), did I think that on a hot summer day I would be walking away from a kiosk, driven away, and rightly so?

What have I seen in my life? I'll begin with what I just saw. As I was walking along the asphalt path that follows the Kremlin wall, a sparrow quickly moved over it, or more accurately, skipped across it. It was alone on the asphalt in the middle of a large patch of brilliant sunlight only slightly darkened by a single fallen leaf—a small, solitary sparrow that quickly hopped almost sideways over the gray surface capable of repulsing a large cloudburst.

Then it reached the green slope and vanished in the high grass and wildflowers.

That's what I just saw.

Much earlier I saw a mortally wounded bandit lying in the street, his chest raised up like a mountain. That happened on Deribasovsky Street in Odessa when I was eighteen. I don't want the reader to seek in my book any preconceived analogies or significant interconnections. If they occur on their own, that's fine and their affair, but I'm consciously furthest of all from any wish to engage in trite philosophy, beginning with a sparrow, then jumping to a bandit.

One may safely assert that the overwhelming majority of people pays no particular attention to the starlit sky.

How often have you seen someone lift his head to gaze at the stars? Or how often has someone come up to you while you yourself were gazing at the stars and, after guessing which star you were admiring, then shared that admiration with you?

Most people living in the city probably don't realize that the sky has virtually the same appearance for whole periods of the year, that it's a motionless pattern. More likely, they think it changes every evening, that every evening a new stellar rocket takes off to scatter itself across the firmament.

Sometimes you yourself walk along oblivious of the sky, though it hangs above you like a blue spangled cap pulled low over your forehead.

Maybe the book I'm now writing is none other than the story of how it's always been my intention to visit an observatory.

When I think about the cavemen, they seem to me closer in time than, say, the people of the Middle Ages do.

Why is that? Perhaps because they were naked, because they gnawed on bones, because, being without fire, they suffered from the cold and from fear, because, unlike the people of the Middle Ages with their fantastical dress and their polemics on religious themes, they were more human—precisely human, truly human.

Strange too seems the relatively rapid development of man's understanding of clothing, the appearance of his taste for it.

The Roman togas, some scarlet, some with golden bands around the hem; the beautiful hair and crowns of the Gothic kings; the headlong, almost decade-by-decade variation in the outward aspect and color, in the very essence of clothing in the Middle Ages and the dawn of the new era, if only red hoods in combination with matching red notched collars covering the shoulders, or the long pointed footwear of the pages and their hose, one leg lilac, say, and the other in motley, stripes, or spangles—it's the virtual birth of fashion.

Of all superstructures, art appeared earliest—the attention to beauty, the ability to create and to serve it. Homer compared dressed hair to a hyacinth, and perhaps Greek women did specially arrange their hair that way—hyacinth-fashion.[59]

When after reading a great deal of Morozov, I smugly announced to the critic Dmitry Mirsky that the ancient world had never existed, that son of a grand duke, that exquisitely courteous fellow who had long resided in London, that good-natured soul struck me across the back with his stick.[60]

"You say that to me, a historian? You . . . You . . ."

He turned pale and his black beard disappeared into his mouth. All the same, to win somebody over with a stick is physically and above all morally offensive . . .

"Yes, that's right, the Acropolis wasn't built by the Greeks but by the Crusaders!" I shouted. "They found marble and . . ."

He walked away from me without listening, in his frayed trousers and carelessly worn old London hat.

We made our peace over a bottle of wine and the chicken they prepare so expertly in shashlik restaurants by baking it between two very hot bricks, and he explained the nature of my, and therefore Morozov's, ignorance. I agreed with him that the ancient world had existed, although many of the Schlüsselburger's insights are still illuminating to me.

Be that as it may, the very fact that Morozov created his own system for negating the ancient world is brilliant. Even if the system itself is ignorant, the very fact of its creation is, I repeat, brilliant, if you take into account that he was incarcerated in Schlüsselburg Fortress for twenty-five years, that is, was in essence deprived of contact with the world forever.

"You have deprived me of the world? All right, then! Your world didn't exist!"

The laying of roads really was a marvel of conception and technology.

Before there were none. Ravines, mud, rolling earth, heaps of rocks, and instead of a direct route, undergrowth and the meanderings of nature—that's the sort of path people used to follow. Even the Greeks with their state system and their art. It's hard to reconcile in one's imagination the Greek toga, the verse of Sappho, the architecture of the Acropolis, the grace of the myths, Socrates and his trial—it's hard to reconcile all that with the absence of roads. Nevertheless, there weren't any. How did they carry on trade? How did they even wage war? How could they march in formation? They walked in a throng, and while part of a detachment was emerging from behind a knoll, another part remained stuck in a marsh. What moved along that undulating trail full of mudholes and piled with rocks? Carts behind teams? Horsemen? You'll never make sense of it.

The roads of the Romans were such a mighty invention that they have survived to the present day.

Who built them? Slaves? What did they live in? Barracks? Under the open sky? But what if it rained? How is one to imagine it all? Very well, they didn't much care about slaves: they beat them with whips and bought them and sold them, but in that case how could the slaves work productively? How were they fed? Did kitchens come to them? Where from? What did they look like? Did the slaves carry their food with them? Or did they eat the fruit of nearby trees? How did they keep them from eating it all at once? You'll never make sense of it.

What tools did they make the roads with? Were there such things as a Roman shovel, pick, and crowbar? For leveling, rollers are needed. What was the Roman roller like?

Is one to imagine hosts of slaves scraping virtually with their hands? With what then? Were there enough tools for everybody? They sweat, they're hungry, they shout, they fight, they urinate and defecate, they die.

Who escorted and guarded them? How was the escort fed and what did it sleep on? You'll never make sense of it.

Do I want fame? No. Rather than fame I'd like to travel around the world. It's even odd to imagine that there is another world, that there are such things as bullfights, for example. The matador, having performed some pass of the *corrida,* suddenly turns his back on the bull as if forgetting about it and walks with his hands on his hips toward the president's box. He doesn't know what the bull is doing behind him; perhaps it's racing toward him on small, unsteady hooves.

Yesterday in the "News of the Day" on Sretenka I saw a foreign chronicle. Slender little figures of Indonesians were running about in helmets and carrying submachine guns, a fire was burning, and the flames billowed and smoked—a giant bonfire of paper and other materials that had been thrown from a multistoried building . . . It was the looting of an international commission on peace in Vietnam.

The contemporary cinema does the newsreel in very epic fashion, using the devices of artistic cinematography (wide-angle views, close-ups). The air was gray with smoke and the helmets gleamed in it: the gray air, the gray asphalt, the swirling black ribbons of smoke.

I sought out that newsreel for the sake of a slice of Spanish life included in it: a bullfight (that it was included I had learned from a newspaper). And then it began. A title or a voice-over, I don't remember which, announced that bullfighting has survived in Spain to the present day and that scenes would now be shown of a fight in Madrid involving a famous matador.

First I saw a section of arena, a sunlight-flooded coliseum of sorts, which, since it was shown in wide-angle view, resembled a piece of watermelon teeming with seed-people. Then two almost naked Spanish women bathed in sunlight and carrying fans flashed by in close-up. Then, at midrange I saw a picador on his horse, which he forced to remain in place and compactly and elastically paw the ground as it waited for the bull. The black bull, with two small beribboned swords stuck in its back so that it looked like an injured insect unable to fold its dragging wing cases, ran with its back to me in the middle of the empty arena. And then the frame was filled almost to its full extent with two figures, the matador and the bull. My heart began to pound with fear and delight. So this is what those matadors, those *espadas* do! He stood very close to the bull—touching its body, in any event. He was entwined with its body which ran around him in pursuit of the cape with which he, the famous matador, was playing. In those few instants, while before me shimmered that dark, heavily breathing frame with the matador and bull set in motion within it, I felt mysterious and very powerful forces in my soul. I was at once a woman in love with the matador and, on the contrary, one who in that moment despised women more than anything else, and all the time my heart pounded, and I was ready to cry out along with the ancient arena.

What would Mayakovsky have said to me about that, Mayakovsky who upon seeing a bullfight thought it a shame that a machine gun hadn't been fastened to the bull's horns so it could shoot at the spectators.[61]

Franklin had already consciously begun to live a cultural life virtually contemporary to our own in the era when Peter, then Anna and Elizabeth were ruling in Russia. Just think: Franklin's moral principles, his printing press, his lightning rod—and Elizabeth's cutting out of tongues.

When you read tendentiously selected facts, his personality seems astounding. He was in his own way a "peaceful Napoleon." The same all-consuming energy, though directed toward peaceful ends.

Then you suddenly come across his gloating over the Indians' attachment to alcohol and their subsequent annihilation . . . What historical narrow-mindedness! He calls the Indians a pitiful tribe and expresses the view that it would be better if Providence should replace them with hardworking "cultivators of the earth." With whom? The planters and their slavery?

He really was a discoverer and a leader of the new bourgeois world then coming into existence. The expression "ça ira" belongs to him, by the way. When the French asked him his opinion of their revolution, he said,

"Ça ira!" ("It will work out!")[62]

The most absorbing reading for me is about the French Revolution. There's something close to my soul in those events. It's odd, but although I've read about the French Revolution most of my life and am particularly fond of the subject, I still lack a clear idea of it—if, say, I should have to take an examination. There's only a crowd dressed in striped pants carrying pikes, only the yellow walls of the Parisian houses of the day, only the silhouettes of the Convention members sitting with their backs to the windows. Only patches of color: Bonaparte with his fantastical appearance, Barras's fluttering hat . . .[63]

An important expert on all that died a few days ago: Tarle.[64] By the way, although the obituary calls him an outstanding artist of the word, his writings leave no artistic or poetic impression of the kind, say, produced by the works of Thiers, Mignet, or Louis Blanc.[65] Rather, one has a sense of compilation.

Thiers was opposed to Robespierre, and in his brilliantly written history he portrays him as the vile, bloodthirsty soul of the terror, a darling of women, a fastidious prig, a sanctimonious hypocrite, and a lover of oranges. Louis Blanc, on the other hand, was an admirer of Robespierre and says it is those who overthrew him who were the ringleaders of the terror, and when you read Blanc, you begin to pity Robespierre, especially when wounded in the jaw by a pistol bullet from the gendarme Méda, he lies deserted by all on a table in the city hall and wipes away the blood with the holster of his pistol. Imagine touching that wound with the holster, probably sewn with metal thread. He was the ruler of a France that had already begun to shake the world.

Thiers's favorite is Napoleon. From his description of the Egyptian campaign, I have the impression of having been told nothing less than a fairy tale about a young hero for whom the waging of war and thoughts that outstrip the ages are equally possible.

After an operation against the Turks ending in their complete rout, Kléber puts his arm around Napoleon's waist—around that slender waist of the revolutionary era girded with a broad sash—and says,

"My general, you are as great as the world!"

Departing Egypt to take power in France into his own hands, Bonaparte left the same Kléber behind as his deputy. One should recall that the French had no fleet, since it had been destroyed by Nelson, and that they were thus doomed to remain in Africa, perhaps till the end of their days. It was no easy matter to assume command of that army. Kléber, who loved Bonaparte, was placed at its head and soon afterward fell to the dagger of a zealot.[66]

Rarely is any reading as fascinating as that about Napoleon. In some salon or other while still a young general in the period of his courtship of Josephine, he performed an improvisation portraying the devil by making faces and flashing his teeth. The lady in whose memoirs this scene is described says that the improvisation came off very well because with his dark face and white teeth he really did look like the devil.[67]

Usually he's depicted with a pale white face. Stendhal writes of a uniform pallor that produced nonetheless, as he notes, an impression of health.[68] Hippolyte Taine in his book *Napoléon* (one barely known to us) says that in the past Napoleon's ancestors were, in all probability, Saracen. He says there are many Saracen graves in Corsica. For Taine, Napoleon is a Saracen, an Arab. He had a dark face (as the above lady attests) but for the legend's sake they made it pale. Napoleon's Arab ancestry is also used to explain his cruelty in relation to Europe, his casual shedding of European blood. The idea is, at any rate, a talented one.[69]

Whatever the case, Stendhal, who had stood next to him, so to speak, writes, as I've already said, of Napoleon's pallor. What do we know about it?

Canova's bust of him in the Hermitage is charmingly European, elegant, pensive, and vaguely doomed.[70]

"Look," Kataev said to me, "you can't help but recognize Napoleon in it, can you?"

Yes, it's mournful, that marble head, and the features you're accustomed to don't show through immediately. At first, it's only a sad person aware of his doom.

After him, Canova, Rossini, Byron. After him, a phalanx of magnificent victories for youth. Beethoven? Balzac? Lermontov? One might say that mysterious destiny appealed mainly to youth, that it took youth under its protection and blessed it. Is that true? But he wouldn't have seized power, after all, if it hadn't been for his brother. Is there any point in lumping the youth Lermontov together with a youth who ordered the saber slashing of three thousand Egyptians on the banks of the Nile? Perhaps those other youths surrounded that swarthy Italian face like a garland?

No, it was he, after all, who summoned the poet Herder to a meeting of dukes and kings in some German city, and when the poet turned up dressed virtually in slippers for lack of any other shoes, the emperor talked only to him and gave his attention only to him for several hours.[71] No, he really was a marvel, a profoundly European, even an Atlantic one, all in the picturesqueness of moderate distances and the names of capitals, peoples, mountains, and rivers.

We shall return to him again. He continues to make a stir somewhere behind us. Makes a stir to this day.

I have been glancing back at Napoleon behind me my whole conscious life. What is it that's so attractive about that destiny? It's that it is nothing less than a symbol of human life with its youthfulness, its striving for the future, and its end still striving for some horizon—the sunset or the island of Saint Helena in the distance.

Very likely we enjoy reading about Napoleon because it gives rise to a sense of immortality. That victory of youth evokes a vision of the endlessness of the future, of immortality. And that indeed is why we prefer the successes of younger famous people, the successes of the young and not the old. With their wrinkles and yellow eyes, the latter will die anyway, whereas the former may be standing on the threshold of an era of immortality.

I never saw the pyramids. How strange that they exist. How strange that Bonaparte engaged in battle at their feet. Just imagine the tunics of the officers of French revolutionary times amid the desert's yellow.

All my life my gaze has been turned toward the sunset. It's difficult to imagine anything more appealing to the sight than that great wall of fire.

Does one have to compare the sunset so feebly?

The Greeks saw it as the fire in which Phaëthon perished. The sunset probably belongs to those earthly manifestations that may be compared to anything at all. There a city is piled up, there towers grow, there long roads are laid out. Sometimes it's the Bible—Ezekiel's vision with an enormous guitar of sunbeams, sometimes it's a lyrebird, and sometimes it's a fleet of aircraft silently moving away into the distance with greetings from us to the country of friends who have left us behind.

The opinion existed (in the nineteenth century) that the spider could walk on air. And it's true that the filament it spins is imperceptible in the air, so that it looks as if the spider is actually striding through empty space. What is a spider? What sort of wonderful machine is it? Try to imagine one the size of our own machines—what parts won't you see, what articulations! And from that machine issues a thread that it has itself produced.

It looks like a figure eight, the spider, a figure eight carelessly drawn by someone.

Sometimes you'll see a fly weighing several tons caught in a spider web. That's right, several tons, if you imagine the whole drama on the scale of our dimensions. The heavy silvery blue body of the fly hangs in fetters incomprehensible to us . . . How can they be strong if in the daytime when they're being spun we can't even see them—something merely glimmers all of a sudden.

Since a parade's in progress on Red Square, a picket has been placed at the entrance to the Bolshoy Kamenny Bridge to keep people from crossing over to the center of town on the other side.

On the picket's right flank is its commander, a tall police major with a sturdy build and a long, very interesting, even peculiar face. Either an actor with traces of greasepaint or a sort of double for the generals of 1812. The embroidered collar of his dress tunic, the dark blue tunic itself, his ruddy face and blue eyes. Though he looks ferocious, it's clear he's kindhearted. He's a head taller than everyone else, and not just one person but in fact everyone else—the whole picket line, the whole crowd—and his large head with its inordinately long and straight occiput that imparts a rather blocklike appearance to it is visible from all sides.

His job is to let no one through. He's besieged, for the most part by people who are slightly drunk. He asks to see your identity papers. If you live in that direction and nearby, he'll let you through.

Witte cites the story of how, when the Emperor Alexander III was being escorted out of Berlin, Wilhelm II, then still crown prince, rushed to take from a Cossack a cloak the latter was holding ready to give to the emperor.[72] He had decided to give it to the emperor himself.

This is the ancient idea of venerating the chosen one, of deference to the leader, the sovereign. It is an idea of unquestioning discipline, of joyful abasement in the service of a superior.

Vasily Vasilievich Shkvarkin was telling me about the so-called *Zuck* and how it was practiced at the Nikolaevsky Cavalry School when he was a student.[73] A senior cadet could force an underclassman to do the most incredible things. The junior cadets didn't in the least protest; on the contrary, they performed every absurdity with enthusiasm, even if it caused them physical suffering.

"How could they?" I asked, sympathizing with the junior cadets. "Why, that's awful! How could they agree to it?"

"Yura," Vasily Vasilievich said to me, slurring the "r," "nobody forced them to submit to the *Zuck*. Upon entering the school a cadet was asked whether he wished to live according to the *Zuck* or not."

"And he could refuse?"

"Well, my goodness, of course he could, but if he did, he might not be accepted into a decent regiment. Then it was to the back of beyond."

The hot weather's here. The sun now sets in absolute stillness and immobility of light, as if the heavenly ocean were becalmed.

Some cinematographers had picked up an ill-informed account of the nonrotation of the earth about its axis told by someone as if it belonged to Einstein. Nodding their heads and exchanging the solemn gazes of ignoramuses, they discussed the idea around a table at the Hotel National.

How I've aged! How terribly I've aged in the last few months! What will become of me? Today I ate a cherry without the usual sense of rapture. Even those slowly rolling little spheres have suddenly broken loose—and just try to catch them.

You used to want to compare them—their form, their taste. You wanted to imagine sparrows pecking at them. You thought they were a cherry rain, slightly sweet and very, very fresh.

Evidently I'm turning into a graphomaniac. Hurrah! Recently something started to happen to my handwriting. I'd write first with one kind, then with another—straight, slanted, then very slanted. Sometimes I would suddenly lose the ability to write with pen and ink. I could only write with a pencil. And, oddly enough, with a pencil my handwriting became precise, round, and erect, almost leaning backward, while with a pen the lines at once got messy and smudged, taking on a repellent appearance. And in addition to that, much of it disappeared without a trace, literally slipping off the page. Oh, what torture that was!

And then a fact was added that still further impaired an already impaired ability to write—I quit smoking. Whereupon the link between head and hand completely broke down. It seemed I'd lost the miracle of cursive writing forever. And because I was writing without smoking, my heart beat painfully . . . I remember writing a sentence in Golitsyn and then leaping to my feet and running out onto a dusty green country road among the geese and the goats. What agony! What torture! It got to the point where I was writing no more than a sentence a day. Only one sentence, which tormented me with the fact that it was only one sentence, that it was short, and that it had come into being not in creative but in physical torment. It seemed that, covered with rimples, it was running after me, that it got caught on a tree, that it was smoothed out on the wool of a kid, that it was running after me again, that it got stuck on the label of a quarter-liter bottle. That was delirium, that was talking to myself, that was agony and heat—not smoking and losing the ability to write . . .

All the same, what sorcery it is! Why, when I'm writing for myself, do I write easily and well, but when I'm writing for publication, let things drag on and force out the words?

It's easy to imagine a day in Florence or Venice in some very remote era. Summer, the blueness of the sky, the gilt of the cathedrals, statues . . . The same *David,* let's say, in the Piazza della Signoria.[74] It's possible that Michelangelo is crossing the square, the Michelangelo of whom the young Raphael said that he walks "gloomily, like an executioner." Money changers, soldiers, merchants, artisans, children, women with their hair in golden snoods. In a word, people, people in no way unlike ourselves, the same people with two arms and two legs and two eyes and motes that fly into their eyes on windy days, people like those who yesterday were waiting at the entrance to the Bolshoy Kamenny Bridge.

Yet those people were certain the sun revolves around the earth. It never occurred to any of them to suppose that that was merely an optical illusion. Everyone lived according to the system of thought wherein the earth was the center of the universe.

But did any prince consider himself an ignoramus because of that? Or did any Pico della Mirandola?[75] Or did any young mother posing for Titian regard herself as less happy because of it? Or less beautiful? The Polish priest hadn't yet revealed the great wonder of orientation.[76] The most intelligent people still believed in the music of the spheres, but did they think about, did they lament the fact that they were behind, that their education was on such a low level? By no means. For every age views itself as standing on the pinnacle. Thus, someday someone will look back on our own age much as I'm looking back on that of Florence, and will, like me, entertain the idea that in that age—just imagine!—people lived for only fifty years. Well, he'll say, were they any less happy and beautiful than we who live for three hundred?

It's amazing that Savonarola recruited children to assist him. Cohorts of juvenile informers, confiscators, and destroyers of treasures. Then, as a bonfire raged, consuming pictures by Botticelli, the children and old men would dance around it.[77]

When Kepler offered his astronomical treatise to a publisher and the latter refused it, Kepler answered with a rejoinder that deserves mention whenever it comes to mind.

"I can afford to wait another century for readers," such were his approximate words, "if God himself has waited six thousand years for an observer."[78]

That is, he considered himself to be the first observer of the diamond theater on display in the heavens. And it's true that if he was the first to see its plan and mechanism, if he was the first to see the clashes of that spectacle, then he was its first observer. Before him people had merely looked without comprehending.

He was one of the last astrologers. Incidentally, he prepared a horoscope for Wallenstein.[79]

Kepler proved that the heavenly bodies move in the figures of a conic section: circles, ellipses, parabolas, hyperbolas. Has that been revised by contemporary astronomy?

Kepler's remark about the celestial theater is mentioned by Delacroix. Very likely he got it from the same source I did. He mentions that source in another connection. It's Edgar Poe. Poe has a cosmogony, *Eureka,* and he cites Kepler's remark there.

The book *Eureka* is indescribably magnificent, poetical, brilliant. In the margins of my copy, which came from the library, there are occasional comments by a contemporary reader, someone familiar with the subject. And those comments are a complete vindication of Poe's conjectures, an expression of delight in them.[80]

Once as I was about to cross Arbat Street at the Arbat Gate, a voice resounded in my ear, ordering me to halt. I understood more quickly than I saw that I had been stopped by a high-ranking police officer.

"Halt!"

I stopped. Rocking from side to side, two automobiles hurtled in my direction. It wasn't difficult to guess who was in the first. I saw the car's interior, dark as in summer when the shutters are closed, and in it, especially bright amid that darkness, indeed with a brightness of almost spectral dissociation, the band of a military cap.

In an instant it all disappeared and the world resumed its course. And so did I.

The Golden Shelf

THE GOLDEN SHELF is the one you keep exclusively for your favorite books.

I've long dreamed of such a shelf. And precisely a shelf is limned in my dreams—not a whole bookcase but a single shelf, a single story of a bookcase, if one may put it that way. How does one acquire such a thing? Probably you have to order it from a carpenter. Why do I restrict myself to a dream? Because it's in fact hard to call a carpenter, consult with him, describe to him exactly what I have in mind. Anyway, I don't call him, and the dream remains unfulfilled. Perhaps that happens because it's not very easy for a golden shelf to become a reality. It is, after all, a golden shelf, of which there aren't very many in the world. At least, I've never seen one in any home.

Sometimes I imagine a simple shelf of rectangular design; sometimes, on the contrary, I see something elaborate, and not merely elaborate but a sort of gewgaw, with little twisted columns at the ends.

Perhaps I don't acquire that shelf because there isn't any gold paper for sale? It's true you can't buy it now . . . I remember the embossed gold sheets that so adorned my childhood. What were they sold for? To make Christmas decorations, I think. The sheet was as large as a normal sheet of writing paper, and its reverse side, which in this case you want to call its lining, was white. White and somehow strange, as if a bit downy, just a bit . . . As I've already said, the paper was embossed—with something like the flowers on a frosty window, only those flowers are either silver or light blue, whereas the patterns on the paper were gold. But in outline they were the same.

It's paradoxical, but the most remarkable books, the ones we continually reread in the course of our lives, are forgotten, are not retained in the memory. It would seem that it ought to be the other way around: the book that has impressed us enough to be read more than once should be remembered in all its details. But that doesn't happen. Obviously we know what the book is basically about, but each time the details are unexpected and new, and not merely the details, but whole parts of the overall construction. This is unquestioningly so: we read remarkable books each time as if for the first time . . . And therein lies the amazing destiny of the authors of remarkable books: they have not departed, have not died. They remain sitting at their desks or standing in front of their writing bureaus; they are outside of time.

Shelley says that the wonderful quality of the Greeks consists of the fact that they turned everything into beauty—crime, murder, lack of faith, any bad characteristic or action.[1] And it's true; everything in the myths is beautiful. Phaëthon's disobedience is turned into the fiery fall of his steeds, into the myth of the sunset. The gods' vengeance on Niobe is turned into beauty too: her children are destroyed by arrows, ruthlessly, one after another. Terrible though it may be, the event is still beautiful in form, especially when we realize the arrows are the sun's rays.

Here the idea obtrudes itself that art, if the artist transforms everything into beauty, is somewhere at bottom immoral. And in fact while describing, say, the death of a hero, the artist does make him die as expressively as possible, removing that pitiable event to the realm of beauty. Isn't that immoral? Isn't immorality bound up, for instance, in the dying delirium of Andrei Bolkonsky as that delirium takes the form of an edifice of needles erected over him, a delirium that is in fact an invention of Tolstoy in the realm of beauty?[2] In the very attempt to depict, to adorn the delirium of a sick man, isn't there something immoral?

But perhaps by bringing suffering into the realm of beauty, the artist compensates the sufferer for his agonies with some higher value?

(On Dante.) At first you know about him only what everyone else knows: the author of *The Divine Comedy,* died in exile in a parvis in Ravenna, the love for Beatrice: "Bitter another's bread, steep another's stairway."[3] And of course in my own case the fact that from childhood on that tiny figure descending the spiral of a crater clad in a red cowl with notched edges has never left my imagination . . .

Then, picking up your courage, you start to read, you read to the end, and before you is a wonder! You never thought, you never supposed that it was so superb, so incomparable. They deceived you who said it was dull. Dull? Good Lord, there's a whole fire of imagination there!

Not to mention the precise and tender poetry, the melancholy phrases, the wonderful epithets . . .

We'll recall that Dante descends into Hell alive, not as a shade but in fact alive, as the same person he was on earth at the entrance to Hell. All the rest are shades, but he's a human being. Virgil's a shade too, Virgil, Dante's guide in Hell. Gustave Doré, who illustrated the *Inferno,* makes no distinction in his drawing between Dante and the shades. The shades have the same appearance; they don't glimmer and nothing shines through them. And the author himself doesn't describe them in any special way; he merely calls them shades, in the sense that they're dead and not people anymore. Doré, it's true, depicts Virgil as slightly more powerful than his guest—as if, say, a statue were standing next to a person. And Dante does from time to time press close to Virgil, seeking protection at his breast.

The demons—pickets or patrols of some kind—that Virgil and Dante keep running into in separate groups recognize at once that Dante's alive, that he's a human being. Oh, how they want to grab him! But they aren't allowed to; Virgil's presence prevents them. For them, it's mysterious, unclear, yet somehow unquestionably powerful and responsible. If not for Virgil, things would go badly for Dante. Dante understands this and is mortally afraid of the demons, who openly rage at him.

And then the two, the dead poet and the live one, suddenly lose their way. Virgil is alarmed; as for the live poet, he is terrified. After all, his escort could in fact disappear at any moment, called away for some reason by a higher power. And Dante would then be alone. Alone in Hell, where even the names are horrifying: the city of Dis, the Malebolge or "evil fissures."[4]

A bridge had served Virgil as an orientation point, so to speak. It was supposed to be right there, that bridge. But it wasn't. Perhaps they had taken the wrong path from the start? The picket of demons—simply a foul, drunken band—keeps turning up.

"Is there a bridge nearby?" Virgil asks.

"There is!" one of the demons replies. It should be remembered, by the way, that they have wings. Imagine a dozen winged monsters winking at each other as they answer Virgil. Yes, that's exactly what Dante writes: they wink at each other.

"There is a bridge! There is! It's over there! Go that way!"

The bridge isn't there either (it has in fact been destroyed), but the demons want to put the two travelers into a panic and utterly confuse them. Incidentally, the demons have nicknames. Like thieves and murderers have. And they produce obscene noises. One made, Dante says, "a trumpet of his arse."

Dante sees the demons winking and accurately judges the meaning of their behavior, but what can he do? Virgil follows the path indicated by the demons and fails to find the bridge . . .

I don't have the book in front of me and can't remember how the adventure ends . . . I'll cite only the extraordinary reason devised by the author to explain why the bridge wasn't there. It had collapsed during the earthquake that shook Hell when Christ descended into it.[5]

What power of invention!

It's hardly surprising that when passersby met Dante on the streets of Florence, they recoiled in holy terror:

"Dear God, he was in Hell!"

In one of the cantos of the *Purgatorio* is the story of a moving bas-relief carved out of a cliff. The bas-relief depicts the mercy of Titus.[6] Either it speaks or it moves, but it is in any event alive. Dante, in order make sure his eyesight hasn't deceived him, moves off to the side and looks at the bas-relief from there. Yes, it's moving. A colossal bas-relief carved out of a cliff. That's the kind of imagination you find in Dante: a huge moving scene the size of a cliff!

Dante wonderfully depicts the first appearance of angels on the path of a whole group of souls ascending through Purgatory. The sinners become aware of them all of a sudden. There are two of them. One descends a little lower, the other remains above. Both take their seats on rocks. They have the sorts of faces, Dante says, that may be compared to swords glinting in the sunlight.[7]

A mysterious and incomparable poetry emanates from the *Purgatorio*. About that I shall write and write.

I would like to bring this great author nearer to the Russian reader. I would undertake that task, of course, not only from a desire to render him an exceptional informational service, so to speak, or to make him better educated; more than that, I would like to share with him the thing of beauty I hold in my hands . . . What could make one happier than sharing something beautiful?

Paradise is a forest, according to Dante. The crossing from Purgatory to Paradise is unmarked. Suddenly everything becomes brighter and safer. A stream, almost a river, running through the forest is depicted. Surrounded by elders and dressed in garments of white, green, and red, Beatrice appears in a chariot drawn by griffins. Dante sees all this reflected in the river. He meets her while standing on the other side of the river. She thanks him for having loved her but reproaches him for the vanity he showed on earth and for his intrigues.[8]

According to Dante, Hell is populated not only with sinners; confined there as well are those who were remote from Christ as a result of their not having been historically contemporary, if one may put it that way—the devils of antiquity, for example.

Newborn infants who died unbaptized are also in Hell. But only in the Hell of the innocent, not the one of sinners. This is a special place in Hell, the city of Limbo, a place of eternal twilight and cheerless repose.

Dante puts the great poets of antiquity there too.[9]

There was an announcement in today's *Literary Gazette* of the death of Mikhail Lozinsky. He translated several Shakespeare tragedies and *The Divine Comedy*. One of the joys of my life is linked to his name; I read Dante for the first time in his translation.[10]

I don't recall I ever saw him. Probably I did see and meet him, even though I can't remember having done so. Now he's in Paradise. Do I have the right to such dispensations? After all, according to Dante, poets reside neither in Hell, nor in Purgatory, nor in Paradise. They're nowhere—in the city called Limbo in the midst of twilight. Dante encounters a group of poets there, among whom is Homer—"with sword in hand," Dante says.

Eternal memory to a poet who retold a great work in another language.

I'm glad my delight in the author of *The Divine Comedy* is shared by such a magnificent writer as Oscar Wilde.

Truly, a magnificent writer.

His manifesto holds no interest for me; one could easily skip it without fear of losing anything.[11]

He wrote *The Picture of Dorian Gray*, about a bad man who remains immutably young while the image in his portrait changes into that of an old man who is all the more frightening since the original, as I've said, is a bad man who has committed crimes.

He wrote the tale "The Birthday of the Infanta" about the tragedy of a dwarf boy who falls in love with a princess, and the tale "The Star-Child" about an evil boy who doesn't love his mother, a beggar, because she is ugly, although she is beautiful in spirit.

A whole series of remarkable articles on art (including the one on Dante) issued from his pen.[12]

Persecuted by society and destitute after serving a term in prison, he died in Paris, where he had rented a pitiful room from a landlord who, despite the fact that the deceased owed him a considerable sum for the room, was the only person to place a wreath on his grave.

Wilde's portrait depicts a man with a heavy face and small eyes—a late-Victorian Englishman. That Englishman, by the way, wrote a play in French: the famous *Salomé*, in which a king, while watching his stepdaughter dance, lusts for her, as a result of which his wife, the girl's mother, lets fly unflattering jibes—jealously yet haughtily, fully conscious of her power over him.

It is impossible to speak of Wilde—especially *The Picture of Dorian Gray*—and not be reminded of Edgar Poe. The Wilde novel derives, of course, from Edgar's "William Wilson." The same theme of good and evil in the form of doubles. It was Edgar who was the first to address that theme in that way—doubles.

Again a cold spell, a northerly wind, storm clouds, or rather that which with perfect accuracy is called cloudiness. These out-of-season changes act on the psyche with such force that, waking up on a morning turned suddenly cold and gray, you immediately begin to think about life with a heart-rending sadness, to sum it up, expecting nothing more. The weather changes act on you so forcefully that it's as if you had suddenly aged ten years. And then, amid that cloudiness, a small blue clearing will suddenly appear, and it seems . . . No, nothing seems. There's still no clearing.

Yesterday I was walking down Gorky Street with Boris Livanov.[13] His intelligent views on Hamlet. "After all, I've been working on the role for five years," he says.

"Take Laertes or Polonius . . . What majestic figures they are in their own right. Yet next to Hamlet they're nothing."

"Majestic?"

He quite properly answered that Polonius is by no means a comic character—narrowly sycophantic, an eavesdropper, and so on. One should remember that the dead king loved him. As for Laertes, he is at the very least a Cid.

"But next to Hamlet he's a fop. Simply a fop. And Horatio? Why he's an Erasmus from Rotterdam. But Hamlet instructs him. That's the sort he is; that's how much higher he is than the others."

Livanov is making a movie in which he plays Lomonosov.[14] "I'm tired," he said. "Yesterday they incinerated my face."

At last a clearing. Only since it's very close to the sun, it isn't blue but something on the order of a widening patch of sunlight becoming ever brighter until at last it permits a sheaf of rays to pass through . . .

Why am I writing all this? Sheer graphomania! Livanov was talking about *The Cid,* in which I especially like it that Rodrigue captures "two kings" in battle. Another might have said "three." That's strictness of taste. They aren't kings, of course, but probably sheiks or something like that, but in French, and for Rodrigue, they're kings. And it's good that they're kings; it's grander, clearer, more exact.[15]

About these details. It seems to me, and the idea gives me pleasure, that I sometimes see in other artists details that other observers pass over, even though those details are very important for the artists and very noticeable to them. For instance, I think the "two kings" were a pleasant and very important detail for Corneille. I have a confirmation that my responses to artists do have a place in this sense. Thus I noticed that in one of his screenplays Chaplin calls our contemporary world "the age of crimes."[16] Nobody singled out that phrase in the screenplay, only me. And now, while talking in my hearing about meeting Chaplin in London, the director Gerasimov suddenly remarked, though unaware of its meaning for me, that Chaplin had said he made the movie for the sake of that very phrase.[17]

The village barber gave him a basin to use as a helmet, they turned up a breastplate and lance that were lying in some garret, and they found a mare that would, they said, prove to be a magnificent mount for a knight . . . No, that's wrong. He himself saw a helmet in that basin, they didn't look for the breastplate—he reverently lifted it out of the dust of the garret, and he himself chose Rosinante as his steed. That's the point: nobody imposed that mania on Don Quixote; rather, he imposed it on those around him. He imposed it on Sancho Panza, at any rate.

Gustave Doré has greatly assisted in the popularization of famous books among later generations. It's rare for anyone to visualize Don Quixote differently than as Doré depicted him. Or Gargantua. Or the *Inferno.*

Who was his prototype? Rembrandt?

Yes, for Doré illustrated the Bible, too. And the fairy tales of the Brothers Grimm. And something else I've forgotten at the moment . . . *Paradise Lost* and *Paradise Regained.* What were they—copper etchings? Were those astonishing compositions actually drawn directly with a stylus? Or were they drawn first in pencil on paper?

One can imagine the Paris of Doré's time and Monsieur Doré himself dressed in a duster and thinking about the evening's cancan at the Folies Bergères as he sits at his work table with a board between his lap and the table edge and sketches the fiery tomb of Farinata. And Dante with grave, frightened concern gazing at the tomb. It takes an imagination of genius to decide, for example, what the fat-bottomed infant Gargantua looks like, and not only when he's naked and blowing in the rear ends of his rams but also later on when he's dressed in hose and probing his nannies.

It's interesting that we writers hold Doré in higher esteem than his fellow artists do. For some reason they wince. It's not Picasso who winces, of course, but the half-baked cubists.

Doré received enormous fees. Thousands of francs for each panel. And how many such panels . . . Yes, and *Paradise Lost* too. How many in *Paradise Lost* alone! Obviously I've got the figures wrong. No publisher could justify these.

> My mind . . . gives birth to so many chimeras and fantastic monsters, one after another, without order or purpose, that in order to contemplate their ineptitude and strangeness at my pleasure, I have begun to put them in writing, hoping in time to make my mind ashamed of itself.
>
> Montaigne[18]

It is a bad business if there are mistakes even in the main words you always see before you in your brain, so to speak. It's all right if letters drop out as the words are written down in cursive, but if those words that had once stood majestically like battleships at anchor should themselves start making faces, then, I repeat, the business is rubbish.

Incidentally, it's not "Montaigne" in the new book but "Monteigne," with an "e." And traced in the portrait's background is the word, "Montagne." Isn't that a mountain?

I recall in regard to that name my sister's school friend Irène de Montagne Rouge . . . My goodness, I even remember her rather noisy appearances in our home—the laughter, the ruche, the tossing down of her gloves, the giggling with a glance in my direction . . . And all of it in a dark cloud of gossip and sin, the cloud of her charming and bitter notoriety as the kept woman of some rich man . . .

In the essay "Of smells" Montaigne permits himself a magnificent jest about how in his youth he brought kisses home on his thick mustache.

I thought Montaigne was thick sheeplike wigs, stocking-sheathed calves, and crooked shoes. No, he's much earlier. He's just after the St. Bartholomew's Day Massacre.[19] As may already be clear, he wears a mustache and a jerkin and has no wig whatever; on the contrary, he's bald. Then it truly is amazing. In Russia at the time were Ioann the Terrible and maybe Boris Godunov.[20]

I haven't read much of him yet, just a few pages. But already one has the impression that the Encyclopedists began with him . . .

He's a sage, Montaigne. It's strange to find such subtle ruminations in a book written in the sixteenth century. Of course, I'm yielding here to the erroneous impression that the quality of the human mind has been improving in direct proportion to the increase in the calendar date. In the first place, the date hasn't been increasing all that rapidly—it's less than five hundred years since Montaigne, which isn't really that long, is it?—and in the second place, words were spoken in Greece and Rome that were perhaps more intelligent than any that have been uttered in all the subsequent reaches of calendar time.

Clearly, only mind concerned with the mastery of the material world—with science and technology—has been developing. Mind concerned with the mastery of itself has not changed.

What we designate by the name "Egmont" was for Montaigne a tragedy recently played out in Brussels . . .[21] Maybe it really wasn't so very long ago. Maybe the fact that they beheaded their victims instead of, say, shooting them is what makes some events seem so remote to us?

Montaigne cites examples of people faced with death who without any wavering of self-possession give instructions for the disposal of their remains.[22] Thus the Bohemian leader Jan Vischa left orders for his body to be flayed after he died and his skin stretched over a drum. The Emperor Maximilian, distinguished during his lifetime by exceptional modesty (he never allowed a servant "to see him in his privy," Montaigne puts it) left instructions that underdrawers be placed on his corpse. Could he have been a hermaphrodite? The idea may be right: the emperor was very handsome—"with singular bodily beauty," Montaigne says. Also cited by Montaigne are instances of the careful arrangement of one's own funeral rites.

Montaigne doesn't reveal himself to be much of a believer. Even though there is in these ruminations something about what occurs after death, he speaks least of all of the soul. That's all the more strange since the era in which he lived not only continually referred to religion but was imbued with a sense of its terrifying aspect.

How frightening is Montaigne's comment that once you've lived a year and seen the change of seasons—winter, spring, summer, fall—you've seen everything. You won't see anything new again!

That's like something Ilf once said: "Let's go, they won't show us anything else here."

By the way, I don't think they'll show me anything else either. However, it's possible it's just fatigue and a lack of fresh air.

It's worth noting that, in addition to everything else, Montaigne is a critic of poetry. The frequently encountered quotations from Greek and Roman poets attest not to scholastic erudition, not to the author's desire to pay tribute to his enthusiasm for classicism per se, but rather to the fact that he sincerely loved poetry.

And he judges it with exceptional tact.

I too would like to write an article in which an appropriate place (interesting for the reader, that is) might be found for the quotation of Russian poets—not one quotation or two, but a whole torrent of them.

I'd include Esenin's striking lines,

I am glad that I've kissed women,
Trampled flowers, and lain in the grass,
And never, like our little brothers,
Beaten fellow beasts on the head.[23]

The first two lines hardly seem exceptional; on the contrary, they might be found in any poet. To trample flowers, lie in the grass, kiss women, and be glad of it—there's no poetic depth; it's banal. But to consider oneself happy for not having beaten fellow beasts on the head—that's unusual. Only a poet could reveal that to us in ourselves. And only a poet could call the beasts our little brothers.

How many similar quotations would one want to cite. There's nothing more pleasant, by the way, than sharing beauty with someone, than pointing out to the reader one or another beautiful thing that he, from inexperience or merely from inattention, might happen to overlook.

Montaigne lived before Napoleon. It would be interesting to know what he would have said about him. But that "if" is a child's word, a game.

How utterly charming is the little article on Cato, the purpose of which, as Montaigne says, is to establish a competition among four poets who praised Cato. Montaigne quotes four lines, commenting on them with great skill.[24]

Sometimes I'm drawn to do the same thing, to find occasions for citing a series of remarkable Russian lines. To bring them to everyone's attention. I don't forget to do that whenever the occasion presents itself. And I'll do it now. For example, the attributes Mandelstam found for a peninsula in a poem enumerating geographical forms:

And ethereal its sculptured peninsulas.[25]

I think comparing a peninsula to a sculpture is very good. We'll recall that Michelangelo wanted to make a statue from a cliff . . . And in Dante, in the *Purgatorio,* there's a bas-relief cut out of a cliff.

Incidentally, Montaigne mentions a ruler of antiquity (Cambyses?) who in a rage challenged a cliff to individual combat.[26]

I read *Werther* and wept bitterly as I recalled my own life . . . How strange that I was young! You see him—tall, wearing a blue swallowtail coat, boots, and yellow breeches. Strolling, or rather dashing, around the city's outskirts at night in turmoil, he has lost his hat. He rides horseback. Visually, something like Lensky, it seems to me. No, that just evokes his horse and boots. And then why Lensky and not Onegin? No, it's silly.

It's magnificently written. Not an epistolary novel but a collection of letters from one person to another: from Werther to Wilhelm. Suddenly just before the hero's death the editor intervenes, his text little differing from Werther's. It's all slightly naturalistic, especially the final scene. The situation itself is very individual and naturalistic and therefore singular and photographic. It isn't generalized. All the same, since love, passion, and poetry lie at its basis, one would have liked some generalization.

In short, what can you say? It's superb.

Bonaparte took *Werther* with him in a field chest on the Italian campaign. You can imagine how popular it was.

Ossian is mentioned: Werther reads him out loud to Charlotte. I found that part tedious. Why the vogue for Scotland? Walter Scott, Ossian . . . And then Bonaparte's fondness and taste for Ossian. The foggy shroud, the flying moon, the large women with unbound hair.

"*Werther* has already been written, my love."[27]

Let's try writing by hand. By the way, when Gogol wrote—no, probably later, let's say when Herzen was in London—you could have heard discussions about who wrote with what.[28] One said that of course he wrote with a steel nib. Another: "What do you mean? Why, I only write with a goose quill. Can one actually write anything with a steel nib?" In a word, just like discussions today about writing by hand or on a typewriter. As if it mattered. "Do they really write with their hands?" Michelangelo asked. "They write with their heads!"

It would be interesting to specify when the transition to steel nib actually took place. Did Stendhal write with a steel nib, for example? What about Hugo? What did Lev Tolstoy start with, a quill?

What did the steel nib look like? Where did it first appear? In Birmingham?

We forget that goose quills weren't, so to speak, a natural thing either, but a kind of manufactured item. They were sharpened by special craftsmen who gave them the simple and convenient exterior of short little tubes virtually the size of our fountain pens although without any nibs on the end.

Obviously it's absolutely unimportant what you write with. You could even dictate. When images of any kind come from the lips of a great man, he isn't writing them; they're in the air.

True, you sometimes sense a link between head and hand whenever a page gleams white before you. True, to write by hand is to write consecutively, in a run . . . As for the typewriter, I waste a lot of energy each time lifting and moving the clumsy thing. It may be that influences the course of my work: I get tired more easily, I feel the desire to rest sooner . . .

I knew several graphologists. One of them, Zuev-Insarov by name, plied his art from a little table at the Uranus movie theater on Sretenka. A great many who came to the theater stopped by the table while walking around the lobby and asked the graphologist to determine their personalities from their handwriting. Zuev-Insarov, a severe, dark-haired young man in a black jacket and, it seems to me now, black glasses, wrote down his conclusions on sheets of postal paper.

He put together a description of me too—accurate, in my view.

I started to grasp something of that art. It was clear to me, for example, that if someone writes quickly but still remembers without thinking to make in a single flourish, if one may put it that way, the astonishingly complicated connections among the separate letters, then he obviously has the ability to organize . . . With poets those connections are extraordinarily beautiful. Take a look at Pushkin's handwriting: it seems a fleet is under sail.

It was also clear that if each letter stands alone, then the handwriting's owner is somebody with a high opinion of himself. In fact, even in cursive writing such a person will manage to write each letter separately, as if remembering each, as if holding each in high esteem . . . The standard for such a hand is Esenin's. I saw some stanzas he had copied out in alizarin green ink. Each letter was rounded, almost a circle, and each stood by itself, green against the white paper like a bush against the snow.

Another graphologist was named Verov. He had a skewed little beard and was disheveled and shabby . . . He told me that if he were given only a sheet of typewritten paper, he could still determine the writer's personality. He also said he could determine not only personality from handwriting but even how many rooms a person had in his apartment . . .

I don't recall under what circumstances I first saw the typewriter. It's possible that miracle had already become fairly commonplace by the time I was able to gaze through windows. In any case, I don't remember any day filled with amazement and exclamations in regard to that little machine.

Perhaps I first saw it through a window of the Trapani Steamship Company on the corner of Karantinny Street and Stroganovsky Bridge. It was known by one name then—Remington. The young lady who knew how to operate that machine and who sold her labor on it was called a *remingtonistka.* One of the rooms in Lev Tolstoy's house at Yasnaya Polyana had a similar name: the *remingtonnaya.* In addition to a great deal else, *Resurrection, Hadji-Murad,* "The Living Corpse," and "The Devil" were all typed there. Not bad nourishment for the first steps of that little Moloch.

I don't recall the advent of the typewriter being heralded in any way, as other miracles of that kind were. The appearance of the cinematograph doesn't seem to have been anticipated either. Tolstoy's name is connected with the cinematograph too. He regarded inventions with approval; he even wanted, it's said, to write a screenplay for some contemporary company. See what an innovator he was! Tolstoy, incidentally, was in fact among the very few to be captured by the cinema at its dawn—as if thanking him for his support. In any event, praise! Through the shimmering film of that era as if through a continuous rippling of water, we see Tolstoy's carriage drive up to a station, and in the carriage sits a gentleman in a black broadcloth coat and a black hat with an enormous quantity of gray hair on the broadcloth and around his face . . . That's Lev Tolstoy. Students are running about and shinnying up a pole. Because of the speed of the film, everything is intensified. All wag their elbows—Tolstoy, Sophia Andreevna, the students, the constables . . .[29] The carriage turns foppishly, then everything disappears.

Just think, I too might have seen Tolstoy when he was alive. Those virtually my contemporaries did. One lady told me that once when she was a little girl riding on a streetcar with her mother, her mother whispered that the old man sitting in front of them was Tolstoy. The streetcar proceeded down what is now Kropotkin Street but what was then Prechistenka. Suddenly the old man stood up to get off. And the lady said,

"As he walked toward the exit, the entire streetcar rose to its feet."

You shouldn't write a story standing up. Yet more often than not that's how I work. Gogol, by the way, also wrote standing up. Annenkov splendidly recalls his meetings with Gogol in Rome while the latter was working on *Dead Souls.*[30] Gogol had just finished the Plyushkin chapter, the one, it follows, where the garden and the birch tree that looks like a broken column are, where the allusion to the beautiful third sister is, and where the roadway planks that move like piano keys beneath a passing carriage are . . . Gogol, Annenkov recalls, was delighted with what he had written, and suddenly setting off down a Roman lane on his haunches like a Cossack dancer, he twirled the shaft of his folded umbrella over his head.

Gogol wrote standing at a writing bureau.

How much have Pushkin and Gogol overshadowed almost everyone else who wrote at that time. The same Annenkov, the Aksakovs, and many others who even today remain overshadowed for me . . .[31] My goodness, Herzen! The Herzen who remarked of Nicholas I that his forehead sloped rapidly backward.

Herzen wrote magnificently (in a purely descriptive sense). Here I'll find the passage with the depiction of the old monkey with a cold that lived on the corner of a stove in Herzen's childhood.

Of books dedicated to a survey of one's life, *My Past and Thoughts* is obviously the best. What a marvelous book has been written in the Russian language! There doesn't seem to be any aesthetic evaluation of it in our criticism.[32]

(Reading Tolstoy.) I'm unable to visualize Andrei Bolkonsky's appearance. According to Tolstoy, he's handsome, dark-haired, and short with small hands. There's no impression. Bezukhov is large, fat, and wears glasses. In the scene where he becomes enraged, he picks up a marble slab from a washstand and is ready to kill the person he's infuriated with.[33] Physical strength. There's an impression. Probably he's wearing knee breeches and stockings. The corners of his collar stand erect against his cheeks. The greatest impression is made by Speransky. The unpleasant laugh, the white hands. And his "good wine now walks in boots," said after taking an unfinished bottle from his guests and recorking it. For sheer authenticity, the dinner at Speransky's may be the best scene in the novel.

How is *War and Peace* read today? We, I recall, approached that period gradually on the stairway of age: "You need to read *War and Peace,*" someone would say. I read it in the time of first love. I didn't want the girl I loved (all in moonlight—oh, you could hold in your hands a single strand of one of her curls on which lay a single beam of light), I didn't want her to "betray" me as Natasha had "betrayed" Andrei. Yet that's exactly what she did. I tore a sheaf of pages from *War and Peace,* the ones about Natasha's love for Andrei and her abduction by Anatoly, and sent them to her for consolation. It's astonishing that such a thing actually happened in my life, that I supposed in complete confidence that someone could be consoled by literature.

Reading, for example, Shakhovskoy's memoir of the first days in Moscow after Napoleon's departure, you have the sense that Tolstoy failed to tell something, that he failed to convey certain peculiarities of that year, those days, that style.[34] It was all more picturesque, as everything older is. That's exactly right—it was all more antiquated, if one may put it that way, all more ancient, more remote and fabulous . . .

I think Tolstoy erred in *Anna Karenina* when after choosing Levin as his hero with his philosophizing, his antistatism, and his search for the truth, he failed to make him a writer. The result is that he's merely a stubborn, spoiled person, an *enfant terrible,* just the sort of person, by the way, that Tolstoy himself would have been had he not become a writer. Sometimes Levin seems vain, sometimes merely fatuous . . . And all because he isn't a writer. What is he in fact, if he isn't a writer? A special landowner? What's a special landowner? If he's intelligent, a philosopher, if he sees the evils of society, then why isn't he with the revolutionaries or with Chernyshevsky?[35] Why is he, after all, against the progressives (and to be frank, Levin isn't very sympathetic to the emancipation of the serfs)? If he's intelligent, then why isn't he a writer, why isn't he a Lev Tolstoy? What is he? An eccentric? Merely an eccentric?

What ultimately is he preaching when he sings that hymn to mowing? I must mow. Why mow? I must invent an analysis of infinitesimals or compose the music of Beethoven, but not mow.

He's just preaching gymnastics.

How did Tolstoy stand in regard to property relations? There's no evidence in his early notebooks that would bespeak a neglect on his part of the material side of existence. Rather, he was parsimonious. What are credits and debits doing in the diary of a great man? There's Tolstoy's remark about Napoleon in which he denigrates the latter's majesty, taking him to task expressly for his crediting and debiting, for his "fussiness," as he calls it. Did Tolstoy notice that he himself wasn't crystalline pure in that respect? His brother Nikolenka was pure—not fussy and without a property assessment of life. Remember how much moral effort his so-called simplification, his rejection of publishing rights cost Tolstoy . . . Why in fact did there have to be a special role for his wife, with whom he was forced to struggle? If he wanted to simplify, then he would have done so; it isn't that difficult. He would have lived from the beginning in such a way that it wouldn't have been necessary to repudiate or simplify anything. That wasn't required? True, it wasn't, but then neither was it required to circle around and about that which is unattainable for you, that which you cannot do.

The stationmaster in whose room and on whose bed Lev Tolstoy expired was named Ozolin. After what had happened to him, he became a Tolstoyan and later shot himself.

What an incredible fate! Imagine living quietly at home in the bosom of your family, minding your own business, and not anticipating any particular events, when one fine day Lev Tolstoy suddenly pops in out of nowhere carrying a stick and wearing a peasant coat—Lev Tolstoy, the author of *War and Peace,* who lies down on your bed and several days later dies there. That would indeed be something to make you lose your way and shoot yourself.

One of the more striking circumstances, if one may put it that way, in *War and Peace* is when Pierre Bezukhov, who had never revealed his secret (his love for Natasha) to anyone else, reveals it to a drunken, vulgar invader in burning Moscow . . . Just so: they're sitting and drinking in a strange house, and Pierre tells Major Ramballe of his love. The major, however vulgar, however drunk, however crude (he is, moreover, an invader), appreciates what Pierre is saying; he understands that Pierre is in fact speaking of a pure love.

"Yes, yes," he exclaims, "*les nuages!* Clouds!"

If I were writing a screenplay for a movie of *War and Peace,* I'd begin with that scene: Ramballe and Pierre in the strange house. I'd start with Pierre's declaration. That would shorten the novel by half. The *nuages* would become a montage of brief images of what had happened before 1812, images of Natasha and everything connected with her.

It's odd that although Tolstoy's style with its piling up of coordinate and subordinate clauses exists, so to speak, in plain view of everyone—that although it's essentially the only style in Russian literature characterized by license and a distinctive infelicity (several other "thats" issuing from one "that," several subsequent "whiches" from one "which")—no one has yet provided an explanation, despite the demand that young writers write correctly, of just why Tolstoy wrote the way he did. It would be necessary (and it's strange no one has done this) to write a dissertation on Tolstoy's peculiar "illiteracy." Someone once observed that Tolstoy knew about his violations of syntactic rules (he constantly spoke of having a "bad style") yet felt under no obligation whatever to avoid them. He wrote, it's said in this observation, as if no one had written before him, as if he were writing for the first time. Thus, even Tolstoy's style is a manifestation of his rebellion against norms and conventions, whatever they might be.

The acceptance of syntactic imprecision allowed Tolstoy to cope more easily with the difficulties of rendering thoughts and describing things or conditions. The other writers of Tolstoy's day were extraordinarily bound by prohibitions against the subordinating conjunctions "that" and "which." Remaining within syntactical limits, they sought other means of constructing sentences, and their work is the more significant for their having found them. But syntax is hardly important when Tolstoy writes. Only he, by the way, wrote that infelicitous Tolstoyan language of his; no one else ventured to adopt it.

Just as some of the loftier achievements of technology and medicine are identified by the word "miracle," so that there are miracles of technology and medicine, so may literature's highest achievements be identified, thus permitting us to speak of the miracles of literature.

It seems to me that the description in one of Tolstoy's Caucasus stories of the sky over the heads of some soldiers who are passing at night through a narrow ravine belongs to the miracles of literature. It is said there that the winding strip of night sky filled with stars that the soldiers see above them as they pass between the ravine's two cliffs looks like a river. It flows over their heads like a river, that dark band twinkling with an infinitude of stars.[36]

It would be worth making a selection of a hundred such miracles. For what reason? To show people how others have been able to think and see. Why show that? So that those who are unable to think and see in that way may nonetheless respect themselves at that moment, realizing that to the extent they are human, they too are capable of much.

(Turgenev.) What a pinnacle of artistry "The Living Relic" is![37] What a story! It's all in shades of sunlight mixed with the darkness of the dwelling, which is so characteristic of summer; it's all in descriptions of summer things and conditions: honey, wasps, beams of light, forest animals. And the dream that Lukerya recounts is summery too: death with yellow eyes at a fair. But the best thing in the story is Lukerya's sudden joy as she recalls the time a hare came into her cell of torment. It sat down on its hind legs, resting a moment, and gazed at her . . .

"Like an officer!" Lukerya says, remembering her own beauty, remembering love.

Pushkin has some lines that seem inconceivable to us for a poet of his era.

When here to this proud grave
You'll come to bow your curls and weep.[38]

"To bow your curls" is the result of heightened attention to a thing and uncharacteristic of the poets of those times. It's too "close up" for the poetic thought of that era, which, though capable of creating powerful images, still could not do so without a tinge of rhetoric: "and star speaks with star."[39]

Isn't it a recollection of the portraits of Bryullov?[40] Or the rendering of a fleeting impression received by the poet while gazing at his wife, whom we know to have worn curls? Whatever the case, it's a step by the poet into another, later poetics. It wouldn't be surprising if someone, even someone who knows poetry, should disagree that the lines do in fact belong to Pushkin.

"What do you mean? It's some modern poet. Blok?"[41]

It is our right, after all, to select from the whole of Pushkin the lines we admire most.

And let at the sepulchral entrance . . .

The "o" is repeated five times in succession: *grobovogo vkhvo-* [sepulchral en-]. You descend the steps of the vault into the crypt. And, yes, inside the vault there's an echo.[42]

In a happy reading of the lines "There the ravishing Rossini,/There Europe's favorite, Orphé!" I noticed that the words "Europe's" and "Orphé" were in a certain way visually similar. I examined them more closely and realized that the word "Orphé" is to a considerable degree a palindrome of the word "Europe's." In fact, "Euro" *[Evro]* read backward produces "Orvé," which is almost "Orphé." Thus, in the line beginning with the word "Europe's" and ending with the word "Orphé," a mirror has, so to speak, been placed.[43]

We still don't know how to read, but already we hold *Eugene Onegin* in our hands.

When I was a small child, Pushkin was published, just as he sometimes is now, in a one-volume edition. In those days it was a thick folio-sized book with illustrations arranged four to a page in the form of a window—yes, in the form of a window where each pane is a picture.

There were also illustrations that took up a whole page. For example, the floating gallows from *The Captain's Daughter.* Oh, how frightening it was to look at that picture!

The Nicholas of Pushkin's day was quite unlike the figure since found in illustrations, the movies, and on stage. He had no mustache. There's a bust by Vitali, who was Pushkin's, Bryullov's, and Glinka's contemporary, in which Nicholas is represented with no mustache and a sharply modeled Roman face.[44] The mustache very likely turned up later after it had made its appearance in Europe. So that the image of Nicholas glaring with terrible eyes from behind his mustache was undoubtedly concocted later on to strengthen the image of Pushkin's "oppression."

Perhaps the best lines of poetry in the Russian language are these by Fet:

In my hand—what a marvel!—
Your hand.[45]

Further on in the poem we find "and on the earth are two emeralds, two fireflies," but these lines are enough.

There is, by the way, such old and general meaning in them that they might be taken as the epigraph for any book involving human activity. *War and Peace*, for example, or *The Divine Comedy*.

Fet sits in his portrait like a Jew, even a rabbi, with a scruffy beard he might well be scratching.[46]

It's strange to imagine he was a great Russian lyric poet. He was a cuirassier and a bear hunter. It was on a hunt at his estate that a bear mauled Lev Tolstoy.

Fet is hidden by the figures of Pushkin and Lermontov. But he was no less important a lyric poet; he merely wrote differently.

What wonderful names there are in Ostrovsky's plays. His talent seems to display itself with particular grace in them. There's a young man in love with an actress who's been carried off by rich people. He's called Melusov. Both "small change" [*meloch'*] and "melody" are in the name. There's a merchant who, though a cad, is urbane and liked by women. He's called Velikatov. Both "giant" [*velikan*] and "delicacy" [*delikatnost'*] are present. Combined in the names are the spontaneity of a find and craftsmanship, and therein lies the charm of these by-products of the art of a writer of genius. The names are like flowers . . .

The widow in *The Last Victim* is called Tugina. "Tuga" is grief [*pechal'*]. And she does grieve. She could have been Pechalina, but Tugina is better. Her seducer's name is Dulchin, and that suggests both "deceiver" [*dulia*] and *dulce*—"sweet" (since he's sweet to her).

These sounds really do seem like a flower bed to me. Perhaps that's because Ostrovsky gave one of his merchants the name Margaritov (derived from "daisy").[47]

A beguiling impression of excellent literature, humor, and art has remained with me from *The Frigate Pallada*. I'm not even talking about the material of the book itself: the voyage round the world described in it and described so well that you want to call it the best travel book ever written.

Goncharov had his own stateroom. On the island of Madeira he was carried around in a covered sedan chair and drank, as he stresses, genuine Madeira.

How strong our literature is if a writer as splendid as Goncharov was setting down his literary opinions and tastes barely by the end of its first decade.[48]

In *Oblomov* a woman is depicted from whom the hero, exhausted by his madness, seeks comfort (and the laziness and inactivity of Oblomov are by no means "national" but characterize him as someone who is in fact mentally ill, just as the author himself had been). The woman is a wonderful figure, and it seems likely to me that Tolstoy duplicated her in *Hadji-Murad* in his portrayal of the officer's wife who suddenly falls in love with the hero.

A. Panaeva's memoirs are childishly written, in a professional sense quite feeble.[49] Letters are written like that, without a single vivid portrait. The Turgenev probably comes off best. Her attitude toward him was hostile. How much more effectively, by the way, did Koni portray Turgenev—the scene in Paris at the Viardots' house where Turgenev is getting ready to go out for breakfast in some worn-out overcoat that to the memoirist's amazement is missing several buttons.[50]

Judging from what Panaeva writes, Dobrolyubov was in love with her.[51] He asks her to place her hand on his forehead as he is dying.

Gogol makes an appearance in the memoirs. There's a special place setting for him at dinner and a special pink wine goblet. He says almost nothing at all, then goes to bed.

Gogol is virtually a patriarch for the whole group (Nekrasov, Turgenev, Panaev). But he wasn't yet forty. How old were they, then?

In "Viy" Gogol says that the little *panna*'s father is forty. Elsewhere he says,

"The old man started to cry."

It can't be that the young Gogol considered a forty-year-old to be an old man. Most likely he forgot that he'd made the little *panna*'s father only forty.

Panaeva's information about Nekrasov's wealth comes as a complete surprise. He was very rich. Returning home after playing cards, he told Panaev that of the evening's winnings he had only thirty thousand left, although he had in fact won about a hundred and fifty!

After dining he would dress to go to his club. He rode around in a carriage.

I. Panaev's memoirs of the same figures and era are written at an incomparably higher level: manfully and professionally.[52]

Once a book by Sheller-Mikhailov fell into my hands, a novel from the *Grainfield* edition of his collected works.[53] I started reading the book, an account of some misfortune involving a monetary legacy in some bureaucratic or academic milieu . . . It was briskly written but there wasn't a trace of charm or magic. Weddings, promissory notes, intrigues, a widow's tears, dissolute sons . . . Then turning the page, I suddenly sensed that the lines were melting away before my eyes, that the room was disappearing, that I was seeing only what the author described. I myself was almost sitting on a bench in the rain and the falling leaves just as the person the author was talking about was sitting, and I myself was seeing a sad, sad woman coming toward me, just as the one sitting on the bench was seeing her . . .

Sheller-Mikhailov's book had been mistakenly bound up with several pages from the *Grainfield* edition of the works of Dostoevsky. The pages were from *The Idiot*.

I had no idea I was reading a different author, but I almost cried out,

"What's this? My goodness, who wrote this? Sheller-Mikhailov? No! Who then?"

Whereupon my gaze fell on the startling name of Nastasya Filippovna. And there it was again in another place—a seemingly lilac name that here and there caused the printed lines to shimmer.

There's an enormous difference between an ordinary writer and a great one.

I ran into someone at the Writers' Club barbershop whom I had long known by sight and who turned out to be the same deputy director of the Vakhtangov Theater who had just sent me a letter. He said that Remizova had arrived, and that, as far as he was concerned, everything in regard to *The Idiot* was the same as before.[54]

That means I should hear from Remizova today.

If the business really is going to get started, then I'll have to find a copy of *The Idiot* and quickly read it through. I'll get it from Kazakevich.[55]

I never thought I'd be so hard at work on Dostoevsky (I'm writing an adaptation of *The Idiot*). Even so, I still can't make up my mind how I feel about him: do I like him or not?

The principal line in his treatment of the human personality is that passing through the sense of self-esteem. He imagines no more important force in the human soul than that. He attributes that personal, tormenting quality to man in general, but especially to the heroes of his works . . . It's impossible to imagine that Ganya, who so dreams of becoming rich, won't crawl into Nastasya Filippovna's fireplace after the burning money. Nevertheless, although he falls down in a swoon, he won't crawl. The presence of self-esteem, stronger than the craving for money, delights Nastasya Filippovna.

Incidentally, to bring a healthy and impudent young man down in a swoon when he's on the verge of fulfilling a dream is very good, very inventive.

I waited to see how Nastasya Filippovna would react to Ganechka's collapse—in an ordinary practical sense. She exclaims,

"Girls, give him some water, some spirits!"

Also very good.

With what puzzled disdain would the author regard my homage. Although in a letter to Princess Obolenskaya (who had asked his permission to adapt *Crime and Punishment* for the stage), he wrote in reply to her praise that it is for the sake of such opinions that writers in essence create their works.[56]

Nikolai Vilyam-Vilmont told me that according to evidence from the author himself there is in the plan of *The Idiot* a theme from Dante (the passage through the circles of torments).[57] I still haven't read anything about *The Idiot,* nor have I looked at any of the many adaptations already done. I'll read them after I've finished my own. That seems the best procedure to me: to solve everything along the way, spontaneously, with a fresh eye, trusting to my own imagination.

Ganya's twenty-seven. You get hints that he's handsome, a dandy. In the scene at Nastasya Filippovna's he's clearly dressed in a swallowtail coat. What did the coats of that day look like? And the dandies of that time, what were they like? Where will Akimov, who will probably design the production, get his material?[58]

Nastasya Filippovna is in all likelihood dressed like Anna Karenina. Is that right?

The Petersburg of *The Idiot* is nothing at all like the Petersburg of *Anna Karenina.* I won't be saying anything new to call the first fantastical, the second realistic. Although Dostoevsky remarks very realistically of the trotters rushing about the streets of Petersburg that "their shoes resonate upon the pavement." (Oh dear, no! If you listen carefully, there is in that description an echo of "Nevsky Prospect"; it is of course akin to the devil's lamp and the carriage horses stretching out their legs. Verify all this.)[59]

Sometimes Rogozhin thinks no less "grandly" than Myshkin does. The common and mercantile disappear. When Myshkin tells him about the "eyes" that had been watching him at the station, Rogozhin asks,

"But whose eyes were they, then?"

That's quite in keeping with (in the present instance) Myshkin's own delirious thinking: "Whose eyes?"

Rogozhin didn't have to ask. Since it was in fact he who had been watching the prince at the station, it would have been more appropriate for him to have kept silent—he might have been frightened.

But a great artist is always correct.

By the way, working now on the speeches for one or another scene of my adaptation, I sometimes move, if one may put it this way, a line or two away from what Dostoevsky has indicated. I depart rather far (it seems to me in such cases that I'm achieving greater theatrical expressiveness) and each time, however correct I thought my departure to be, I still return to the line from Dostoevsky I had abandoned. He always turns out to be more correct.

There's something slightly inane about diaries intended to produce material for quick publication that will appeal to the reader.

The best diary is by a certain Pigafetta, the secretary or some such of Magellan's expedition.[60] Properly speaking, it's a nautical log that contains personal experiences as well. Pigafetta records how once, when they had all gone ashore to meet with some natives who had come to trade, he found himself with nothing to offer in exchange for gifts—no pieces of glass or anything like that. But he did have a playing card, a jack. His comrades made fun of him (obviously there had been a card game the day before, and Pigafetta had lost or given away all the "valuables" he had prepared for trading and then had picked up the card from off the floor). Yet this Pigafetta got more for his jack than the others got for their things—nearly a whole cow in addition to some sheep and chickens. How much does that jack reveal to us of the colorful shipboard life of those explorers!

The thought often occurs to me that it wouldn't be a bad idea to recount on a special sheet of paper—actually, several sheets would be required—all the plots of literary works that have struck me. I really should get around to doing that.

How many plots are there? It's hard to give an immediate answer without first writing them down. Two hundred? Probably two hundred. No, less than that. One hundred. One hundred at once? The first to come to mind is *The Prince and the Pauper.* Actually nothing comes to mind by itself—a whole whirlwind bursts forth.

Some effects in literature are prepared with exceptional skill.

Among the plot lines in *The Prince and the Pauper* is one connecting the young king in distress with a certain young nobleman whose fate is similar to the king's: he too has been deprived of his property . . . True, the king finds himself denied his right to the throne, while the nobleman has merely been deprived of part of the hereditary lands he is entitled to, but they are nonetheless drawn together by anger over an injustice. The young nobleman grows fond of the boy. Like everyone else, he regards the boy's claim to be king a mark of insanity. But the young nobleman patronizes him, pretending he really does acknowledge him as king. However, to the extent that the young nobleman agrees to accept what he views as the boy's mania, there arise certain inconveniences for him. The king, for example, will not allow him to dine with him . . .

"Forebear! Wouldst sit in the presence of the king?"

As a result the young nobleman is forced to eat his dinner cold. The inconvenience is, I think, eliminated in the following way: the young king falls into the hands of a half-crazed religious fanatic who, hearing that the boy calls himself king and the son of Henry VIII (who had sequestered church property), has decided to stab him in order to take revenge on his father, or rather, on his father's memory, since Henry VIII is already dead. The young nobleman saves the boy from the fanatic's vengeance.

"Such service demandeth rich reward," the boy says. "Name thy desire."

"That I and my heirs, forever, may sit in the presence of the majesty of England," the young nobleman replies.

The young king solemnly proclaims that Miles Hendon (for such is the young nobleman's name) and his descendants shall henceforth be granted the right to sit in the presence of the king of England.

The king's friend is pleased; at least now he won't have to stand behind the boy at dinner and will be able to have his own while it's still hot.

"Yes, that's very good indeed," we note, even when reading the book for the tenth time, although as if for the first time, as always happens with truly remarkable books. "Yes, a charming story. How often and in how many different ways you remember it."

We are thus completely satisfied with that story as it stands, satisfied with it as something that exists in finished form in the narrative, never suspecting that . . . But listen further.

Toward the end of the novel Miles Hendon is suddenly separated from his favorite, who has somehow disappeared. Our hero grieves for a time, but his grief soon gives way to extremely important matters having to do with the fact that in London the coronation day of the new king has been set, a king who is young and, it's said, good . . .

"Why not go and get speech of him and beg for justice against those who have wronged me and deprived me of my inheritance?" Miles Hendon thinks.

He hurries to London . . . Then he enters the cathedral where the coronation is already under way and sees that the king really is young and, apparently, good.

Our hero approaches the place where the king is standing and is astonished to recognize in him the friend with whom he had not long before shared a misfortune.

"Is it a dream? . . . Or is he the veritable sovereign of England, and not the friendless poor Tom o' Bedlam I took him for?"

And then the young nobleman remembers the right granted to him, and pulling up a chair, sits down in front of everyone. There is general consternation, and he is seized.

"Touch him not," a voice is heard from the throne, "it is his right!"

That's what we didn't suspect. A story that in itself had seemed merely an adornment to the narrative actually turns out to have been preparation for the brilliant finale . . .

It seems to me that the whole move is one of the best plot inventions in world literature, that it belongs among the first ten.

Did Mark Twain already know of the finale when he was writing about the cold dinner? Or was it from the cold dinner that the finale unexpectedly emerged?

How much it is to carry off such a move! What incomparable craft![61]

Besides *The Prince and the Pauper* and the books about Tom Sawyer and Huckleberry Finn, Mark Twain wrote a number of other excellent works, if only *Life on the Mississippi* and *A Connecticut Yankee in King Arthur's Court*. From his pen also came a host of stories and articles on a variety of themes linked to criticism of the capitalist system and American philistinism. But the main value, the greatness, of Mark Twain's work lies in his having written *The Prince and the Pauper* and the Tom Sawyer epic, in his having created books that have become popular reading for children and youth thanks to the impression they have made on generations, books that are the equal of *Robinson Crusoe, Gulliver's Travels,* and *Don Quixote,* or the novels of Jules Verne and the fairy tales of Hans Christian Andersen. It wasn't an easy thing to add new books to that few-volumed and proudly exclusive library . . . Mark Twain did, and that makes his figure in literature a uniquely splendid one.

In outward appearance he resembles the gentlemen of the time of the war between the North and the South—the mane of hair, the thick mustache, the frock coat, the seemingly rumpled trousers . . . You are reminded too of the old-fashioned illustrations in the novels of Jules Verne. A member of the Gun Club?[62] There's laughter in his eyes. He's about to tell a joke. Thus is he taken by many to be a humorist.

Well, what of it? Humor is pervasive in world literature, starting with the writers of antiquity. It's unfair there's no muse of humor. Actually, all nine represent it. Even Melpomene, the muse of tragedy. Even Clio, the muse of history.

Just as imaginative power, analytical force, and the skill to name things differently and toss off vivid images characterize great writers, so does a sense of humor. The serious Balzac, the serious Zola, the passionate Hugo, and the fearsome Edgar Poe all shine, when they wish, with humor.

Not to speak of Dickens, Chekhov, and Gogol, those geniuses of humor . . .

It seems to me, for example, that the ability to delineate a character's exterior appearance concisely, instantly, in a few strokes, as great writers do, depends in large measure on the presence in them of a sense of humor.

It's funny, I seem to be defending humor . . . It needs no defense. I'm speaking this way in order to lend more weight to the opinion that Mark Twain was a comic writer, an opinion that sounds a bit superficial in the mouths of those who don't know him very well. Yes, humor does play an enormous role in the works of Mark Twain, but as with other great writers, it is used to ridicule the bad and adorn the good. With his truly immortal humor, he is gracious to the world.

More about his humor . . . It is to him, Mark Twain, that perhaps one of the funniest lines ever spoken belongs. When the press suddenly began spreading false stories that he had died, he announced in the paper that "the reports of my death are greatly exaggerated."

Mark Twain was not a humorist but a great phenomenon of world literature, one of its luminaries, for he put his genius into the service of man, into strengthening man's faith in himself, and into helping man's soul develop in the direction of justice, goodness, and beauty.

I remember the powerful impression Rostand's *The Eaglet* made on me in a theatrical production in Odessa with Victor and Marius Petipa.[63] The first played the role of the Duke of Reichstadt, Napoleon's son; the second, Metternich. I was sitting surrounded by girls and ladies in a red box seat and gazing at the almost cream-colored stage, at the golden legs of the chairs, and at the duke in his no less cream-colored tunic and black patent-leather Wellington boots . . . How could I not feel bliss?

Metternich drags the poor Eaglet to the mirror . . . The latter holds a candelabrum in his hands, and the almost falling candles burn and smoke. Metternich drags him to the mirror in order to show him how weak, pitiful, and degenerate he, the bearer of Hapsburg blood, looks. The young duke, grasping the truth of his tormentor's words, hurls the candelabrum into the mirror. The noise of breaking glass, darkness. It was something you could never forget.

Actually, it isn't Rostand's *Eaglet* we know but Shchepkina-Kupernik's. The play's in verse, and as always happens with verse translations, there's much of the translator in it.[64]

Rostand was held in high regard when he lived and worked. Vrubel was fascinated by him. The image of the Faraway Princess was one that made my youthful heart beat faster. *Cyrano* brought me to tears. Then, in the time of first love, I thought I was Cyrano.

"I shall perish at the end of my commission."

That line from the ballad improvised by Cyrano during a sword fight was repeated quite often in my youth. I still like him, that long-nosed cavalier leaping onto a chair, that dwarf with the huge nose, that poet, dashing fellow, and expert fencer . . . In my youth I imitated Rostand (or rather Shchepkina-Kupernik); I wrote a comedy in verse.[65]

There's a photograph of Rostand wearing the short uniform jacket of the Académie Française with an embroidered olive branch on his collar. He has a mustache that sticks out like two spikes and he's consumptive . . .

When you're reading a dramatic work, you wait with particular interest to see how a character will react to this or that event contrived to astonish him. After all, a talented playwright doesn't have to limit himself merely to exclamations in depicting such a reaction:

"What? Really? What are you saying?"

I once crept up on such a place . . . Banquo's ghost appears to Macbeth. The first time Macbeth is merely startled and says nothing. He approaches the throne again, and again the ghost appears. He remains silent. Then the ghost appears a third time . . .

"Well," I wondered, "just how will Macbeth react?"

It would be difficult to imagine a more accurate one.

"Which of you have done this?" he asks.

Knowing how insecure his position is, he has every reason to suspect the lords. It is indeed possible that they have arranged the apparition—that one of them has dressed himself up or has dressed up an actor.

"Which of you have done this?"

But the lords have no idea what he is talking about.[66]

It's customary to speak of Tolstoy's aversion to Shakespeare. Yet from the way he recounts the content of the first scene of *King Lear,* the very opposite is apparent: he likes Shakespeare. "A charming scene might have resulted here," Tolstoy says again and again, "but Shakespeare has spoiled it with his customary crudeness."[67] How could one not appreciate a writer who has such abundant possibilities for creating charming scenes or merely conceiving them?

Hoffmann, describing some student in a story, says the student belonged to the class of people who are unlucky in everything . . . Yes, if he dropped bread and butter, the bread always fell with the buttered side down. One might object to Hoffmann that buttered bread always falls with the buttered side down.[68]

Who was he, that mad person, the only writer of his kind in world literature, with his peaked eyebrows, his slender hooked nose, and his hair forever standing on end? There's a report that he sometimes was so frightened of what he was depicting in his writing that he would ask his wife to sit down beside him.

Hoffmann's influence on literature was considerable. And that includes his influence on Pushkin, Gogol, and Dostoevsky, by the way.

Herzen wrote an enthusiastic article about him.[69]

He sprang into existence, it seems to me, resembling no one else. He was more than a fantast; his work is full of genre scenes and authentic everyday life.

Sometimes he gets confused. It's said he wrote while intoxicated.

Music reigns in his works. Ritter Gluck comes out of the past and stands alive before him, before Hoffmann, listening to a performance of *Iphigénie en Aulide.*[70] His pages abound with conductors, theater curtains, and actresses in makeup.

He was perhaps the first to portray doubles, the horror of that situation—before Edgar Poe. Poe denied Hoffmann's influence, saying the horror he saw came not from German romanticism but from his own soul . . .

Perhaps the difference between them is indeed that Poe is sober while Hoffmann is intoxicated. Hoffmann is multicolored, kaleidoscopic. Edgar is two or three colors within a single frame. Both are magnificent, unique, divine.

He had a cat he was fond of. He drank heavily, growing less human with each passing day. Then once after coming home drunk, he unburdened his heart on the cat. He set fire to it. Is that right? The story about the first, favorite cat is always hard to remember because of its lack of clarity (or because of my own muddle, which can't make sense of the story) . . . In a word, the cat he has destroyed returns to him in the form of another that he suddenly sees on a counter in a saloon. He likes the new cat very much.

"May I have your cat?"

"Certainly."

He takes the cat home. Suddenly he notices a white spot on its chest (the cat had been absolutely black). It seems to him the spot is shaped like a gallows. And so it is: the next day he sees that the spot not only looks like a gallows, but that the gallows has become even more distinct during the night. This frightens and annoys him.

His drinking gets worse. His poor wife suffers from it. He goes down to the cellar to draw some wine from the hogshead. His wife accompanies him, imploring him not to drink . . . When his tankard is full, the cat, which had followed him to the cellar, suddenly jumps and clumsily knocks the tankard from his hand. He grabs an ax in order to strike the cat, but the blow falls on his wife and it is fatal. With diabolical precision he removes a row of bricks from the wall and in the niche conceals his wife's corpse, placing it upright, since that is the easiest way, given the niche's dimensions. Then with the same diabolical care he replaces the bricks . . . Afterward he's pleased that his home is now quiet and that the cat, which with its gallows had reminded him of a ghost, has disappeared . . . The neighbors, however, begin to wonder about the long, unexplained absence of his wife. The police come to search the house and go down into the cellar. He's so sure of his invulnerability that he even allows himself to taunt the police. He says,

"Perhaps she's in there?" and pounds on the bricks concealing the corpse.

Suddenly a monstrous howl is heard. They remove the bricks and in the niche they find the half-eaten skeleton of the woman, the cat sitting on her head and wailing with its bloody maw.

Not realizing it, he had immured the cat with his wife's body.

Can one imagine a more powerful plot? And besides that, America is in it: bars, the police, brick walls, suspicions, mysterious murders . . .

Dostoevsky retells this story of Edgar Poe's in one of his articles.[71]

There's not much that's better written than the scene in H. G. Wells's *The First Men in the Moon* when Cavor and his companion, guided by the Selenites, approach a bridge over a gigantic precipice of industrial character, as they sense, and seeing that the bridge is no wider than the palm of a hand, instinctively come to a halt . . . The escorts with their thin goads, not realizing that the reason for stopping is simply that the bridge is too narrow, regard it as an insubordination, a mutiny. They start pricking Cavor and his companion with their goads, as if saying, "Well, go on! What's the matter?" But the two men can't go on by their very nature. The hopelessness of their situation is aggravated by the fact that if our earth dwellers had attempted to explain to the Selenites why they were unable to cross such a bridge, the latter wouldn't have understood anyway, since the sensation and fear of height were clearly absent in them. At this point Cavor and his companion (who are exasperated by the pricking) decide that the best they can do under the circumstances is to start fighting. They seize golden fragments lying scattered at their feet and hack away at the Selenites left and right.[72]

A wonder!

It resembles Dante: the Selenite-demons, the passage across a narrow bridge—it's one of the torments of hell. And there's the same compelling reality as in Dante, the *reality of the fantastic.*

Wells has always been my favorite author. And how sad I never got to tell him of my esteem. I didn't have the good fortune to do that, although besides his first visit to Moscow (when he talked with Lenin), he came again in 1934.[73] But I was in Odessa at the time.

How could one not be delighted by the masterful inflections in *The Invisible Man,* for example.

"Remember I can see your face if you can't see mine," the Invisible Man says to Ayde, the colonel of police who had foolishly decided he was stronger than the Invisible Man because he had a revolver.

He's majestic, the Invisible Man. Why? Oh, about that one could write and write.

Then he's lying on the ground, felled by a navvy's spade, and gradually he becomes visible to the surrounding crowd—increasingly human, increasingly pitiful. There was a movie about the Invisible Man. Did Wells write the screenplay?[74] The movie's inferior to the novel; it's poorer in essence. In the movie invisibility is acquired by means of medical injections that also doom the Invisible Man to madness, so that the reason for his insanity is physiological and of a lower order. In the novel he becomes enraged and goes mad from isolation, from the fact that he is one against many, a reason, it follows, that is historical and of a higher order. *The Invisible Man,* it seems to me, is a novel about the anarchists who were shaking the era in which it was written. Yes, yes, that's certainly correct; it's an artistic depiction of anarchism . . . (In "The Stolen Bacillus" Wells depicts anarchism directly: the narrative's anarchist hero steals cholera bacilli from a laboratory in order to infect the entire city of London.)

Wells has a story ("The Door in the Wall") about someone who, upon opening a green door met in childhood, found himself in an ineffably beautiful garden where a panther was playing with a ball on a flowering lawn . . . Although that happened in early childhood, at the dawn of his life, the memory of the wonderful garden has so possessed the soul of the hero that despite the passage of years he still seeks the green door. He is now a mature man who has reached a high position (he is a minister), but the ideal to which his soul constantly returns is the dream of finding that door. And then it seems to him that he sees it . . . There it is, there's the door. He opens it and steps over the threshold, but beyond is no panther playing with a ball on a lawn, only darkness. It turns out he has entered an excavation and fallen.

The story is thus about the discord between the pure strivings of youth and the subsequent lapse, it would seem, into thrall to a daily routine that brings about the loss of that purity . . . It seems to me that "The Door in the Wall" could have been included among the stories chosen by the author of "Notes of a Billiard Marker" for his *Circle of Reading.*[75]

The presence of such a story among the works of an author of fantasy novels about technology is interesting for the way it characterizes his poetic imagination. And the fact is that to interpret a great technology coming into being in the world and to write about it did indeed require a poet. For that reason the fantasies of Wells stand before us as the myths of a new era—myths about man and the machine.

If we say that in the capitalist world technology oppresses man, then that oppression, that fear of man before the machine, has of course been best expressed by the author of *The War of the Worlds,* a novel with a scene in which a dazed person in a suit jacket and crooked tie cowers against some wretched urban wall, staring in terror at the steel antenna of a Martian moving toward him through the rubble . . .

To offset a too great extolling of Wells, Jules Verne is usually brought forth. It was he, after all, who first started to speak in literature of technology. That may be, but what is Captain Nemo, say, next to the Invisible Man? The Verne hero is a diagram, the Wells character, a living human being . . . What could be more conventional than the figure of Paganel? He's virtually a comic figure from an Offenbach operetta. I worked at one time on a dramatization of *The Children of Captain Grant* and finally had to give up the task because the characters would in no way come to life on the stage . . . It was necessary to invent an entirely new system of dialogue, a whole new vocabulary, but when I tried to do that it produced violations of the novel along other lines . . . I shall be told that there are in fact adaptations of Verne things like *The Children of Captain Grant* . . . That's so, but there aren't any living people in them; they're fairy tales. And with that phrase one may define the novels of Verne: they're fairy tales on technological themes. It would be ridiculous to disparage Verne's genius, although the human side holds little interest for him, a fact even he emphasizes by frequently making his heroes cranks and eccentrics (the members of the Gun Club and the same Paganel) or melodramatic villains (Ayrton) . . .[76] Thus Verne's novels fail to acquire those qualities by which, in contrast, the novels of Wells are distinguished: the qualities of reality and epic. Reading Verne, we never forget that everything is invented, but reading, say, *The War of the Worlds*, we fall under the spell of a strange idea: it suddenly begins to seem to us that there really was a time when the Martians attempted to conquer Earth.

Wells was a modest person with a not-very-high opinion of himself as a writer . . . L. Nikulin was present at a conversation in which Wells remarked that it was Gorky who was really a genius.[77]

"Whereas all I have is a well-organized brain."

He's a little like the people who appear in Wells's fantastic novels—*The Invisible Man* or *The First Men in the Moon* . . . Little English clerks in bowlers and narrow ties who run in every direction to escape the marvel that has emerged from the world of future technology, or, on the contrary, who come running to look at that marvel and perish. He was born in the same era. If he's sixty-odd now, then he could have stood among the bicyclists who gathered around Cavor's sphere just after it had fallen from the sky. Yes, for he was a boy at that time and lived in England. We know something of his biography. We know that his mother was an operetta actress, and we know that he started out in a pantomime troupe in England and went on tour with it to America. Just what sort of troupe was it that aroused such interest that it was even invited to go on tour in another part of the world? We are unable to imagine anything here, since in our time those troupes had already ceased to exist.

And so, Chaplin is akin to the little people of Wells. It's significant that like them he too was frightened of technology, that because of the machine he too was unable to find happiness.

Among Mirabeau's last words were some to the effect that if the sun isn't God Himself, then it is in any case His cousin.[78] When you read about the death of a great or at least historically important person, you always want to understand what he died of from our own point of view. Much then was called fever or gout. Phlebotomies were performed for almost everything. Mirabeau died within a few days. It's unclear from what. A stroke? No, he remained coherent till the end. What is now called a heart attack? He had an enormous crimson head, like a wineskin, with edemas.

Has something happened to me or hasn't it?

I don't feel like going to shows I have a chance to see, new shows I still haven't seen. Thus I didn't go to a Chinese opera that delighted Chaplin when he saw it. Thus I haven't torn myself away for the international football matches. Thus I didn't go to the new Picasso exhibit.

Obviously something has happened. What? Age? That's possible. Although it does sometimes seem to me that the disappearance of interest in the new, the refusal to take it in, is occurring because I've grown interested in creating my own things.

I'd probably tear myself away for the new Chaplin movie if it were shown here . . .[79]

What interest I took in everything when I was young and just beginning my literary activity. I remember going to the movies with Ilf to see German expressionist films with Werner Krauss and Conrad Veidt or American ones with Mary Pickford and the Talmadge sisters.[80] It was at the Uranus Theater on Sretenka which I now pass by with complete indifference, not even glancing at it . . .

The first time I saw Charlie Chaplin was in a picture that seemed unusual to me. Yes, just so; everything was new and unprecedented: the subject, the treatment, the hero, and above all the humor, although we, the moviegoers of those times, weren't without considerable cultivation in that area. No, that kind of humor had never been seen before. An odd, very funny little fellow, as it seemed to me then, with the large hairy head of a tailor, who, as he passes a poet walking along with an open book and daydreaming about something, puts a rotten egg on the page. Whereupon the poet slams the book shut. Horror, stink, but chiefly dismay—before there had been poems but now what muck! Why didn't it ever occur to Charlie Chaplin to play Edgar Poe? Nothing comical there? It would have been possible to find it. The short film I've just recalled was showing in Odessa at the Odeon movie theater when I was eighteen and in the throes of first love. I didn't take very much interest in the phantoms drifting by on the screen, or rather, in the awkward little fellow moving there, but, as you see, he did stick in my memory. I remember that when I saw the already world-famous Chaplin on the screen for the first time, I recognized the little fellow in him at once.

In regard to the opinion of foreign critics that invention is alien to our literature . . . Once in my youth in an issue of *The World of Adventures* (not

The World of Adventures that came out in Soviet times but the old supplement to the magazine *Nature and People*), I read a story by some unknown Russian writer with the following subject (I stress: by an unknown Russian writer whose name I can't remember).

An engineer (also with a Russian name) constructs a time machine capable of going into the future as well as the past. Once while he is busy with calculations in his study, his two sons enter the workshop where the apparatus stands completed . . . Hearing voices, he rushes to the workshop, but alas he's too late: the workshop is empty, with neither machine nor sons, who have departed in it. Where have they gone? Into the future? The past? The engineer is in despair. And then begins the construction of a kind of magnet with the power of, so to speak, drawing the machine back from the vastness of time wherever it may be, in the past or the future.

Listen to what the writer has contrived . . . For many years the engineer works on the construction of his magnet. Then it is completed . . . He turns the levers and steps back in fright: a Roman in beard and armor falls to the ground before him with a crash . . . The two men stare at each other in silence.

"Father," the Roman whispers.

The name of his son breaks from the engineer's mouth . . .

"Is it you?"

"Yes, it's me!"

"But where is your brother?"

There follows a pause during which the engineer, seeing his son's confusion, begins to guess what has happened. And then the son says,

"Father, I was Romulus."

The magnet's operation thus produced the lightning during the discharge of which the great Romulus, in his time a fratricide, was taken up to heaven.

In terms of invention, the story is brilliant. At the same time, the Russian author has added humanity to his inventiveness.[81]

From birth the boy was held in conditions that kept him from knowing what the world looked like—literally: he never saw the sun.

A kind of experiment, the whim of wealthy people . . . And now the boy has grown up, has become a youth, and it's time to carry out what has been planned. The world still hidden from his eyes, he is taken to one of the most beautiful places on earth. The Alps? There in a meadow where cyclamen are in bloom the blindfold is removed . . . The youth, needless to say, is overwhelmed by the world's beauty. But that isn't the point. The story concentrates on how this human being who has never seen the sun will behave while watching a sunset. The sun begins to set. Those conducting the imperious experiment watch the boy. But they fail to observe that he's watching them. The sun has already disappeared . . . What happens? What happens is that the boy says to those around him,

"Don't worry, it will come back!"

That's the sort of writer Grin is.[82]

He's underrated. He's been linked to the symbolists, although everything he wrote was filled with faith in precisely the strength and possibilities of man. And if you like, the note of irritation that permeates his stories—and that note is undoubtedly there—had as its reason his dissatisfaction with the fact that people are not as wondrously strong as he had imagined them. It's interesting that even he had a false idea of himself. Since he had begun as a writer for the young in the company of other Soviet writers with roots in the prerevolutionary past—a past, moreover, in which he had belonged to bohemia—in order not to lose confidence in himself (a slightly embittered confidence), he held tight like a charter of rights to the critical approval he had once received from critics who were champions of art for art's sake. Thus he said to me with pride,

"Aikhenvald wrote about me."[83]

I have no idea what Aikhenvald said. Grin did in any case link himself to the symbolists. I remember a characteristic skirmish of my own with him in that regard. Around 1925 his novel *The Shining World* came out in *The Red Grainfield,* one of the magazines published at the time.[84] It was about a man who could fly—like a bird, although he had no wings but was an ordinary person who flew without the aid of machinery. The novel enjoyed wide interest among both ordinary readers and literary people. And there really were magnificent things in it. For example, the panicked flight of the audience from a circus at the moment when the novel's hero, demonstrating his ability to fly, suddenly after several running turns around the arena begins to rise from the ground and take off in full view of everyone . . . The audience is unable to tolerate that unearthly spectacle and rushes out of the circus. Or this striking detail, for example: after leaving the circus, he flies through the darkness of an autumn night, and his first haven is a lighthouse window.

When I expressed to Grin my delight at his having found such a truly superb theme for a fantastic novel (a flying man!), he was almost insulted.

"What do you mean, a fantastic novel? It's a symbolic, not a fantastic novel! It's not a flying man at all; it's the soaring of the spirit!"

No praise seems sufficient for his inventiveness. Here you straightaway yield to a marvel. Even if it's a story about a man who, because he's an insurgent, has had to abandon the town where his family lives and take up residence in another town at the opposite end of the arc formed by a gulf separating the two towns—about how a friend once galloped from the abandoned town to the man with the news that his family had fallen victim to a fire, and that if he wanted to find his wife and children still alive, let him at once mount his, the friend's, horse and gallop to the other side of the gulf, to the other end of the arc. The friend dismounts and holds out the reins, but the insurgent is nowhere to be seen. Where has he gone? The friend calls to him and then looks for him . . . He isn't anywhere. Nothing remains for the messenger but to remount his horse and return home. Arriving there, he is astonished to meet the insurgent already in the town and coming out of the hospital.

"I managed to part with them."

"Wait," asks the friend in amazement, "you came on foot? But how did you get here before me? I galloped along the shore for two whole days . . ."

The other, it turns out, had not walked along the shore but crossed over the water!

That's how strong human beings are, according to Grin. They are able, without even realizing it, to walk across water. Where's the symbolism or decadence in that?[85]

Sometimes it's said that Grin's work is an imitation of Edgar Poe and Ambrose Bierce. But how can you imitate invention? After all, you still have to make it up. He doesn't imitate them; he's their equal and no less unique than they are.

The presence of a writer like Grin in Russian literature is phenomenal. And the fact that he is a Russian writer allows us to take issue with those foreign critics who contend that plot and invention are characteristic only of Anglo-Saxon literature. For here, after all, is a writer in our literature who has created plots so original that in seeking to define the full extent of their originality, you're inclined to compare them to such primordial circumstances as the movement of the planets over our heads.

Grin lived out his last years in Old Crimea not far from the town of Feodosiya. I never visited his house; I've only been told about it. His room was whitewashed, and there was nothing in it except a bed and a desk. And one other thing . . . On a wall of the room—the wall the owner faced as he lay in bed—a piece of a ship had been fastened. Listen, Grin decorated his room with the figurehead that is sometimes used to support a bowsprit. Clearly, it was only a fragment of a statue, only its head (had she been whole, that wooden maiden, she would have lain across the whole room, perhaps across the whole house, even reaching the garden), but the head was enough. On the wall where in other houses people hang photographs, this man splashed the sea.

I want to write something easy, not difficult. Difficult is when you write thinking someone else will read it. The branch of syntax, or rather its birch rod, is always threatening you. Easy is when you write down what's taking place in your mind both in essence and grammar.

How I like Maeterlinck! His *The Deceiver* (is that really a good translation?), his *The Blind*.[86] Blind people, led by a sighted priest, suddenly begin to sense that something has happened. It's that their leader has died, died in their midst, although for a long time they don't realize that that is what has happened.

He had the drooping, slightly roguish mustache of a folklore warrior. He was Flemish. The first time Stanislavsky saw him, he was wearing a chauffeur's jacket and cap and standing next to an automobile. He was one of the first motorists. He wrote a whole essay about the car, at that time still new . . . It's a man's first impression of that new technology one would like to call technology in the name of speed.[87]

He's called a decadent. But he was a warm, joyful lover of nature and animals, was, with his automobilism, one of the first poets of just that form of technology that, had he been a decadent, ought to have horrified him.

In the years immediately after the Versailles peace several remarkable German novels appeared. They were called expressionist. Their authors' names were Werfel, Perutz, and Meyrink.[88] They were, you might say, novels of fantasy. But it wasn't a fantasy that sharply diverged from everyday life, from the commonplace, the way Hoffmann's fantasy does, for example. Real cities and real people figured in that expressionist fantasy, although something strange happened that thrust those real people into terrible situations. Perhaps more than anything else the fantasy resembled Dostoevsky, whom the expressionists regarded as their spiritual father, by the way. Yes, it resembled Dostoevsky with his scenes like the one where Raskolnikov rushes about the stairwell. It was a fantasy born of the alternation of light and dark, of the appearance in one's path of a barrier, a corner, a turn, steps . . .

It would have been hard not to surrender to the charm of those writers, especially for someone just starting out, someone not raised on Russian literature, someone only recently arrived from Europe-like Odessa.

I notice I now avoid recounting any serious thoughts that occur to me. Apparently I'm afraid they won't come off. Or maybe I'm just tired.

I've started reading *Hedda Gabler*. An inane young scholar has married the daughter of a General Gabler—a demonic sort of woman, it's shown at once, who by her marriage to him has made a sacrifice, as it seems to her. He tells the aunt who raised him that Hedda won't agree to a conventional bourgeois life. Incidentally, the room in which the act begins is all in flowers (the heroes have just returned from their honeymoon) . . .

Why retell all this? Everybody knows the story.

The end of the act with the pistols is a little surprising and abrupt. Hedda comes off a bit too frightening.

When I was little I would see those words over and over on theater bills: *Hedda Gabler.* I think she was played by Komissarzhevskaya.[89]

Thomas Mann nicely observes in one of his stories how during a village ball the children kept dancing even after the music had stopped.[90]

A detail in the style of Russian writers.

Some of Thomas's cerebrations are beyond me, but in image and epithet I'm no weaker.

Thomas Mann is dead. There was a mighty clump of them, a grove, a dozen oaks, one after the other: Wells, Kipling, Anatole France, Bernard Shaw, Gorky, Maeterlinck, Mann.

And now he's dead, the last of the great writers.

The Magic Mountain is his. There's a place in it where a certain mystic working with a medium calls forth at the request of several independent, intelligent, and wealthy people staying at a sanatorium the spirit of a young man who has recently passed away there. At first the spirit fails to appear . . . Then the young man's ghost suddenly begins to materialize in the air.

Seeing it, someone cries out.

Then another of those present calmly remarks,

"I've been aware of it for a long time."

The hardest thing, something given only to outstanding writers, is this reaction of the characters to a frightening or extraordinary event.

Yes, there are exceptional things in *The Magic Mountain.* If only the basic premise: he has transferred the feverish world of humanity, or at least of Europe, to a tubercular sanatorium in Davos, thereby compressing, generalizing, and heightening all the thoughts and anxieties of the world within the limits of a small group of people who actually are condemned to death.

In it a young man in love with a woman accidentally sees X rays of her lungs in the office of a doctor who is also in love with the woman and who has had some success with her, and this causes the young man to feel with particular passion both his love for the woman and jealousy of that omnipotent rival who has the ability to look at her lungs.

I don't much care for Bernard Shaw. Everything's contrary, tricky, affected. Whatever he's preaching, whatever he's inveighing against, I don't care. There's only one thing I value in a writer: he's an artist, an inspired artist. Herzen also preached and inveighed, but to do so he didn't need to conjure and speak contrariwise. He worked like an artist.

To me, Wilde's much more likable than Shaw. That isn't even the word—likable. He's incomparably higher. Without Wilde world literature would, I think, be poorer; without Shaw it would remain the same.

Not even to mention the great Wells.

I saw Shaw in person. It was in Moscow in 1931 (I think) at a banquet arranged in his honor by State Publishing. He was sitting at the head of a table covered with a white tablecloth and eating raspberries which he took with slender fingers from a large bowl. In keeping with the European fashion of the day, he wore no tie, just a summer shirt with an unbuttoned, well-starched collar.

Among the guests was Mayakovsky, whom I remember not at the table but entering a doorway somewhere at the end of an angled corridor, and then coming down that corridor toward the room in which I was standing. He was wearing a hat and carrying a stick and he saw me. His eyes, with their white whites and the black circles of their irises, stood out in the darkness of the corridor, and that both pleased and frightened me.[91]

Karel Čapek is a magnificent writer and a towering achievement of the Czech nation.[92]

He died young . . . We have information that it was an unnecessary death, a sudden illness whose progress might have been checked if measures had been taken sooner . . .

He was among the first to turn his attention to the machine—his artistic attention, as Wells did in *The War of the Worlds* . . . To the machine and its significance in human life, to the machine as a philosophical, historical, and moral phenomenon. Belonging to his pen is an inspired work written expressly about man and the machine: *R.U.R.* It is a play in which "robots" have been given artistic reality for the first time. Čapek was the first writer to think of making characters out of artificial machinelike people. They function among living human beings who, though their masters, are still fatally dependent on them. Karel Čapek was in the forefront of introducing that new character into world literature, a character still vague and fantastic, yet oddly vivid, mysterious, and interesting.

We know that Alexei Tolstoy borrowed the story of Čapek's play, reworking it to be sure, and on its basis wrote his own *Revolt of the Machines.*[93] Čapek's poetic power and image are enhanced even more by the fact that another artist, also strikingly individual, found inspiration in his idea, gave his attention to it, and was enchanted by it.

Čapek never abandoned the theme of the machine; he thought about it continually and remained within its power, as befitted an advanced artist of his day. Quite so, and it should be stressed: Čapek, that most gifted Slav, was an advanced artist of his day. While Marcel Proust, let's say—and we have no wish to diminish the importance of that writer—was searching for lost time, was glancing back in nostalgia and yearning for that lost time, Čapek pursued time moving forward, gave it careful scrutiny, and saw that the main thing in it was the interrelation of man and the machine . . .

He wrote *The War with the Salamanders.*[94] It is a novel about fascism, a political system that turns people into machines, into slaves. Salamanders perform the action in the novel, but we understand that in the guise of salamanders Čapek is depicting depersonalized, pitiful human beings who have lost their full value from having been placed in the conditions of a fascistic state with its "stifling of genius," its attempt to render the human spirit uniform, its requirement that man in fact become a soulless machine.

The novel is brilliantly fantastic, and moreover in the highest and most skillful sense of fantasy, when it begins to resemble reality, as we see in Dante or the author of *The War of the Worlds.* There is in Čapek's novel a whole series of ideas, discoveries, and inventions . . . It is a truly distinguished work of the prewar era: unique, original, reminiscent of Rabelais and Swift.

Čapek's works are imbued with a wholesome, earthy, robust humor, the humor of a son of Slavic culture . . . We know a great many of his stories, sketches, and miniatures on genre themes and the themes of art. They are humorous in the mode of Chekhov, where the humor becomes a constructive principle, organizing the material in the most expressive and edifying way . . .

Now that the historic name of Karel Čapek is being recalled, it would not hurt Soviet readers to reread his books. They have been published here in large editions with affection for this splendid writer.

Sometimes he is very subtle and refined . . . He is acquainted with all the mysteries of craft, for he is on the level of world writers, this Karel Čapek, our brother by the roots of language, a man of lofty mind and talent, whose great soul always belonged to the oppressed.

Hemingway's artistic power is exceptional. On almost every page of the two-volume translation of his works issued by State Publishing—and there are more than a thousand such pages—there is, it seems to us, something capable of engaging the reader's admiring attention.[95]

How superb, for example, is the scene from the novel *A Farewell to Arms* where battle police pull from the mob fleeing along with the retreating Italian army certain old, decorated officers who in the given instance can't help but retreat, and, if one may put it this way, demagogically execute them. It wouldn't be too bold to say that the scene is written near the level of the famous battle scenes of *War and Peace*—for example, the one where Bagratiön walks at the head of the regiment near Schön Grabern . . .

In another book is an episode concerning an argument between the doctor of a dressing station and an artillery officer.[96] Surrounded by the horrendous conditions in the dressing station after a battle, both men are in a hysterical state and insult each other, until in a rage the doctor splashes a dish of iodine in the officer's eyes. The scene's tempo, color, and shifts in perspective are so strangely good you are not sure whether you're reading a book or watching a film or dreaming or present at an actual event. Or, to take another example, how could one fail to recognize as magnificent the place in the novel *To Have and Have Not* where we are shown the slow movement of a vessel drifting out of control because its four passengers have been slain and its captain is gravely wounded and dying. They've killed each other. The reasons are not at all romantic but rather the result of cruelty, greed, and fear . . . Imagining that vessel of dead men, anyone reading these lines who was not familiar with the book would assign the episode to romantic costumery and the past, but the corpses and dying man on the vessel are wearing suit jackets and raincoats, their hair is combed and slicked, revolvers lie scattered about, and the vessel itself is none other than a motor launch . . . Horror wafts all the more from that picture because it is indeed contemporary and derives from gangsterism, a monstrous phenomenon rampant in America.

In depicting the scene, Hemingway reveals his true power as an artist. The dead men's motor launch, he writes, was accompanied by little fish of different species, and when a drop of blood fell through one of the holes made by the bullets, some of the fish immediately rushed over to it and swallowed it, while the others, being less adroit, were on the other side of the boat when the drop fell and thus failed to regale themselves.

One would also like to tell how he portrays the lion's charge in "The Short Happy Life of Francis Macomber," for example, or the terrorizing of a lunchroom in "The Killers" by hoodlums in too-tight overcoats like those worn by variety-show buffoons, or the death of the boy in "The Capital of the World."

Wonderful, too, are the autobiographical stories where the modest figure of his father, a country doctor who practiced among Indians, is tenderly described.

Already present in the stories is the theme of fishing, which occupies a very large place in Hemingway's work, appearing in virtually all his writings. In wartime at difficult moments he recalls going fishing in his youth and makes a mental journey back along the river of youth in his homeland. There's a story called "Big Two-Hearted River" in which nothing happens except that a young man, the author, sets up a tent, prepares breakfast for himself, and then fishes for a trout. The love of fishing is of course Hemingway's private affair, but once it has been set down on paper, it comes to stand for love of the world in general. It has been transformed into incomparable depictions of nature, man, and animal and plant life and has therefore become an affair of literature.

By the way, it occurs to me that the tale *The Old Man and the Sea,* essentially written on the theme of the impossibility in the capitalist world of the poor man "to have," is also a reflection of Hemingway's love of fishing, a love that has been combined with nostalgia for lost youth and transformed into a tale about the quest for a giant fish.

Hemingway regarded the rich with extraordinary aversion. One need only acquaint oneself with the portrayal of the yacht owners in the novel *To Have and Have Not:* ostentatious culture, recognition only of the power of money, unbridled sensuality, coldness of heart—such are the qualities with which Hemingway endows those who have managed "to have" in a world where there are those who "have not." Or the obnoxious pair of American millionaires in the story "The Short Happy Life of Francis Macomber" . . . And there's the article called "Who Murdered the Vets?" It's an impressive document that characterizes Hemingway as someone who hated the rich and the power of wealth. With Dantean force he depicts the results of a crime committed almost carelessly, almost inadvertently, by the government and entrepreneurs.

Hemingway's sympathies lie with those who "have not." His friends are simple people, the humble masters of their trade, of whom there are so many in America. Consider with what affection, with what an outpouring of artistic regard he describes the Negroes and Indians. "Indian Camp," in my view one of his best stories, is in fact dedicated to praise of the Indian's spirit, his purity of heart. An Indian, hearing how his wife suffers, how much she is in agony as she unsuccessfully tries to give birth, cannot endure the pity, the sympathy for the woman's suffering, and the consciousness of his own guilt that overwhelm him, and cuts his own throat.

With his criticism of the rich, his heartfelt love of the poor, and his organic rejection of racism, Hemingway is undoubtedly one of America's leading writers.

Hemingway's writing style is the only one of its kind.

Sometimes it seems he could have cut some lines . . . For example, why describe how a taxi drove up and how the waiter who had been sent for it rode standing on the running board? For the action of the story it has no significance at all. Or is there any need to dwell on the fact that a group of Indians who have nothing to do with a story taking place in a railroad station have left the station to board their train? Or is it important to give a detailed picture of how a bartender makes a cocktail: first he poured this, then he poured that, then he left, then he came back with a bottle, then he poured something else, and so on? If, say, the hero had been poisoned by the cocktail, then it would have made sense to isolate the moment . . . But the scene lies outside the plot. It would also have made sense to dwell on it if the author had wished, say, to tell us how cocktails are made. But that isn't Hemingway's purpose either. Indeed, another would have cut such passages. But Hemingway doesn't cut them; on the contrary, he uses them extensively, and the peculiar thing is that you read them with particular gusto, with a sort of pleasure that considerably elevates your mood. What's going on here? It's that sometimes we readers hire taxis too, that sometimes we too have to wait for a train, that sometimes cocktails are made for us too. Hence our pleasure. We begin to sense that our life is dear to us, that it's good to hire taxis, wait for trains, and drink cocktails. Undoubtedly, that technique consisting of the fact that besides managing the plot the author is also with his peripheral vision, so to speak, keeping an eye on life's little things—on how the hero shaves, how he dresses, how he chats with a friend—undoubtedly, we shall say, that technique is vital and optimistic, since it stimulates in us, as we have already more or less indicated, an appetite for life. The honor of first use of that technique unquestionably belongs to Hemingway. Many Western writers now use it, including Remarque, Saroyan, Faulkner, and the remarkable Pole Jarosław Iwaszkiewicz.[97]

Hemingway's range is extremely broad. He's capable of touching every string of the reader's heart. Yes, even of provoking tears . . . Do we not cry when reading the passage in *A Farewell to Arms* about Catherine's death? Truly, how we pity her. How moved we are by her desire to cope with childbirth, to give birth . . . How much the feeling of guilt about something, about the fact that she has not coped and is dying, that comes to her at the onset of death—how much does it tear at our hearts. It is a very great achievement in artistic terms, a masterpiece.

Hemingway can also touch the strings of delicate emotion, of tenderness. Read the story "Wine of Wyoming," where an elderly couple receiving guests is portrayed.

The already-mentioned story "The Capital of the World" is absolutely superb. From nothing at all, from a mere two or three pages of dialogue, there emerges an actual, living image of a boy. And there is no limit to the pity evoked in us by the author, pity for the boy who perishes as the result of naïveté, of desperate, vain courage, and of boyish eagerness.

Hemingway considers it essential to elicit pity and tenderness for those who are good, to arouse sympathy for them.

When you want to determine where the roots of Hemingway's writings lie, it's not English, French, or American literature that comes to mind but in fact Russian writers you recall: Turgenev, Chekhov, and Lev Tolstoy. Tolstoy especially was an inspiration. Even Hemingway's effort to demolish literary canons stands in a kind of dependence on the legacy of the author of *War and Peace,* who amid firmly established literary traditions came forward with a new form, one for which no definition was found, although for simplicity's sake it was called epic.

It is possible that Hemingway's dislike of precious writing emerged by itself, just as it did in other writers of the era in which he began. But finding that same dislike in Tolstoy, he could not help admiring him.

"It is a very good story," he says of Tolstoy's *The Cossacks* in *The Green Hills of Africa.* And he repeats it: "It is a very good story."

A great writer doesn't imitate, but near the base of this or that work by someone who at the beginning of his career has been attentive to another already-departed master, you will invariably see the light of the one who has passed away. Thus, now and again at the base of the works of Hemingway, you will see the light of the Tolstoy of *The Cossacks,* the Sevastopol stories, *War and Peace,* and "The False Coupon" . . . If one should put it more exactly, that light is Hemingway's love of Tolstoy.

Obviously, these are cursory, superficial notes . . . But if the phenomenon you are writing about is the power of thought and imagination that a major artist represents, then you will, whatever you write, remain a dilettante.

I've never fished. Probably it's very interesting. One can imagine how pleasant it would be, after the city, work, and quarrels, to breathe in the fragrance of a river . . . I have seen how bulbous float, one half red, the other white, resting on the water. It sits on the completely flat surface, one so brilliant it dazzles the eyes.

Hemingway described fishing without any embellishment—moment by moment, gesture by gesture, thing by thing, thought by thought.

In Odessa they fished not in rivers but the sea. Floats figured there too, but in the sea they were somehow harder to make out. Their trousers rolled high, the fishermen walked along the edge of the sea, stooping beneath the overhanging cliffs. Afterward on a back road there would appear a rapidly walking dark-haired man hurrying somewhere in those same rolled-up trousers, barefoot, in his hand a bough of bullheads for sale. The bullhead was a little monster with an enormous head that truly was bull-like, although with fans around the ears . . . Kataev has given a good description in his *A Lone Sail Gleams* of how Madame Storozhenko sold bullheads at the Odessa market and how she bought them from her suppliers, those same bare-legged, dark-haired people who hurried down back roads in eager expectation of calls from the windows.

Is the abundance of imagery in Bunin really necessary? "The Gentleman from San Francisco" simply overwhelms with figures and reading the story becomes tedious. Each by itself is magnificent, to be sure, but as you read the story you have the impression of being present at a performance where exceptional skill is being demonstrated—in this case, the description of things. Besides the development of the theme and the exposition of the ideas, something else is going on that has no direct bearing on the story itself. It's just that show of proliferating imagery. It diminishes the story's value.

After all, we writers know that everything resembles everything else and that the power of prose isn't in colorful language.

Bunin observes that rain falling on a newspaper dropped in a garden path chirrs. Certainly it does chirr; you won't say it any better. That is, you don't have to say it any better. It is, in the language of mathematics, a necessary and sufficient definition . . . But is there in fact any need to single out from the narrative a detail that in and of itself is a work of art and that inevitably diverts attention from the story?

We are faced here with the larger question of how to write. A story is not, in the end, the unfolding of a series of images and epithets . . . There are wonderful stories not at all filled with imagery and details. Although Gogol did make wide use of comparisons. There are swans flying against a background of blazing sunset that look like red shawls; there are roads crawling away into the darkness like crayfish; there are rickety boards of a roadway set in motion like piano keys beneath a passing carriage; there is a waiter's tray on which teacups perch like seagulls . . . Gogol compared a thing covered with dust three different ways: first it was a carafe that seemed, because of the dust, to be clad in a sweater; then it was a dusty chandelier that resembled a cocoon; and finally it was a man's hands that looked gloved after he had taken them out of the dust.[98]

Bunin writes in one of his fragments that whenever he met a fifty-year-old person, it was as if some fearsome creature stood before him. Now, writes Bunin, he's already that age himself. The fragment is signed, "Alpes-Maritimes, 1925."[99]

I met him in Odessa on Ekaterininsky Street in . . . In 1915! That is, when he was forty years old. Later on when at a gathering of actors, writers, and poets he banged his stick at us young people and already seemed beyond any doubt a spiteful old man, he was only forty-two.

But he really was an old man then. And not merely an old man, but a spiteful and bony one—a grandfather!

Should one write as Bunin does?

He's a pessimist, a spiteful, gloomy writer. All right, the village was an awful place in his day, but when you read the horrors depicted by him, it seems he's counterfeiting other people who were sincerely distressed by those horrors in order, as the phrase has it, to make his mark in the world.[100]

What does he want? I don't know. For him the landowners are unquestionably decent. The kulaks aren't, but the landowners are. Did he think elimination of the horrors would come from the landowners?

Even the pessimistic Chekhov believed that in two hundred years, "life will be beautiful."[101] There's no faith at all in Bunin. A yearning for departed youth in regard to the fading of sensuality . . .

His cogitations on the spirit merging with eternity or whatever seem on occasion merely silly. The celebrated "Gentleman from San Francisco" is bleak, though; the images in it are piled up ad nauseam. A critique of the bourgeois world? I don't think so. Rather a personal fear of death, envy of the young and the rich, even a kind of servility.

His ability to describe precisely is truly astonishing. Although the girl with the tender pimples on her naked back, the daughter of the gentleman from San Francisco, comes from Tolstoy's "After the Ball."

I've read magnificent things in Bunin. It's said in the description of the way the blind musician is dressed in "Rodion the Lyre Player" that his canvas shirt was bound at the neck with a red ribbon, Slavic-style.

The images are marvelously precise. There's an endless profusion of them, not one of which makes you question or wonder about its accuracy. In the story with the dying peasant at its center, it's unclear where they come from. Who sees them?[102]

In "Rodion the Lyre Player" there is a magnificent Ukrainian folk song about an orphan and his stepmother.

Ivan Bunin is from the impoverished petty gentry on the verge of ruin. It's already the era of the decadents, of Blok, Vrubel, the "World of Art," and soon afterward the war.[103]

The rhapsodic reminiscences of hunting. Excited dogs, the wind whistling and howling in the barrel of a gun, the landowners with their unbuttoned long-waisted coats, the dead wolf on the drawing-room floor, its teeth bared, its pink blood oozing.

In Chekhov there are at least a hundred times fewer colors. Why? Was he unable to see them? Or did he think it impossible to name them? In the story called "The Mire," the heroine smells sweetly of jasmine and that's all, yet the story is unbelievably vivid.[104] Chekhov, incidentally, modernized animistic imagery in a certain way. He could, for example, say of debris blown from the pavement by the wind that it flew off so rapidly that it was as if it were ashamed of itself and wanted to hide as quickly as possible.

You won't find a single figurative expression of that kind in Bunin.

Chekhov is much stronger than Bunin. Why?

If it weren't for the fact that the trees have already blossomed, it would be like March. The turbid gray sky, the clouds that resemble carts, the instability in the temperature, the shivering cold . . . In a word, just as bad as this fragment.

In the Chekhov museum are his collar, cravat, pocket handkerchief, and muffler . . . The cravat is light blue, a ready-tied bow with long straps for fastening round the neck. The handkerchief little differs from contemporary ones, and the muffler could easily be found in a shop window on Stoleshnikov Lane.

The departure, the absence, of a certain life that once existed but now is no more is felt with such force in that house that for a few moments the silence becomes almost tangible.

All the judgments I hear from the lips of lovers of painting seem new to me. Before such people I am an inferior, someone gazing up from below. For me, it's always something new I need to know; I'm always at school when talking to experts on painting. I experience nothing of the kind when I'm talking about literature or reading about it. Even if it's the opinions of great writers—of Lev Tolstoy, Pushkin, and the like. There's nothing new for me here. I know it all myself. Here I'm not at school, or if I am, then it's among the teachers.

What artists do I like? I can't answer that. Enthusiasm for one or another of them has for me no character of pure delight in painting as such. Rather, I make literary and historical associations. Color, line—what makes me pause? Titian? Raphael? I don't know. I know something about painting, but I'm unable to judge it. When Michelangelo's name is mentioned to me, I think with great interest not of his works but of the fact that he painted "The Last Judgment" lying on a scaffold with the paint dripping in his face. When I think of Van Gogh, I see not a lilac bush but a man who cut off his ear with a razor.

Of course, it's impossible not to grasp the wonder that Botticelli is our contemporary in his sense of line.

The little pictures by Leonardo set in the altar at the Hermitage are hard for me to appreciate, since in the first place I'm unwilling to believe they were painted by Leonardo, and in the second I'm only able to admire the scarlet lacing on the breast of the Madonna . . .[105]

Raphael's Madonna emerges from between the folds of what appears to be a green curtain drawn to the left and right, barefoot, her garments blown to the side by a breeze. To me it seems that "Raphael's angel thus contemplates divinity" is about angels contemplating the Sistine while resting on their chins. Pushkin, who had never been abroad, obviously knew the picture from reproductions.[106]

There's an optical illusion there. The angels, leaning on something terrestrial, are gazing straight ahead, and although she walks behind them, we are convinced they see her.

The golden tint of Titian's paintings . . . What is Venice? Who built it? Why is it a fairy tale incarnate? People went about in masks. Who thought that up? Who thought of the gondolas? The singing on the gondolas?

The golden Venetian women. Are they Slavs? I ought to read a history of Venice. Bonaparte looked at the canals from the point of view of an attack on the city. It's all in light blue ripples reflecting the gold of its cathedrals. Actually, I haven't seen any of it. But there is Canaletto. In him, incidentally, Venice isn't as fantastical as you imagined. A broad expanse.[107]

Byron lived there. Edgar Poe wrote an incomprehensible story about Venice.[108] Rousseau served in an embassy there. How many fabulous, strange lands there were that knew their own qualities: Venice, Toulouse. A certain feature of human consciousness emerging then: dressing in outlandish clothes, constructing filigreed houses, composing amatory codes. A lot higher stage of culture than our own. More elegant, in any case.

And just think, in the midst of it all Titian and Giorgione with their Floras and Ledas.[109] A kind of divine barbarism, a kind of paradise.

There's a bust of Catherine II by Shubin in the Tretyakov Gallery.[110] Her expression is vague. She gazes as if from the remoteness of time, a beautiful face (which doesn't correspond to reality).

She was, in all probability, small but portly. Surrounded by lacquered parquet and by diamonds, candles, young blackamoors, and playing cards—small, too, and made of an almost powdery satin. Probably it was all very beautiful. The medals on high-ranking officials and generals gleaming in the candlelight.

Suvorov runs into a hall and flings his hat at a young blackamoor. The fallen hat slides across the parquet. The blackamoor takes to his heels.

Catherine predicted Bonaparte's rise and Caesarism. She got up at six and immediately sat down to write at her desk. A writing woman, a habit and fondness for writing, graphomania. Her favorite dish was pork with sauerkraut—German.

How touching is Van Gogh when he writes to his brother, a paint merchant, that he, the brother, might also learn to paint—after all, it's not such a difficult thing! This is at once a rejection of the view of himself as someone extraordinary and an apology for his easy money, as it might seem to almost anyone else.

Just as touching is his admiration for artists whose names aren't even remembered anymore. Certain Dutch artists who were his contemporaries and whom he considered vastly superior to himself, indeed to compare himself with whom would have been for him the height of dreaming . . .

"If only I could paint like that one!"

Not only is he a great artist but also a remarkable writer. Read how he describes his picture *The Night Cafe.*[111]

First he cut off his ear, then he painted his portrait without an ear, then he shot himself.

The piano's shadow on the floor of that cafe has remained with me my whole life, no less vividly than have the black lances in Velázquez's *The Surrender of Breda.*[112] They are, moreover, the drawings of a madman—those little human figures in the night cafe that seem to be winking and breaking into grins.

It seems to me it would be a good thing for the Soviet reader to read through Delacroix's *Journal.* The book was published in Russian in 1950—a long time ago—and one has to assume that the critics noticed it and that they very likely wrote about it. Belated though it may therefore be, we still want to have our own say . . .

Eugène Delacroix is the artist who painted the very popular picture *Liberty Leading the People* about the revolution of 1848.[113] It's the one, you'll remember, with the Parisian gamin in the foreground standing pistols in hand next to an immense female figure in a Phrygian cap . . . In front of them is the body of a young worker, and all around are the figures of rebels holding their weapons at port, puffs of smoke, and flames. Either a barricade or an attack . . .

As you read Delacroix's *Journal* you immediately begin to sense the nearby movement of a physical body. It's not a journal but life itself restored by the incantations of the mind. So much the worse for me then to observe that the book is already half read. He's still making his entries, and although he's ill, like the rest of us he still thinks that it—death—won't happen to him. But I have only to turn over a certain number of pages and he's no more, that Delacroix, who so loved to eat and paint.

His is a powerful mind, and moreover one that entertains questions not merely of art but of morality, life, and death.

He has, by the way, extremely interesting things to say about Michelangelo. The Italian was a painter, in Delacroix's view, a painter and not a sculptor. His statues are presented to us *en face;* they are contours filled in with marble and not the result of thinking in terms of masses. One cannot, Delacroix observes, imagine Moses or David from behind. Perhaps (and here we're expressing our own view) there were in fact in Michelangelo breakthroughs into something new that was still uncharacteristic of his century, something indistinct and romantic that only Delacroix could recognize? Perhaps Michelangelo had already seen the swirling figures that would later emerge from beneath the chisel of Rodin? In any case I want to defend Michelangelo even from Delacroix. Let's remember who he was. Even the smallest detail of his biography is able to astonish: not long before he died he painted Death carrying a coffin on the wall of the spiral staircase of his house.

Shall we end today's entry on that somber note? Better to recall something pleasant. What then? Here's what. Once as I was returning home along the dark streets of an Odessa still under blockade by an English cruiser, a few sailors in machine-gun belts who were apparently completing some operation suddenly ran out from behind a corner and disappeared down a side street. Then one of them ran out again and asked me which street they had gone down—what its name was . . . And I remember he called out to me,

"Little brother!"

I was the sailors' little brother. In what way haven't I been addressed in my life—even as "maestro"! "Bravo, Maestro!" the Bulgarian orchestra leader Panteleev called out to me at some poetry reading in Odessa. Yet whenever I feel low it's just that greeting fluttering near my shoulder that I recall:

"Little brother!"

I put off reading a page in Delacroix's *Journal* that was a whole article on art so as not to read it carelessly, in passing . . . Less and less of the *Journal* remains. The author is nearly sixty years old, and everything he writes now is magnificent in intelligence and subtlety. Sometimes he may be faulted for the writerly desire to tie everything up in a concluding flourish, to show that he is in fact a writer . . . Well, even that works splendidly for him. Thus while delighting in one of Raphael's pictures but at the same time aware of its faults, he observes that "Raphael is graceful even when he limps." It's an arrant phrase, a typographer's tail piece, yet how good!

I was at Kazakevich's, who's always the epitome of intellect, education, and temperament. Could he write a good play? It's precisely that form of literature—and it's even strange to call such a miracle of created event literature—that is at once a test of rigor and the flight of talent, of a sense of form and of everything singular and marvelous that in fact constitutes talent.

When Mozart was composing his music, the whole world was completely different from our own. He composed by candlelight, perhaps by a single thick candle not hard to imagine with its tongue flickering whenever anyone opened the door. He was dressed in a green silk caftan and wore a peruke with curls and a pigtail wrapped in black silk. He sat at a harpsichord as if made of chocolate, and there were no electric lights in the street; rather, there burned . . . We can't even imagine without hesitating just what burned there. Torches? Lamps with whale oil?

In short, it was still before Napoleon. Or even before the Great French Revolution, a time when it hardly occurred to anyone to be astonished at the existence of kings. A different world, an entirely different world.

And what Mozart composed, we in our different world, as different from his as an old man is from a baby, now remember, repeat, sing, and pass on to one another . . . We touch the levers of our machines, switching on the current, so that the golden gossamer created by his brain will never disappear, so that it will always exist to be passed down to the next different world . . .

He suffered from twitching as a child and was, as people now say, given to seizures. He's handsome in his portraits, but it's more likely he had a large nose and was of small stature. His appearance was probably most expressive when he was a Wunderkind: small, big-nosed, in convulsions. It's odd to imagine there were taverns, drinking bouts, frivolous ladies, and fisticuffs in his life . . . At the Prague premiere of *Don Giovanni* he proposed that in the last act just before the statue makes its entrance, Don Giovanni sing Cherubino's satirical ballad from *Figaro* in order to amuse the Praguers, who were very fond of the latter opera. I haven't read Mozart's letters. Have they been preserved?

I listen to Beethoven's Ninth constantly.

How could Lev Tolstoy attack that work, Lev with his love of the heroic, with his sky above the wounded Andrei?[114] Isn't that the same thing? Probably from envy, or rather not from envy but from a demand that there be no visions of the world but his own . . .

It's a symphony about the history of the world at a given stage, as they say. The bass drum and timpani go off just like the cannon of those days, the stubby cannon with the double reverberation of the kind that Bonaparte later became fond of. The execution of the royalists in the parvis of the church of Saint-Roch.[115] Perhaps all that is in the Ninth Symphony. It's history, in any case. But what would cannon be doing there? It's not an illustration, after all.

Instead of an enormous throng of musicians, old, speckled with ashes, and dressed in baggy vests; instead of piles of music books, whole forests of double basses, whole storms of bows, and much, much more, if only the din of music stands, coughing in the hall, and the chirping of instruments being tuned—instead of all that you hold in your hands a record that squeaks elegantly when touched, a black record with a garland glinting from it every second. The result's the same: the same Beethoven symphony, the true embodiment of which is ultimately unknown—it's the above-described chaos of the orchestra, and a record, and the grand piano of Beethoven himself, and before that simply the breeze or the sound of a cuckoo or Napoleon's crossing the Alps.

Oh, this compilatory itch! Reading or learning about something, you want to retell it at once. Stendhal suffered quite literally from the urge. He recounts whole works.[116]

I want to tell of Hector Berlioz and his unrequited love for an opera singer. Like one spellbound, he would stare at the stage while she sang. He visited Petersburg. Toward the end of his life he became mentally ill with a black melancholy.

I want to tell of Franz Liszt, who in every city he performed in invariably found himself a lover, a woman he would place under lock and key in order to avoid lamentations when it came time for him to depart. Heine calls him a brilliant fool and says that it was Liszt himself who had wreaths sent to his concerts. Was he really such a fool, then? He came to love Russian composers, by the way, and popularized Glinka in Europe.

He played two grand pianos, not simultaneously obviously, but moving back and forth between them, since they stood, if one may put it this way, back to back . . . This was done so the audience could see him from all sides, so to speak.

As he neared old age he became a monk. Or was it an abbot? In any case, there's a portrait of him in a cassock, old, his hands folded on his knees, and his face tossed back—an old, toothless face with the hair brushed up off his forehead.

Now he's called Ferencz Liszt, since he was Hungarian.

I never heard Shalyapin while he was alive. Only on records. It's very pleasant to listen, pleasant in a physical way. Sometimes it's as if you're hearing a bell, sometimes as if not one person but a whole choir is singing. But only physically, for the ear, in the sense that Stendhal understood pleasure from music.[117] The modeling, expression, and so-called play of the voice are all within the bounds of ordinary theatrical convention, timbre, and meaning. Of course, when a robust person of enormous size with a beautiful voice weeps theatrically, it is in any event curious.

He died relatively young in Paris—at sixty. He's buried at Père-Lachaise under a stone with the inscription, "artiste lyrique," which in the French style means an opera singer.

There are many legends about him.

I've aged and don't much feel like writing. Do I still have the strength to produce metaphors? Sometimes I want to check on myself in that area. Rimsky-Korsakov wrote that once he was suddenly stricken with the fear that he could no longer produce melodies. He tested this by setting himself the task of composing something that depended above all on melody and soon became convinced he could still produce them . . .

I imagine Rimsky-Korsakov only in terms of the portrait (Serov, Repin?) in which he looks like someone already dead—with a long translucent beard and fragile brow.[118]

He was a naval officer who circumnavigated the globe.

I remember the powerful impression *Scheherazade* made on me when the artist Sokolik sang parts of it to me in Odessa when we were young.

"Hear that? That's the ships calling to each other," said Sokolik. "Do you hear it?"

And really the ships were calling to each other. I became acquainted with symphonic music for the first time then. It entered my mind as a kind of still unmastered condition that nonetheless affected me strongly.

No, I'm unable to write and don't want to.

What a majestic letter Tchaikovsky wrote in regard to the young Rachmaninoff's transcription of *Sleeping Beauty* for four hands![119] He, the author of a work another composer had recast in a different form, reproved that composer for lack of audacity and initiative and for an excessive deference to authority (that is, to himself, to Tchaikovsky). He would, in other words, have been pleased if Rachmaninoff had treated his work more destructively!

Somebody once said that metaphor is all that will remain of art for eternity. It's pleasant in that regard for me to think I'm making something that might last an eternity. Why ultimately is that pleasant? What is eternity if not a metaphor? After all, we know nothing of nonmetaphorical eternity.

One thing I know for certain about myself is that I have a gift for naming things differently. Sometimes it comes off better, sometimes worse. What that gift is for I don't know. People need it for some reason. A small child hearing a metaphor even in passing, even with half an ear, will emerge from his game for a moment, listen, then laugh approvingly. That means it's needed.

It seems to me that I'm merely a namer of things. Not even an artist but simply a kind of apothecary, a packager of powders, a roller of pills. Tolstoy, preoccupied with moral or historical or economic considerations, tosses out images along the way. I turn everything toward the image.

I recall that Kataev enjoyed ordering me to try and find a metaphor for one thing or another. Whenever I succeeded, he neighed. With what inner echoes precisely of recognition, of approval, does Tolstoy recount Baudelaire's "La Soupe et les nuages" even though he wants to demonstrate its "worthlessness."[120] And with what admiration does he speak of the "ant brotherhood" of his brother Nikolenka, also in essence a metaphor.[121]

I opened a metaphor shop in my old age.

An artist I knew made me a sign. On a rectangular board the size of a small tabletop that had been covered with light blue oil paint, he wrote that name in carmine letters, and since the sign was in light blue oil paint and carmine letters, if you looked at it sideways the daylight was glancingly reflected in it and it seemed very beautiful. If you looked at it at an even more oblique angle, you had the impression of someone in a light blue dress eating cherries.

I was convinced I would get rich. I did in fact have a stock of magnificent metaphors. Once the shop almost caught fire because of one of them. It was a metaphor about a puddle under a tree on a fall afternoon. The puddle, it was said, lay beneath the tree like a Gypsy woman. I was returning from somewhere and saw smoke tumbling out of one of the shop's windows. I poured water from a coal bucket onto a writhing tongue of flame, whereupon it became clear that the blaze had in fact been started by that metaphor.

There was another time when I had trouble driving off some sparrows. Cherries were involved again. I had a metaphor about how when you're eating cherries, it seems to be raining. The metaphor proved so true that those cherries of mine attracted sparrows intending to peck them. I was awakened one day by chirping in the shop. When I opened my eyes, it turned out to be sparrows. They were hopping and quickly turning about on the windowsill, on the floor, and on me. I started to wave my arms and they flew off in a flat but swift little cloud. They'd given my cherries a considerable pecking, but I wasn't angry with them, since the cherry that's been pecked by a sparrow even more resembles a cherry—the ideal cherry, so to speak.

And so I supposed I'd get rich from my metaphors.

The customers didn't buy the expensive ones, however. The main purchases were figures like "pale as death" or "the time passed tediously," just as images like "shapely as a poplar" were grabbed up at once. But those were cheap goods, and I couldn't even make ends meet. When I realized that I myself was having recourse to such expressions as "making ends meet," I decided to close up shop. And one fine day I did just that after taking down the sign. Then tucking it under my arm, I went off to the artist's to complain about life.[122]

It's warm and humid. It's like April, only there isn't that soaring of the spirit that takes hold of you in April, nor is there that sudden appearance of blue in the sky, nor ice melting like sugar cubes . . .

Vladimir Narbut has some splendid lines about April.

A blessing to you, April,
To you, young kid of the heavens.

"Young kid of the heavens" is very good indeed. True, he later changed it to, "To you, fire poured upon the earth . . ." Of course, there's no saying how much better "young kid of the heavens" is than "fire poured upon the earth."

The whole poem is magnificent. A strange sort of thing, comprehensible only to the poet, yet troubling to the spirit.

Of you, of you, of you I want
To speak with sleepless verses.
Above us the owl-moon tells our fortune,
And our name and in parting is three.

Seeing spring (or April), he sees signs of the Zodiac—the lamb and the owl . . . I know, I know, the owl isn't a sign of the Zodiac. But it almost is, or it could have been. In any case, the poet has populated the vernal sky with animals.[123]

Oh, these animal metaphors! How much they have meant to poets!

Velimir Khlebnikov gave us a series of animal metaphors that is perhaps the richest in the world. He said, for example, that elephants make faces like mountains in an earthquake.[124]

Khlebnikov had no material relations with the world whatever. He would write out his poems on little scraps of paper, spilling over onto whatever scrap happened to turn up next. The scraps were then stuffed in a sack. Mayakovsky attests that Khlebnikov did not, when reading his poems to anyone, in many instances even consider it necessary to read to the end. He would say, "et cetera."[125] A mathematician's son, he occupied himself with a kind of mystical blend of history and mathematics, among other things attempting to prove that great events occur every two hundred and seventeen years. (I saw those calculations of his in published form: they were called *The Tablets of Destiny* and were printed on the shabby, yellowish, yet somehow pleasant paper of the period of War Communism with big poster-sized letters and a virtual lilac bush of figures.)[126]

Reading his poems takes more effort: everything's all jumbled together, disordered, in a heap. But incomparable beauty may suddenly turn up:

The somber marching of infantry,
The murder by spear of a king,
Dark blue fields and the deluge of stars
Are, like nightfall, obedient to numbers.
The years of war, the shrouds of plague,
I added and subtracted in my mind,
And a respect for numbers grew,
The rivulets leading to a channel.[127]

Or, addressing that connoisseur of Greek and Roman verse, the symbolist Vyacheslav Ivanov:

You, whose intellect flowed like a hoary waterfall
Down into the pastoral life of the first antiquity . . .[128]

Once you get a general impression of his poetry, it is precisely the Slav you see in it, and moreover a Slav for whom Slavdom extended all the way from the North to the Adriatic.

Once when Dmitry Petrovsky fell ill during some trek or other they were making together, Khlebnikov suddenly got to his feet to continue on his way.[129]

"Wait, what about me?" Petrovsky asked. "Why, I could die here."

"What of it?" Khlebnikov replied. "The steppe will bury you."

In fact, the steppe buried Khlebnikov. We don't know where and how he died or where he's buried . . . Not long ago Petrovsky died too—a Cossack eternally holding a pipe between his teeth who never, so it seemed, looked you square in the face but always peered at you over his shoulder or from behind that pipe.

The verse of the Chuvash poet Yakov Ukhsai is very rich in metaphors.[130] Once I was given his long poem "The Divide" for review, and I found miracles in it. The sun is so close to the earth at sunset, he says, that even a rabbit could reach it in a jump. He compares a cow to a chess rook, a running horse as seen by a coachman to a brook, and potatoes to the foreheads of sheep. The tiny horns of lambs are waxen, and the horns of a ram are like wheels. And, finally, the boots of a fop are to him yellow ducklings.

Jules Renard has some short compositions about animals and nature in general that are very like my own.

Once, describing some flight of mine, I spoke of how I had put my face to a tree—to the face of a brother, I wrote. Later on, I said that its face was long, wrinkled, and that ants ran over it . . .

Renard has something similar about trees: the family of trees that takes him to itself, recognizing him as one of its own . . . Some things he already knows how to do—how to look at clouds, how to be silent.[131]

The indivisibility of the world has always seemed proved to me in the relations of art. One and the same thing comes to mind at different ends of the earth.

I've been planning to write about animal metaphors for a long time. I mean by that term any figure of speech involving an animal, whether the animal is enlisted for the creation of the image or the image is, so to speak, contained in the animal.

Inexhaustible artistic possibilities are hidden in any sort of animal. Among its feathers, crawling on its bill, gleaming in its eyes, or caught in its tight grasp . . .

It seems to me, for example, that I could pull from the jaws of any animal an endless ribbon of metaphors about the animal itself.

And not only from the jaws of a tiger. From the bill of a jay or gull. Once I heard someone in a group walking along the beach remark of a gull in flight that it was elegant. "The elegant seagull."

Everybody started laughing, but it seemed right to me.

Also that the gull is an aircraft. That's almost the same thing.

Not once in childhood, nor in youth, nor later as an adult—in short, at no time in my life had I heard the singing of a nightingale . . . For me, it was a lie, a convention, whenever I spoke of nightingales or read about them in the works of others.

And then when in already quite mature years I was living on the outskirts of Moscow, in the afternoon, or, more precisely, at noon when everything was still among the birds and plant life, something suddenly came rolling out of the stillness—an enormous ringing wheel—and then it rolled away . . . Immediately after it came another wheel, and then a third . . . And then all of a sudden the ringing stopped.

Those wheels undoubtedly were golden and higher than the trees. They rolled upright, straight, and then, starting to wobble, they were gone in an instant, as if they had never existed.

I turned to the person standing next to me. He nodded in reply. He'd heard the question I hadn't yet asked, had only intended to ask: was it a nightingale?

And nodding, he answered,

"A nightingale."

Have you ever seen a secretary bird?

It's rather tall, about human size. It seems to be wearing short yellow breeches, white stockings, a swallowtail coat, a vest, and spectacles, and to have a pen stuck behind its ear. It moves rapidly about its cage in a methodical manner, although a bit irritatedly and nervously, like a secretary who has bungled something and intends to justify himself before his superior, if only the latter will see him.

In all likelihood, the representatives of some English firm trading in Africa or Australia were the first, so to speak, to see that bird, and struck by its resemblance to a secretary, they gave it that name with a chuckle.

It could have been called Metternich.

It eats snakes.

I never heard its voice.

They sway as they walk, and since they aren't very high off the ground, when you're on one side of the grass, and they're moving in single file along the other, it seems as if they're riding. A honk is a relatively loud noise; in any case, you clearly have the sense that it's a kind of speech, indeed, a kind of foreign language. Their bills are yellow, as if fashioned from wood like spoons. They ride by you in a businesslike way, undoubtedly talking among themselves and certainly about you; in fact, they even glance at you as they pass by. One can believe that they saved Rome. They look charming once they're afloat. Dipping their heads, they suddenly lift up so much water it seems they're wearing glassy jackets. Now they aren't riding but gliding—white cushions on the flat blue surface. Suddenly they all converge, and then it seems that a white pretzel is rocking on the water.

An animal drama was played out here. A large, mature ginger-colored cat, his fur almost dragging on the ground like a bison's, had fallen into the habit of preying on some pigeons kept by someone. A trap was set and he was caught. However, even though his leg was injured, he set off for home, dragging the whole heavy, clumsy, awful trap behind, still clamped to his injured leg . . .

The drama consisted of the fact that the cat, which had more than once fought with a mixed-breed German shepherd named Chaika and made a fool of her and left her angry, had because of the injury this time blundered while fighting and been torn to pieces by the dog.

I knew well that supercilious cat that resisted my playful overtures almost squeamishly. Fortunately, I didn't see the corpse. The wounds in combination with the ginger fur probably looked horribly and inaccessibly beautiful. It's their, the beasts', concern and not ours that they tear each other apart. It's strange a dog defeated him, that beast of which it's said in Brehm that he is strong and well-armed.[132] True, his leg was damaged by the trap.

Soon afterward I saw the victorious shepherd. She was romping in the courtyard with a puppy, which hopped after her. The puppy tossed up its plump little bottom and looked at me from below, from no higher than the flowers among which I had brought him to a halt—pansies. His shepherd-mother kept to herself in the distance, watching him. No one would have guessed that not long before she had torn apart a living creature. On the contrary, she seemed a likable dog, and calling to her—"Chaika, Chaika"—I patted her flat brow with its hot fur that made my palm feel dry. The pansies bloomed, sometimes resembling Japanese military masks; the jasmine, the most beautiful flower in the world, stood quite high; and a woodpecker knocked, a woodpecker I've never seen, although it's been knocking on my door for some time now.

One night as I was going down a dark staircase after leaving the home of somebody I'd been visiting, I suddenly heard a rapidly approaching movement. In that instant when the most likely thing would have been to expect an attack, a blow by something deadly, something warm touched my hand. That too startled me, but the fright already racing from my hand to my brain was turned along the way into tenderness and pleasure. I realized it was the little dog, Jack, who lived in the hallway and who knew me. Thus, instead of my greatest enemy, which by rights I ought to have met, I met my greatest friend.

Little black Jack was run over by a truck.

An American who had spent his whole life in Africa where he hunted animals he would then stuff for Columbia University wrote a book about his life. There are wonderful things in it. I'll come back to that subject, but for now, in order to complete the recollection, I'll report his concern about whether or not one should kill gorillas. That question troubled the society of his day, which had only recently encountered the gorilla for the first time. And truly that beast does look like a human being. Indeed, is it really a beast?

In a word, his concerns are eventually laid to rest: one may kill gorillas. A description of a gorilla hunt follows. The animals appear on a mountain top—huge, rocklike silhouettes, and the hunters are afraid . . . But the gorillas don't have the black stick from which fire comes. A gorilla is killed and dressed. They'll stuff him, and then he'll take his place in a glass case, a reddish-brown creature with long hair somehow reminiscent of a coconut, and attached to his stuffed head, a pendent jaw with crimson gums displayed.

I started petting a cat lying on a chest in someone else's apartment. As was evident, no one had petted him with sufficient feeling, and he surrendered himself to it; he liked it. Clean, elegant, strong, he stood up, arching his back. Then he looked at me several times with friendly attention, and not only attention but approval of the fact that I, an unknown person, had come in out of the dark and started petting him. His triangular muzzle was suspended in the darkness of the doorway at quite a respectable height, and his eyes gleamed with the greenish light with which the planets shine on a summer night.

After petting him, I left. He followed me, first along the chest, then, after softly leaping off the chest onto the floor, at a run down the corridor. I took pleasure in thinking that for a few moments I had bound to myself something very like a tiger.

A fox owner, the journalist Miklashevsky, has died. Why a fox owner? He raised a fox, a wild one that had turned up at his place by accident. In recent years he would appear on Gogol Boulevard with the fox in his arms. It sat with its back to the direction of travel and thus looked over his shoulder. Children ran after them. He would sit down on a bench, the fox continuing to look over his shoulder and the children crowding behind the bench. The fox felt a bit out of place. Its eyes were like a girl's, actually a bit lighter than a girl's, and slightly unmotivated, I would say.

I knew Miklashevsky personally. He told me how once when they had lit their Christmas tree, the fox sat together with the children and gazed up at it as if mesmerized. One can imagine those little eyes with the candle flames reflected in them.

The last time I saw Miklashevsky was about a year ago at the *Literary Gazette.* I didn't know him well. Someone who loved animals, a poet.

Spring began this afternoon.

The cat emerged from a small attic window onto the moonlit leaves of the roof. She crossed the shadow of the chimney, disappearing into it for a moment, then reemerged onto the leaves and proceeded down the slope of the roof, herself casting an oblong shadow in front, then reached the gutter and walked along it, now casting a shadow behind rather than in front, a shadow that this time was more triangular than oblong. There she walked for a time, having at her side a certain distance away treetops with foliage that even a slight puff of wind would cause to release a whole avalanche of leaves, and then she went back up, evidently not wishing to be compared to a whole avalanche.

While walking along the gutter, the cat bent over something lying there, moved it with her paw, at the same time holding the ball of her head down, as a consequence of which it was somehow diminished. Then she walked a rather long time upon the leaves illuminated by the flat yellow lunar light, and entering the shadow of a larger building cast upon the roof of the smaller one, she disappeared without even letting anyone know what color she was.

Large crows were walking about a mown field and eating something. They really do seem sinister—ecclesiastical functionaries of some sort from the time of Louis XVI, bigots, torturers. But looking at them with an ordinary eye, you see only a strong, healthy bird and you have greater sympathy for it.

Suddenly they took to the air above the field and flew off in search of other, richer ground . . . They flew low, in order, apparently, to see whatever it was they needed to see. Their tucked-in legs hurtled over the field and their wings worked efficiently like parts of a new machine—flap, flap, flap . . .

I followed one as it walked on ahead of me. At first it didn't hear me or wasn't afraid, but then it took off, and the stroking of its wings seemed to say, "Oh, leave me alone! Leave me alone! Don't bother me!"

I went to the zoo with the goal of seeing just the tiger. After all, those pictures too, like the ones in oil, are tedious when you see a lot of them at once. And here past the cages, just as there past the frames, you can't hurry once you've taken a look.

And so, only the tiger. Yes, but the tiger isn't just sitting in one of the first cages. The tiger's the high point, a whole section unto himself, the finale of the third act. He's off in the distance, and you have to walk quite a way to get to him. So I was forced to look at other things besides the tiger. I gave the small fry near the entrance a quick once-over. Something tiny was sitting next to its box. A silhouette with ears the size of pansies. Close by, as if on a gigantic cork, a griffin vulture turned ponderously around . . .

Ilya Selvinsky has magnificently described the tiger.[133]

In him, the tiger's muzzle is "golden," "like a sunset," "hot," and "mustached like the sun." (Take a look, the sun is "mustached"—well done!) He says of a tiger that over the summer it faded to "orange," that it was "daubed with niello," that it was "gray on gold," and that it came down "the mountains like a dragon abandoning its temple," the "ridge of its back repeating the ridge of the mountain." Describing the tiger's gait, Selvinsky says that it walked "rippling in the wind, as lazy as a banner," and also that it walked with "a martial stride, its whole shoulder thrust forward."

He exclaims of the tiger,

"Kind one! Clever one!"

"As lazy as a banner" is splendid, worthy of Dante. You have the sense that the poet wanted something more; having seen many vivid images, he felt that there was still . . . that there was still something else. His eyes grew wide, and in the truly bright colors of the tiger, in its velvetiness, he saw "a lazy banner."

It's the damnedest thing! You exchange greetings with someone and talk to him without ever appreciating that thoughts have occurred to him that are perhaps three, four, or even five times removed from the ones that initially prompted them . . .

The most beautiful earthly sound I have ever heard is the lion's roar.

What is it? An explosion, perhaps, or at least a dying roll of thunder . . . You want, in any case, to call it a powdery sound.

What sort of larynx is it that gives rise to sounds of such intensity yet at the same time of such restraint—of such unintentionality, I would say? The sound isn't thrust out very far by the lion but seems to appear only in the vicinity of his jaws. He seems to toss it out, as if it were a short, tattered flame.

I'm late arriving at the circus, and before me in the yellow arena is a young girl in a skirt who is tossing something like bowling pins into the air—she's a juggler—and while I'm watching her tipped-back face and her eyes bouncing behind the pins, a lion's roar suddenly erupts from the wings. Not only does the sound itself enter the arena, but its echo does too, a gust that gladdens the heart and makes you feel tenderness for that soft-footed, sand-colored monster with the wrathful creases on its brow.

What doesn't occur to you standing before the cage of the ape.

When did Europeans first see them? It's unlikely there are any references to them, certainly no pictorial representations, in what has come down to us from Greece and Rome and the kingdoms of Asia.

I was standing in front of the cage of a chimpanzee. I had long been acquainted with that black body, that black oval often seen in the distance through an opening in the crowd, but this time I decided to take a closer look.

The first thought to come to you is that it is a beast of exceptional strength and that it would be a terrible thing to fall into its grip, particularly when you see its upper lip raised in a rage, baring its teeth and pink gums. The second thought is how separately, how apropos of nothing at all, an autumn leaf, carried there by the wind or a zookeeper, lies on the floor of the chimpanzee's spacious cage. The third thought . . . There are numerous thoughts.

When I moved closer to its cage, it came over to me, resembling either a banker about to sit down at his desk or a robber intending to fall on the banker.

A large, plump gray moth, almost furry, suddenly appeared at the base of my lamp. Instantly it resorted to every kind of mimicry, probably sensing the presence of something threatening nearby—me. It undoubtedly compressed itself, shrinking in size, and became still, as if frozen. It had decided it was invisible, or at least imperceptible. But not only did I see it, I even thought, "The fuselage of a moth."

That is, I also saw its metaphorical hypostasis. In other words, I saw it twice . . .

No one has explained to me why moths fly toward the light, moths and all the viridescent ballet that dances around light bulbs in the summertime, all those long ballerinas. I turn off the light and open the window wide so they can fly out, if only by chance . . . I wait five minutes, and already it's as if they're no longer in the room . . . Nothing of the kind. I turn the light back on, and encircling the lamp once again is a round dance of sylphids uniformly rising and falling and occasionally striking the glass of the lampshade as if they're connected to each other by an invisible hoop . . . Why is it so? What is the light to them?

Of wild animals at large I have seen only the . . . really only the mouse and the rat?

Probably that's right. For it has never happened to me to encounter a bear in a country pine wood. Nor have I ever seen a hare scampering along the horizon, nor a gopher, nor a badger.

I shall thus have to be content with the mouse and the rat. I had an encounter with a rat once that inclines me to believe the legends connected with that beast. One bright summer night in Leningrad as I was returning home to the Hotel Europe in a slightly intoxicated state, I saw a rat running at me along the wall, apparently fleeing some persecution. Off in the distance from which it had come, some drivers were laughing and hooting . . . As one would kick at a football, I swung my leg to kick the rat, at once losing my balance and shamefully falling to the ground like a drunk, thereby provoking even greater hooting than before. The rat, unharmed, swept on, disappearing behind a fence and some bushes. After making my way up to my room, I saw below the knee of my trousers the dusty trace of a tiny, delicately toed footprint that crumbled as I touched it. Thus, it's possible the rat pushed me, that one reason for my fall was that the rat had in fact pushed me.

Alexander Grin portrays in one of his stories the whole history of the interference of rats in human life.[134] It's said there that a rat may if it wishes assume the form of any other creature. And in the story the handsome, elegant boy who suddenly appears to the hero and ever so affectionately tries to deter him from a step that is in fact necessary and useful to him is a rat.

I once observed a rat that was unaware it was being watched. We were separated by the thick glass of a store window, and the rat couldn't hear me and thus behaved naturally. Usually, the rat is afraid of us just as we are of it, but here the glass divided us. True, I still had to make an effort to look at it, and true, my heart still rose in my mouth. But I also have to say that there was nothing at all frightening about it: an ordinary little wild beast, brown with brilliant black eyes, that scurried among the price cards and bottles, sniffing and stopping and knocking things over as it moved.

No one believes that my impression was precisely that.

"But the tail?" they ask. "It has an awful tail!"

No, in my opinion the tail isn't awful. A most ordinary tail, the long tail of a little beast, exactly the sort of tail we see in pictures on both the ferret and the marten. It may be that our fear of the rat originates in the fact that upon seeing us, it instantly disappears. Historically, it is known that rats were instrumental in spreading the plague, and from that too comes an ancient dread, one passed down in our memories.

An ultramarine vase with a long narrow neck stands within our field of vision. Although it isn't a vase either, if a bit above the blue neck you can also make out a little crown.

The tail is still furled. He'll unfurl it when he's ready. He almost waits for us to ask him to unfurl it. Sometimes he doesn't unfurl it at all. He drags it behind like a rather dry and unprepossessing bundle of twigs, although some of those twigs are thick, thicker than his blue neck with its iridescent blue scales.

He struts on wide feet.

The ancient world was filled with admiration for the peacock. Kings, queens, generals, and senators gazed at him. Now he's lost his significance as one of life's adornments. In Europe, by the way, his role was and still is performed by the swan. I like the peacock less than I do the swan. My northern European soul shuns the peacock, which somehow seems hot to it. I get a migraine of the soul whenever I see one.

The peacock is the East. It's just as nakedly without shade, without twilight, as are the buildings of the Alhambra, the ornamental designs of the Registan, the verses of the Eastern poets, or the precise and mistless Eastern fountains, whose streams evoke more a sense of precious stones than of water.[135]

The swan swimming away into a greenish penumbra of ooze and willow is mysterious; the peacock stands in the midst of sunlight—clear, docile, yet harsh like the rule of a tyrant.

That dog has probably grown up by now. She loved me very much when she was little, loved me so much that with her jumping she wouldn't let me even take a step. She was a poodle, which, Brehm assures us, prefers the company of people to that of dogs. I shall see her another time, that dog, and I'm sure she will recognize me and again show her love.

Long live dogs! Long live tigers, parrots, tapirs, hippopotamuses, and grizzly bears! Long live the secretary bird in its satin breeches and golden spectacles! Long live everything that is alive—in the grass, in caves, and among rocks! Long live the world without me!

The Extraordinary Intersection

I NEEDED TO GET to the center from the other side of the Moscow River. And so I was considering which bridge to take, the Bolshoy Kamenny or the Moskvoretsky.

Both alternatives were equally acceptable since I was standing on the corner of Lavrushinsky Lane. It opens onto Kadashevsky Embankment just about at the middle, so that the distance from it to the Bolshoy Kamenny or the Moskvoretsky Bridge is the same.

The question came down to which bridge was the more interesting to cross. I thought that if I took the Moskvoretsky, the Kremlin would as it were swim out to me . . . Yes, it would look as if an enormous white swan were swimming toward me, its neck the bell tower of Ivan the Great, its back the cathedrals with the golden plumes of their cupolas. I was about to choose the Moskvoretsky Bridge when it suddenly seemed exceptionally appealing to see that swan swimming off into the distance out of the mysterious shade of the garden, the view that opens to you as you cross the Bolshoy Kamenny Bridge. Shouldn't I go that way, to the left?

A soldier who had come up to me in the meantime probably did so because I looked like somebody well acquainted with the neighborhood, somebody who after all was standing on the corner in the middle of those hurrying by and calmly gazing first in one direction and then in the other.

Was he a soldier?

He wasn't wearing shoulder boards and his garrison cap had no star, yet even though it lacked shoulder boards, his blouse was still an army blouse, and his cap was still a garrison cap: well placed on his head, old, faded, and acquainted with a thing or two in its day.

Even if he had taken up another occupation, he was still a soldier, and no other name could have been chosen for his face, figure, and gait, and for the prominent chest on which the ribbons of his military decorations shone yellow and blue like wildflowers.

As he approached, I anxiously awaited his question. What would the soldier ask me?

I had been thinking about how handsome the Kremlin is, and that reflection on the beautiful had removed me from the mundane. Indeed, it seemed to me that there were only two of us at that intersection—a soldier and a passerby. What kind of question might I expect? Only the kind heard on the roads of war. And so I anticipated some stern words having to do with life's hardships.

"Could you please tell me where the Tretyakov Gallery is?"

That's what the soldier asked me. And it returned me to the mundane. I realized that standing before me was an ordinary Soviet person who had been a soldier but who was now a laborer. It was his day off and he wanted to visit the Tretyakov Gallery. I pointed to a brick wall visible at the bottom of the lane. He thanked me and turned into the lane.

And then a group of children who had stopped nearby a little earlier proceeded after the soldier. Evidently they had meant to ask the same question. Now they knew where the Tretyakov Gallery was.

But an old woman who came up to me a little later didn't know. I pointed out the brick wall to her too.

After standing at that intersection for about an hour, I came to realize that it is an extraordinary intersection.

It isn't extraordinary that on the corner of a lane where a picture gallery is located you're asked about the gallery, but extraordinary that you're asked about it by almost everybody who comes to the lane. A whole detachment of Soviet people goes to the Tretyakov, and obviously on any day. Did I still feel myself removed from the mundane as I stood on that corner? Or was it a very unusual mundanity?

Yes, that's what it was, an unusual mundanity, our Soviet mundanity with its golden Kremlin, its people of warfare and labor, its splendid art, and the smoky clouds of its construction projects—pink, blue, and opalescent.

Those clouds drifted above the river's curve as I quit the extraordinary intersection.

Nowadays crossing a bridge or square, you rarely fail to witness the scene of the amateur photographer taking a picture of a group of his friends.

The group is placed with the Kremlin in the background.

The photographer stands almost in the street.

Indeed, right on the pavement itself.

Sometimes he can even be found in its middle. The policeman pretends not to notice. The cars speeding by do so at an angle.

Wherever it may be, that advantageous point of view.

The group waits patiently. All the more since it has nothing to do but gaze into the distance . . . It gazes into that distance at the dark blue thoroughfare of water, then at another bridge, then at a third, then at a high-rise, and above it all, at a white seagull flying this way toward the bridge . . .

"Ready!" the photographer cries. But at that very instant the eyes of almost the whole group look up, meeting the majestic bird powerfully entering the space above the bridge, and of course it's impossible to take the picture.

"Ahh!" And the photographer even grabs the bill of his cap in vexation. "Come on!"

But he himself gazes admiringly at the gull which has already passed over the bridge, has already cast its shadow on the river, and is now executing a dazzling turn above the young trees on the embankment . . . No doubt once his friends have been photographed, the hunt for a gull will begin—the bloodless hunt of the artist.

How pleasing it is that more and more amateur photographers are making their appearance. It's a common thing now to see a boy or a respectable worker or a colonel with a camera over his shoulder or around his neck or in his hands. Very likely even on a Sunday just about everyone coming toward you will gleam with the eye of a lens, black and shiny like a beetle.

Why is that pleasing? Because it means that an ever increasing number of Soviet people are taking part in the world of beauty and science, of art and exact knowledge. Anyone engaging in photography is at once a specialist in optics, a geometrician, and an artist.

Yet probably not a single amateur photographer thinks, when taking a picture, of what rich historical material his photographs may become after many, many years have passed. In them, in those pictures, the future historian will see how the face of the great country of socialism has changed.

So let amateur photographers do their work in abundance, each attempting to do it well and in his own way, as they record people, their mode of life, their labor, and their path to a brighter future in the midst of events, the natural world, and their own great history.

Much snow has fallen and is still falling and is now on everything—the ground, the trees, the buildings . . . Even the sky is full of it, since it comes into view at a fairly great height.

In cities they clear the snow away now. In Moscow trucks have appeared with technological devices of some kind that swallow it up in a kind of iron maw.

I remember in Moscow when the snow was heaped in piles along the sidewalks and the sunlight glinted in them, producing crimson, green, and yellow sparkles. At night the piles were bathed in moonlight. People rode about in sleighs. The sleighs were small, narrow, and unstable, the driver looked enormous, and the horses seemed the size of horses in monuments. Sitting in a sleigh with a woman, you got up tangled in her hair, which rested on your cheek. Everything hurtled along at breakneck speed and seemed on the verge of toppling over. But with your hand you touched the velvet of the lap robe covering your legs, and the woman was so close to you that it was as if she had always been in your embrace . . .

You always forget that frosts in fact come at the end of November. For some reason you associate them with later on in the winter. No, they come in November. Incidentally, one may regard frosts with less fear if one thinks of them not from the viewpoint of literature or painting about winter, nor from the viewpoint of the everyday attitude toward cold, but as chemical phenomena—if one imagines all those snowdrifts, encrusted overcoats, leaves on the windows, red noses, and frozen rivers as nothing more than the result of a scientific experiment with everything taking place inside a laboratory retort. These, however, are the meditations of somebody warmed by normal domestic life, of a man in an overcoat.

The blazing yellow flame bursting from the torches used in the repair of underground mains looks extraordinarily beautiful in the frost. Actually, it doesn't even burst; it spews out. No, that needs to be put more accurately. It pours out into the air? It rushes out with a rapid billowing? The yellow flame, so brilliant it almost resonates, suddenly reveals its component parts, as if straw were appearing for an instant . . . The tendrils of flame disappear in an instant, and yet they do exist for that instant, and in that truly instantaneous existence you get the impression of a miracle, of an angel's sword. The flame is controlled by a man in an enormous iron mask reaching down almost to his waist. It's virtually a shield, that mask with its tiny, evil eyes. True, behind it is the kind, tired face of a skilled worker, a face as if woven from rope.

From my terrace I can see the stellar dome in the diamond gleam of winter. And in the dome there's a crescent moon with a star just below it. Which one is it?

From my terrace I can see Moscow, which surrounds me as if I were standing at its center on the crest of a peak. In the winter evening the city is one row of lights after another into the far distance. Sometimes there's a patch of seeping neon.

A very warm December, near or above freezing. Generally speaking, I like this time of year when the days grow shorter. The city, now awake but still in darkness and lights, is charming. By the clock it's after eight, yet outside it's still night, although the day has begun to rouse itself, with little lampshades glowing in far-off windows . . . You feel younger and more cheerful and efficient on such nocturnal mornings.

Hidden under the snow accumulating on the ground is a black slipperiness. People fall down, crashing with the full force of their weight on their lungs. Suddenly you imagine the crimson, pulsating bush of that organ in a clump of overcoat, felt boots, and scarf, and it scares you.

In the lane a young fellow with a guitar in his hand is running to catch up with several others who have already left. He runs along waving the guitar, which is of an almost orange color and therefore brightly visible against the snow. After him first runs, then walks a girl with two small braids tied behind who is dressed in little ski pants.

"Where are you going, Victor? Where are you going?"

"Visiting!" the fellow yells, without turning around. "Visiting!"

Obviously a sister. Or maybe just one of the girls from his courtyard whom this fellow, able to joke and play the guitar, can't help delighting.

When did I first see a clock? I don't remember. Undoubtedly there was a moment when I turned my attention to that strange, moving object. I just don't remember the moment.

I do, however, remember learning to tell time. The big hand seemed the friendlier of the two. The other one, the little hand, aloof, persistent, occupied with its own business, wouldn't play with me.

In the years of its existence during my lifetime, the clock has probably changed less than other technological things. In the time, say, that it has taken the telephone to make the dramatic transformation from a large box on the wall to virtually a tube that may be carried around from place to place, the clock has remained more or less the same as it was even three hundred years ago. Perhaps that's because the clock, besides its practical importance, also has importance as a thing of luxury, an object of value, a gift. It has remained unchanged in much the way that bracelets and necklaces have. It may be that there was no need for it to change. A convenient form was found at once, and people soon afterward learned to concentrate the ticking of time close at hand—on the breast or wrist.

Actually, the appearance of the wristwatch was a revolution.

I've never had a watch, have never bought one, nor has anybody ever given me one as a gift. Sometimes I speak pretty words to the effect that my timepieces are in towers.

And it's true, the tower clock is a marvel. Look at the clock on Spassky Tower.[1] It seems like somebody's sitting in a boat and stroking its golden oars.

The tower clock has been a most potent object for metaphorization. Entering a description, it at once imparts poetry, as well as distance, height, and panorama. One can speak of the tower, the birds around it, the clouds some distance beyond it, and the trees and rooftops below. How many time metaphors come to mind as you look at such a clock face above the city! You might even say that you yourself are sitting in that boat swinging the golden oars of life.

Edgar Poe was clearly drawn to tower clocks. He described a little town where every day at the approach of noon the burghers removed their watches from their waistcoat pockets in order to check them against the great clock on the town council steeple.[2]

People come up to me on the street countless times in the course of the day and ask,

"Tell me, please, how can I get to Gorky Street?"

Or,

"Would you be so kind as to tell us how to reach the amusement park . . ."

Or,

"Does it go to the amusement park?"

The last is in regard to the riverboat they see from the Bolshoy Kamenny Bridge. They stop along the parapet and gaze down at it like people entranced.

I had gone for a shave at one of the three railroad terminals—at the Northern, I think.[3]

I stood in line, looking in the mirror. I was heavier then, with broad shoulders, dark hair, and a pale but strong face.

Why was I in such a hurry to get shaved (even rushing off to a train station, since I was unable find an open barbershop in the city on Sunday)?

I don't remember. I do remember riding on a streetcar and standing on the rear platform. And looking at my reflection in the glass. Dark-haired with a youthful if somber gaze.

"Bam, bam, bam!" the streetcar driver was banging his pedal. "Bam, bam!"

The streetcar was going up Pokrovsky Boulevard, I think. No? Up Pokrovksky!

"Bam, bam, bam!"

Then the Kazan Terminal spire came into view. There weren't any tall buildings in that area then. The Kazan Terminal spire. Then a bridge over which a train was running as if having placed smoke above itself in the form of a pillar rushing rapidly into the sky. And finally the square . . .

We had arrived. Then the mirror in which I met my own gaze and scowled, since I liked myself.

I bought a bouquet of sweet pea at an outdoor market and with that wonderful cargo in my arms proceeded along the city's downtown streets.

Since the bouquet was, as I've said, purchased at an outdoor market, it had no special wrapping; the flower-covered bines simply lay, half-spilling, in my arms. True, when I sometimes looked not sideways at the bouquet but downward, so to speak, I thought I saw a round dance of young girls in fluttering dark blue, pale blue, red, and white skirts with something very like polka dots on them.

"Why, look at him! He's so taken with your bouquet that . . . Vovka! Well, what can you say!"

Immersed in my own thoughts, I hadn't noticed that a little boy who was waiting for his mother to buy him some ice cream had suddenly seen a man with a bouquet and been drawn after him.

Those who witnessed the scene laughed.

"He even forgot his ice cream!" one of them said.

Fleeing a cloudburst, I skipped over the first threshold I came to. In a moment it would become clear that I'd run into a cafe, but for the time being I stood behind its double window and shook myself. On the other side of the window the rain fell in columns, and columns they were. They looked like organ pipes.

That Kirov had been killed I learned the next morning at the Hotel London in Odessa.[4] That was twenty years ago. Do I grasp the meaning of this last sentence? No, I don't. Twenty years is the heart of a life, virtually a life itself . . . Isn't that so? Nikitenko says in his diary that it's one-third of a life.[5] It depends on which third . . . It's the middle third that's the most savory . . . Isn't that right? The most savory one?

Incidentally, while engaging in these musings, I've been forgetting that I now live, according to Nikitenko, in the third third of my life.

No, I still don't understand a thing. Obviously, time's a variable quantity. Obviously, it moves now faster, now more slowly. Sometimes, in all likelihood, twenty years may pass more quickly than a single day. In any event, I've noticed with complete accuracy that the hours pass by more swiftly early in the morning than they do after eleven or twelve. One time I sat down at my desk at six, and getting up after what seemed to me to be no more an hour, I saw that by the clock it was already twelve. That is, I had, without realizing it, been sitting at my desk for six hours. Yet in the space of six hours—not in the morning but the afternoon—we dine, nap, dress for guests, and await their arrival . . .

Be that as it may, twenty years have passed. It was only yesterday.

Lydia Seifullina was buried today (April 27, 1954).[6] Small as a doll in life, she lay so deep inside her coffin that however hard I tried I still couldn't make out her face. She was completely covered with flowers, as if she had fallen into a flower bed. A little coffin carried by Lidin, Stupniker, and Ari Davydovich, among others.[7] They loaded it into a small bus from behind, the way it's always done. In the sky a blue patch peeked through . . .

I saw Seifullina about a month ago in the same place, though a little further on—in the courtyard of the Writers' Union. She came toward me with a brisk step that was not only not that of a dying or sick woman but even that of a young woman. It usually happened in the presence of her diminutiveness that even I had to dispatch my gaze from above when looking at her. And I dispatched it from above at that meeting too and met her own gaze flashing like a sickle, a gaze full of youthful feelings of friendship and humor. She did in fact seem young to me.

May she rest in peace. I think she liked me as a writer, that she understood. In the last years I saw little of her on life's highway. For some reason I sometimes thought of her as a being who had already perished, tormented by alcohol and unresolvable passions. No, that meeting in the courtyard of the Writers' Union told me I was wrong. She in no way resembled someone who had perished; on the contrary she was young, as I've already said. Like the blue patch today, the youthfulness of her soul peeked out at me through her old, rather tattered doll of a body. Thus for me did she depart forever—gaily flashing the sickle of her young gaze, as if in that instant cutting through all the bad things that sometimes grow up between people.

One ought to remember that death is neither a punishment nor an execution. Probably influenced by the alcoholism that once held sway over me, just such an attitude toward death has developed in me: it is a punishment.

And maybe it is. But in that case, a punishment for what? And then birth must be a punishment too, with its even more inexplicable "what for?"

A whole series of meetings. The first, barely out my front door, is with Pasternak. He has just come out of his. He's carrying galoshes. He puts them on outside rather than inside the door. Why is that? For cleanliness?

He's wearing a summer topcoat. He is, I would say, lightly dressed as in summer. Two or three rejoinders and suddenly he kisses me. Since I'm planning to write about Mayakovsky, I ask him how. How? He is genuinely confused—how can I advise you? He's charming. Talking about something, he said,

"I speak to you as a brother."

Then there was Bill-Belotserkovsky with an unexpectedly astute observation about the fact that Molière's soliloquies are long and that it's strange the actors of the Comédie-Française he had seen the night before on television hadn't broken them up among several different characters.[8] A long soliloquy of his own about whether or not to have an operation.

Then Vsevolod Ivanov.[9] (All this took place by our building's front gate.) He's young. I thought he'd be older now. No, he's young and wearing a hat. He said he'd written a verse play. For some reason he didn't say what it was called.

Then I ran into Martinson. He said they'd just been talking about me. Where? On the radio. It turns out he's in the new adaptation of *The Three Fat Men.* I was very glad to hear it. I didn't do the adaptation, so I don't know its quality. It seems Yanshin and Babanova are in it too. Very happy news. I wouldn't have done it myself anyway—I don't like fiddling with old things—but it's nice to meet up again with splendid actors who remember you.[10]

And then Kataev rolled by down the middle of Gorky Street in a Zim that looked like an enormous lacquered room . . . I'm inclined to forget my anger with him. It seems to me he's writing better now than anyone, the same Kataev to whom I would bring my poems as a schoolboy on a clear, very bright spring evening with a half-moon off to the side. He liked them very much and asked me to read them over and over while he whinnied in approval. Then he read his, which I thought the height of perfection. And truly there was much aching lyricism in them . . . We were, I think, both gymnasium students, and he received me in a spacious, rather empty apartment where he lived with his brother and his widowed father, a cheerless apartment devoid of any family life, an apartment with no woman in charge. He would accompany me down long, almost rural Pirogovsky Street, then past Kulikovo Field, and new horizons opened themselves to us, and it was for us both a joyful and pleasant time.

The day is windy. I'm standing under a tree. There's a gust of wind. The tree rustles. A muscular wind. It works out in the leaves like a gymnast.

There were a couple of items in *Izvestiya* today that were very intriguing. It turns out that radioelectronic computing machines have something in them called memory tubes. That's already a good distance along the way to the robot.

The other item: the thick, massive part made of wood on a harp, the section of the frame the performer holds against the breast as if embracing it, is called the "sound box." In *Izvestiya* there's a description of an old craftsman at a musical instrument factory who, just as he has been doing for sixty years now, paints a flower petal in gold paint on the harp's sound box. It may be that we're still a long way from the robot, after all.

A year is a very brief span, very brief—the blink of an eye. On that basis, the awe we inspire in ourselves when talking about interstellar space, light years, and so forth seems a bit exaggerated to me. If a year is so brief, must one really be so awed by a distance of several million light years? The kernel of all these monstrous dimensions is, after all, merely the terrestrial year, the human year, the blink of an eye. Several million blinks of an eye—although requiring the possibilities of a giant, let's say, it is nonetheless within human reach. Maybe it isn't so distant, after all.

In an article on interplanetary travel, there was a wistful yet elevated discussion about how, given the fact that at the very greatest speeds the human life span is far from sufficient for getting to even the least remote stars, it will be necessary to undertake that journey by generations, so to speak. Some will fly to the moon, say, and settle there, producing another generation. Others from among those born on the moon will fly higher. They in turn will give birth to new generations on specially constructed stations placed at intervals between the planets and the stars . . . Thus, ever higher and farther into the universe the human species will extend, having already forgotten in much later generations its connection to Earth. This is very solemn, beautiful, and irredeemable.

So this year they've eaten sweet and sour cherries without me. I didn't even see them for sale in the Central Market—by red-haired, blue-eyed Georgians with rosy cheeks, and by Ukrainian women without any particular adornment (although a few were wearing necklaces) but with soft and lilting speech.

Before I became good friends with Alexei Diky, I knew there was a well-known director by that name.[11] I had also seen him act. I remember a play by some Scandinavian playwright called *The Good Hope* in which the main character was a mariner, a powerful man who experienced tragedy—red-haired, freckled, and big-voiced . . .[12] He suddenly entered a doorway dressed in a hooded black slicker shiny from the rain, a gale, and shipwreck, and filling the entire door frame from jamb to jamb, he grieved about something—superbly, fiercely, astounding the audience and arousing sympathy in it almost to the point of tears.

That was Alexei Diky.

After we became good friends, I realized that he was a man who took only his own soul into account, a man who lived according to his own laws. Those laws accorded with the laws of true humanity, with a true understanding of good and evil.

He was diabolically talented.

Humor, taste.

And kindness.

Kindness and a feeling of comradeship. Some manifestations of his spiritual qualities verged on the classical. A magnificent man, handsome, witty, with an extremely subtle grasp of the roots of life.

There are no happier moments than those I experience on a Sunday morning when I go into a pastry shop to buy a torte.

I've chosen a small shop for this weekly ritual. There are too many customers in the big ones. Moreover, the lane on which this particular shop is located is very fine: there aren't a lot of people, there are a few slightly bluish slabs of granite in the sidewalk, and in front of one of the buildings there's a splendid fence whose filigree looks like the handwriting of some famous person who lived long ago. Above all, however, the lane is associated for me with an amazing experience that visits me sometimes and that I call "the world without me" . . . But the reader will allow me to describe that experience another time—it's complicated—and for now merely tell about the purchase of the torte.

The salesgirls already know me. From all sides curly, bright little heads nod to me. It's like entering a greenhouse. Suddenly through a clearing in the verdant undergrowth you see the swaying head of a snake or some marvelous flower . . . It's that way here too, only the undergrowth has been replaced by cartons and vases. There's the same close atmosphere, slightly poisonous and corrupt.

I nod to the right and the left. I know them too: there's Zina, there's Nyura, and there's Liza. The prettiest is probably Liza. Of course, it's a matter of taste, for the truth is they're all charming.

I take a strawberry torte as I always do.

"This one or that?"

This one's a bit larger.

"Let's have this one."

Her small hand, its little fingers poised in the direction of the torte, swims among the masses of confection. With the aid of her other hand, which has swum up the same way, she removes the torte, and there it is before me, that strawberry torte that looks to me like some participant in a fairy tale, some familiar of fairies.

There are always several springlike days in January. Actually, they don't so much resemble spring as suddenly remind you of what it's like.

"Spring," you suddenly say to yourself. "Ah, spring, that's what it's like!"

It isn't spring, of course. There isn't even a hint of it. There's a frost and the snow is crusty, but the sunset is strangely yellow. The veil of distance parts slightly, but in winter, you see, there isn't any sensation of distance. Yet there's distance here . . . a lemon-yellow distance, and something odd happens to the birds, as if they had seen something.

Last night there was a telegram from Animation Films telling me to drop by for the money on the *Three Fat Men* contract, and today there was a letter from an exemplary theater asking me to consider a staging by their company.[13] To think how many years the tale has been on the program of our art. I was very young when I wrote it, part in the little room at the printing office of the *Whistle*, where I lived with the equally young Ilf, part in Kataev's narrow room on Mylnikov Lane, and part at the paper's editorial office in the lulls between verse satires. The room at the printing office was tiny, a floor really, and I wrote stretched out on the floor . . . I wrote on a rouleau of printing paper, flimsy, it's true, but at least there was a whole drum of it. It would roll onto me and I would hold it back with one hand while writing with the other . . . It was amusing work, and I shared my amusement with the merry Ilf.

Once I was awaked in the middle of the night by Ilf's moaning. He complained about very sharp and unusual pains in his abdomen. It became clear that a doctor would have to be found. But where? It was nighttime and we were young and clumsy about such things. I decided to go out and look for a doctor's signboard. Nikitsky Street. Nikitsky Gate. Then Tverskoy Boulevard looking like a train moving off into the distance . . . It wasn't really dark, of course. It was August, an August night, and the trees still had a full breast to sigh with, and everywhere it was beautiful, simply beautiful.

Tip-tap, tip-tap—that was me walking down the boulevard . . . Tip-tap. Raising a dozen branches all at once, a tree pointed the way, and everything spoke to me of the fact that I was young and healthy. I was the only person in the world. Just me. Tip-tap. Tip-tap . . . A doctor. A doctor's signboard. One-two, I was on the landing, one-two and I rang the bell. I was thinking only of one thing: not that a sick person was waiting for help, but that I would now have an opportunity to crack some jokes.

At first I stood in a short line with several other men and women, among whom were both young and elderly people, including, incidentally, one young woman dressed in a sealskin sack coat who was quite pretty, with a haughty expression. I concluded that she was a nurse, since it was a line of people obligated for military service . . .

We were waiting in front of a little window cut in a partition, although I couldn't see what was in the window. I looked mainly at the haughty face of the young woman, well cared for and accustomed to admiration. Next to the window stood a palm tree with leaves that seemed to be cut from iron, so that they resembled the parts of a reaping machine.

Then it was my turn. As it happened, a pale young officer was sitting at the window. I put my draft notification and military service card down on the windowsill, turning them in his direction. After opening my booklet and thumbing through it, pressing down each of its pages with his fingers, he glanced at me with a very courteous look and said he would ask me to wait for a moment while he removed me from the register.

I stepped under the palm tree. Behind me the imagined sister of mercy I had found attractive finished her business and left, although I didn't see that happen, since I caught only the movement of the double front doors shutting behind her. For an instant the bell of her sealskin coat continued to sway before my eyes . . .

"Comrade Olesha," I heard the voice of someone coming toward me from behind the partition. It was the officer from the little window. Courteously, but smiling now, he spoke to me for no more than a minute, at the same time holding out my service card to me. He said that I'd been taken off the register and that as far as work references were concerned, I should know that I no longer had any military obligation.

Thus came to an end my relations with the Red Army, whose birth I had seen with my own eyes.

A dreary spring. Gray, with no breeze.

Albert Einstein died (the day before yesterday, April 18, 1955). I thought he was tall like our Ioffe.[14] No, he was short with lots of hair. None of us normally cultivated people has any idea what Einstein actually did.

The theory of relativity was in fact at the center of attention when I was beginning to feel the power of my own youth and vocation. A short movie (Soviet) was even shown that purported to explain that theory in popular terms. It explained nothing, at least to me. I remember only one scene with a slowly turning globe.

Einstein warned against trifling with the fission of matter.

Yesterday someone was saying that after nuclear tests, waste products are left over that continue to decay in a dangerous way. What should be done with them? The Americans used to dump them in the ocean—also dangerous. Now the wastes are stored in concrete containers. But the radiation escapes from them too.

Today in *Pravda* there was an obituary for Einstein by several of our academicians.

It was neither a Sunday nor a holiday. It was in fact a work day, an ordinary day, and not on the threshold of any events in the atmosphere or history—of spring, let's say, or a visit by the czar. Merely a common, ordinary day in the middle of an already established season.

And yet there was not only turkey for dinner but also the dessert that is linked almost with fairy tales, the dessert it's even dangerous to eat since—who knows?—it might turn you into a dwarf. Plombières!

Thus, in the form of a high-holiday dinner on an ordinary day, wealth and the governing class first presented themselves to me.

"Yura, will you be staying for dinner? Yura's staying for dinner! Yes, he's staying!"

I was about ten at the time and not yet at the gymnasium. I was just a boy in dark blue short pants and black knee socks.

Just a boy.

"Boy!" somebody shouts, unclear at whom, and I too turn around. Will I turn around now when they shout, "Old man!"

Probably I won't. Don't I want to? No, I think it's really more from amazement that it has come so quickly . . . Has it really come?

"Old man! Hey, old man!"

No, he doesn't mean me, that's impossible.

"Old man!"

No, I won't turn around. It can't be that it's happened so quickly.

"Old man! What a fool, he isn't turning around! Why it's me, Death!"

It's comfortable, clean, imposing, and luxurious at the Maly Theater. The woman who takes your pass at the door stands up to do so. It's clear she's following strict orders: whenever you check a pass, stand. And in fact writers as well as actors from other theaters do come there, not to mention highly placed military and civilian officials . . .

You're sitting at a circular table across from Markov and Mezhinsky. Mezhinsky's reading the play.[15]

Maybe I should try to get myself a position at the Maly Theater as an actor? A game of go-betweens. And would they actually help me to get a situation? I'd have a regular salary. I'd wear a wig smelling of glue. Once I got made up as an old man, and a young woman who was fond of me (I too was young) was horrified:

"My goodness, how terrifying you look!"

Now I wear that makeup all the time. But Suvorov was old—was he a freak? All in powder blue, the stars of his orders, and two snow-white forelocks . . .

I know two definitions of the infiniteness of the universe, artistic definitions accessible to any imagination. One belongs to Pascal, the other to Edgar Poe.

Pascal said that the universe is a sphere, the center of which is everywhere, the circumference nowhere. How brilliant that is. It means that everything together—the earth, the sun, Sirius, the planets invisible to us, and the immense space between the bodies—converges in the single point into which we would have to place the leg of a compass in order to describe its circumference. And of course we do not see the endless space beyond the other bodies that are invisible to us, nor the space that lies even further beyond that space, and yet it is all contained in the single, endlessly growing point of an endlessly growing compass . . . But still that compass does not swing into action, for its point is continuously growing, and therefore the compass itself is growing and the circumference is never described. There isn't any.

For an idea of the limitlessness of the universe, Edgar Poe suggests that we imagine lightning traveling along one of the mathematically minute segments of the straight line that forms, just as it forms any circle, the infinite circumference of the universe.

"A flash of lightning itself, traveling forever on the circumference of this unutterable circle, would still," Poe says, "forever be traveling in a straight line."

The great mathematician was, we see, a poet, and the great poet, a mathematician.[16]

All this in the end is merely the senseless expectation of a permit or passport into a land existing not in space but in time—into the land of the past and youth. One cannot obtain such a passport, and the expectation is, I repeat, senseless, although it be paid for with vital fragments of life that are cast off much as you cast off things before any ordinary journey into space. It's all right, we say, we'll turn in a bit earlier tonight, since we're going tomorrow anyway.

But, you see, we aren't going anywhere right now. So why cast off life?

Who would have thought it would be so hard to give up expecting, that it would be so hard to believe that the land you want to set off for has already shifted from space into time?

Sholokhov is fifty years old.

Once on the stairway at the Hotel National I spoke for a long time with a laughing-eyed young man in a cap, not knowing who the young man was. Only later did I realize it was Sholokhov. Obviously, he was modest and polite. He spoke favorably of my critical excerpts, and moreover in an interview, so that it was within the hearing of all.[17]

Today I finally saw a comet for the first time in my life. In 1910 when Halley's comet approached the earth I was ten years old, and on the day, or rather the evening, of the greatest alarm in regard to some disaster presumed to be connected with that approach, Mama and Papa took me and my still-far-from-grown-up sister to Nikolaevsky Boulevard in Odessa, and there where a great many other people had already gathered, I tried to catch sight of the comet that Gorky and Blok would later recall.[18] I saw nothing but the usual star-filled dome of summer. I remember the excited voices of those gathered on the boulevard, I remember the sweet smell of wine on my mother's lips, since she had just been at a restaurant with my father and several other people, but I don't remember seeing the comet . . . It's possible that as small child, I still couldn't discriminate among the different objects shining in the dome. Whatever the reason, I didn't see Halley's comet.

The first comet I ever saw in my life is the one I was watching an hour ago first in the garden and then from the balcony of the House of Creation in Peredelkino near Moscow. Visible in the dark but clear evening, or rather night, sky above the tops of the pines between two ordinary and for me nameless stars was something on the order of a gigantic capsule with its thicker part turned downward, a capsule that glimmered so faintly that its light sometimes seemed to disappear altogether. Knowing beforehand that a comet consists of a nucleus and a tail, you could see a nucleus and a tail here too. Actually, that nucleus and tail were visible even so. But you expect a comet to be very bright, as in the color inserts in encyclopedic dictionaries, whereas in this case its luminosity was almost phantasmal.

In connection with a report on the evening radio that an artificial satellite would be passing over Moscow the next morning between five and six, I lay down without getting undressed and gave myself instructions to wake up at four. I awoke at five. At first it was even hard to imagine how I would be able to get up and go outside. But I did get up and soon afterward I was outside. I decided to walk toward the Bolshoy Kamenny Bridge and wait for the satellite there, since above that bridge there is a lot of open sky edged with buildings only at the bottom. The sky was still dark, although moonlit, with long towel-like, yet translucent clouds. In the south, a large spiked star, which to my shame I couldn't identify, rapidly twinkled. Scattered here and there about the rest of the sky were a few other stars that first disappeared behind the strips of cloud, then reemerged as freshly and confidently as before. I directed my gaze toward the northwest, where according to the report the satellite was supposed to rise—toward the northwest, using as an orientation point a tall building on Smolensk Square. But I understood an aspect of the world, the northwestern one, too much as a single point, failing to realize that that aspect is in fact a whole quadrant of the celestial dome. I had hardly taken a hundred steps when I saw several men coming toward me, talking excitedly, and I realized that I was too late. Those people, it was clear, had already seen the satellite. And so it turned out.

"You're too late," one of them said.

As I was gazing at a point in the northwest with only a tall building on Smolensk Square within my field of vision, the satellite, having risen in a more broadly construed northwest, that is, at a point within a whole quadrant of the firmament, had been moving over my right shoulder, or somewhere off to the right of it.

"What was it like?" I asked. "Like that star?"

"Yes," one of the men answered.

That means it looked quite large. All the same, it's unclear how a sphere the size of the ones sitting on park pedestals can be visible, and moreover bright, at a distance of a thousand kilometers. There's no point in trying to understand anything here, however.

Why indeed has it happened that I was born not in the days when America was discovered but in those when the artificial satellite first made its appearance?

How everything is changing. How it is changing. The voices of the radio announcers are now completely different from those of, say, a year or two ago. I still remember the announcer Pro.

"This has been Pro speaking."

He was the first Russian radio announcer. You remember:

"This has been Pro speaking."

He's still alive. A very, very old man with a vaguely florid complexion and a shapeless hat. All that from old age. He saw me from the window of some public transport and recognized me. We nodded to each other.

Not your ordinary veteran, after all. It's a serious thing—the first radio announcer.

I remember running across a square once in order not to miss a single word of those issuing from the black point of a loudspeaker . . . That was one of my first encounters with that marvel. Wet snow was falling on Soviet Square, the loudspeaker looked like a crow just alighted on a post, and "This has been Pro speaking."

Today in *Pravda* there was a doleful announcement of the death of Fyodor Gladkov.[19]

I saw him about a month ago. He looked very bad and I thought he might be terminally ill. He said he had a kind of spasm in his esophagus—he didn't say in his esophagus but somewhere else—so that his food went down poorly. Obviously, it was cancer of the esophagus, the thought of which occurred to me even then.

He was a decent man, neither a grasper nor a predator. *Cement* was written in a slightly decadent style, although it was the first thing on Soviet labor. Afterward he began to write solidly and well. He was intelligent, mordant, always intellectually irritated.

He was close to Malyshkin, who used to be my neighbor.[20] I saw him often at Malyshkin's, and from those meetings a memory of his merry temperament has remained.

Later, whenever I ran into him on Lavrushinsky Lane near our building, he was always affable and friendly, and I had the sense that we both shared the same trade.

He liked me, I think. Once a very long time ago after I had, as they say, made my entrance in literature and had moreover made it in a sensational way, he came up to me at some banquet—to have a look at me, after all—and said,

"But you're so young!"

He was already the celebrated author of *Cement.*

It is with gravity, respect, and sadness that I mark your passing, Fyodor Vasilievich.

You mourn for youth as you grieve for the dear, beautiful, merry, laughing friends, the whole throng of men and women who have perished with it . . . They're still alive, but none is as he was before. Their hair and eyes no longer shine, the men no longer make jokes or crowd around the telephones in the restaurant saloons, calling the young women to join them. Maybe they don't want anything anymore.

One of the sensations of growing old is that you no longer feel tendrils of the future in yourself. You'd always felt them before. First one, then another grew and started to give off color and fragrance. Now there are none. The future has vanished in me.

All the same, there's the absolute conviction that I will not die. Despite the fact that a great many people, both the young and my contemporaries, are dying off right beside me. Despite the fact that I'm old, I do not for an instant admit the possibility that I too shall die. And perhaps I won't. Perhaps all this with its life and its deaths exists only in my imagination? Perhaps I'm limitless and infinite, perhaps I'm the universe?

I'm thinking about Lev Tolstoy. He constantly reflected on death. Let's recall how death manifested itself to him. He was ill with pneumonia, and when on the second or third day he got worse, he began to breathe noisily, frightfully, filling the whole house with the sound. It's what is now called Cheyne-Stokes respiration, that is, a symptom of impending death resulting from the paralysis of the breathing center and named after the two doctors who first described it, Cheyne and Stokes.[21] With that symptom Lev Tolstoy died. Did his encounter with death at that moment radiate in his consciousness, was it what he had all his life thought it would be? I don't think so. He was merely deprived of whatever consciousness he had, thus ceasing to be aware of what was happening to him. But until that moment he was still alive and reaching for his medicine. His death had nothing in common with the death of Ivan Ilyich and the latter's "give it up" instead of "forgive"—nothing in common with that very earthly, very robust nonsense that Lev Tolstoy invented, having thought a great deal about death and having presented it sometimes in the form of a kind of light, ultimately forgetting that light in that sense is a poetical idea rather than the physiological one that must accompany death.[22] The two physicians, Cheyne and Stokes, knew exact things about death, physiological things. They knew that it is not a light but the cessation, say, of the activity of the breathing center, probably in no way perceptible to the person who is dying.

I'm thinking about Lev Tolstoy the night of December 20, 1959.

Alexander Vertinsky is dead.[23]

I remember his first performances when he appeared dressed as Pierrot, only not in the customary white but in black, stepping out from behind a closed curtain toward the footlights, which cast a lilac glow on him. He sang what he called "Pierrot's arietti," little songs or ballads or, more accurately, poems set to music, yet not subordinated to it as in the song or the ballad, for Vertinsky's "arietti" remained poems despite their distant background of melody. It was original and produced a charming effect. At the time he sang about the city, about the image of it that interested bohemia: perverse relations between men and women, vice, narcotics addiction . . . He rendered his tribute to fashion, reflecting the attitudes that in that era influenced even such serious makers of art as Alexander Blok, Alexei Tolstoy, and Mayakovsky.

Unquestionably, Vertinsky had by then already shown himself to be a very talented person. He enjoyed enormous success with the public.

Later on he joined the emigration, living in Paris and Shanghai, though remaining an artist in his earlier genre of performer of poem-songs. But now he sang of his forsaken homeland and of his yearning for it. He belonged to those émigrés who lived for the dream of return, who were stirred by the image of a changed and, in their understanding, more beautiful homeland. Although their junior in rank, he nonetheless stood with such émigrés as Rachmaninoff, the same Alexei Tolstoy, and later Shalyapin and Ivan Bunin.

Vertinsky's theme now became the word "home" . . . On tour in then nonsocialist Rumania, in Akkerman perhaps, he gazed on the nearby Russian land with sadness and affection and called it "bitter." Seized by a longing for his native soil and by memories of his former life in Russia, he wrote the magnificent lines about the swallows that accompany him to a concert like two schoolgirls.[24]

Alexander Vertinsky returned to his native land and became a Soviet artist, attempting to combine his own genre with contemporary Soviet themes. He enjoyed great success with Soviet audiences too. He started to work as a movie actor.

Here, in this obituary to a departed stage artist and undoubted poet, I want to recall Vladimir Mayakovsky's view of him, which, though I can't remember it exactly, came down to the fact that he, Mayakovsky, held Vertinsky's work in very high regard. I didn't know Vertinsky well, and although I had always meant to tell him Mayakovsky's opinion, I never did. Let that opinion now be known to his friends, his comrades in work, and his admirers. Praise from the severe judge Mayakovsky is no trifle; it could serve as the first line in the epitaph of any maker of art.

It seems to me that despite his frustrations, as the phrase has it, Vertinsky was an important figure of Russian art and, moreover, a unique one. Eternal memory to him.

They put me on the left side at the head of the honor guard. The one lying in the coffin moved away from me into the distance by the great length of his black suit coat and black trousers. Of his face I saw only the yellow hook of his nose pointing into the same distance of his length and visible to me from above, since the dead man was lying down and I was standing over him, or rather over his beginning.

My vision was blurred from the strenuous but unavoidable effort of solemnly standing vigil, and all the strength of my soul was concentrated in anticipation of the change of my shift in the guard. As regards my physical activity, I was in addition to standing also occupied with looking at the hook of his nose and the black extent of his body. And I gazed as well at the other end of the hall at those coming in. Here and there on the dead man lay flowers, including a young white rose with still immature pointed petals . . .

Thus ended Vertinsky's sojourn in my life, a sojourn begun long ago and continuing almost my entire life. I first saw him in Odessa when he was already a well-known performer and I had just graduated from the gymnasium.

For a long time I measured my own life against Vertinsky's. He seemed a model to me of the individual engaged in art—a poet who strangely sang his poems, who was imbued with the words and images of bitter love, who resembled no one else, who was unprecedented, who aroused envy. I made his acquaintance at the editorial office of an Odessa little magazine he had come to visit, stooping in the doorway, a very tall man in a gray suit with a round, apparently bald head that was not at all the kind it seemed he should have had. He was introduced to all of us, including me, but he didn't see me. Since that time and for the rest of my life we never got better acquainted. I am sorry about that. For me, he was a phenomenon of an art whose character I cannot define, yet that for me is sweeter than the rest, an art of the strange and the fantastic.

A certain writer complained to me that in our day it's impossible, as he said, to write a simple story about love, about tenderness, about a young man and a young woman, and about the stars. That's how he put it: "about the stars."

"Technology! That's the only thing you can write about now! Machines! Machines! Machines! But maybe I feel like writing about the stars."

I parted with the writer on a boulevard in the evening. Above us twinkled the starlit sky. He walked away. I remained standing, my head tipped back. The starlit sky shimmered.

I decided to write a story about love, about tenderness, about a young man and a young woman, and about the stars.

We'll try it.

I've never been to a masquerade ball. I do, however, remember the pleasant sensation felt by my hand whenever it picked up a mask. I mean a black woman's mask. Or rather half-mask. The exterior was black and the interior was white, and it was much nicer from that, its reverse side. Those white satin impressions for the nose and cheeks seemed for some reason to take on the form of a smile, the smile of a beautiful young face.

When you threw it, it fell on the table with an almost inaudible tap. It was lightness itself, elegance itself, love itself. It danced, it sang, it gazed at you.

There were perhaps few objects as fine as the mask. It was a woman, a Renoir, a dream, it was "tomorrow," it was "probably," it was "a moment, a moment, wait, just a moment" . . .

Sometimes, when you've hardly closed your eyes, a vision will suddenly enter your not-quite-sleeping brain, or not a vision, but some awful train of thought or maybe even a phrase . . . You experience an instant of incomparable terror. Or is it terror? No, it's already nonexistence itself, already the influence on your brain of cells that have most likely been activated by mistake and that will be called upon only at your death.

But sometimes in the same brain (and this in fact happens toward the end of night, in dreams that occur later on) there appear visions of rural places, of landscapes possessing the incomparable beauty of canvases by Veronese.[25] What then are they? Memories? Images of regret for lost youth? I would even say that one and the same place appears, and when I awake it seems to me that if I should conduct a proper search, I would find that place somewhere in the vicinity of Observatorny and Sturdzovsky Lanes in Odessa . . .

Is it really not astonishing that strange visions make their appearance in our brains? Why should they? What is it that has been called forth to frighten us? Conscience? Or an atavistic memory of the saber-tooth tiger and the cave bear? For that sudden start you experience just before falling asleep, when your whole body shudders virtually to the point of abdominal spasm, has been explained as none other than the memory of falling from a tree in the epoch when we lived in trees and were doomed to perish if ever we fell out of one in the middle of the night . . .

That garden seemed like the extension of a dream. It was because I had entered it at a very early hour on a Sunday in summer when the city was asleep. The quiet, the stillness, the blue of even nearby distances, as always on a summer morning . . . Somewhere close by was the sputtering of water gushing from hoses.

It wasn't really a garden but a small yard by a house, a slightly better-quality yard than usual, a cultivated front yard, although with lots of poppies planted in the so-called Moorish style (right in the grass) and lots of tobacco. There were two or three benches made of green logs and a brick wall running up a hill, as usual forming what may be the most advantageous background for flowers and plants. True, that background is plain, but it is full of reverie, full of a call to the future, even for an old man like me. An iron railing also ran up the hill, and a door was open there with something dark on the other side . . . What was it? A corridor?

I had entered the garden with the idea that it was the extension of a dream. No, it was merely the quiet of morning and the stillness of the little white and crimson heads in and above the grass . . . How can you not start talking to flowers when you're by yourself? "Will everything be all right?" I asked the flowers. "Yes," answered a white tobacco flower. "No," a poppy hurled at me. "No, no, no!" I thus carried from that little garden the memory of the kind, broadly spreading "yes" of the white tobacco flower, and the fiery, tossed-over-the-shoulder "no, no, no" of the poppy.

"No, no, not dreams! If I should begin to occupy myself with that, if I should start to call up dreams with their absurdity, then it would be just a farce. Not dreams, then, but the most real penetration into the material world of the past."

"And the future?"

"From what can I create the future? The past has left behind its glancing reflections; one may catch hold of them and concentrate them, but the future . . ."

He smiled.

"The future is still in the sun!"

He was always returning to the theme of light. The material world is created by light. Call it what you will—quanta, atoms—it's still light, still the sun.

"Is everything created by the sun?" I asked.

"Of course!"

It was possible to believe him, if only because in the end he was saying things known to every schoolchild. It was simply impossible not to believe him, inasmuch as . . .

Inasmuch as he was holding a little device made of glass, actually a glass tube no wider than a pencil. Yes, more than anything else it looked like a glass pencil. He twirled it as you would a pencil, only from the twirling of that pencil came a sound like distant laughter, either in the boat or the garden . . .

On the pencil something like a golden needle appeared from time to time, and distant laughter was heard from somewhere either in the garden or the boat.

"Someone's recalling his youth," he said.

He stopped the twirling of the pencil and slightly turned a tiny dome on it, and we all saw a young woman, herself somehow resembling . . .

Spring is coming round this year with a slowness unprecedented in my memory. The greenness visible today between the buildings and behind them is still far from what is called the first green. It still isn't here, that green; rather, it's only hinted at. Nor does one smell the characteristic fragrance of springtime. Maybe the world has stopped making contact with me? Maybe the possibility of such contact is lost over the years? Maybe it's the schoolboy who smells the fragrance, the schoolboy who conscientiously wants, as I once did, to be done with worries so that not a single spring day shall pass without his full attention.

I need to get out of the city. I'll ride to some station, step off the train, and stand there. Will contact be established then? There was a time when I wanted to devour nature, to rub my cheek against a tree trunk, tearing my skin until it was bloody. There was a time when, finding myself in the country after a long interval, I ran up a low hill and not seeing the cemetery that lay beneath it, fell down full of delight, my face in the grass, the blades of grass that wounded me, and I wept from a consciousness of closeness to the earth and I conversed with the earth.

Rising to my feet, I saw the rural cemetery with its plywood crosses and cardboard photographs, all of it entwined in lilac shoots with a dark rustling oak inclining above.

You're walking around the city . . . It's September, but clear, calm, and hot. And yet wherever you go, the world refuses to accept you. I've been on my way somewhere my whole life. It's all right, I thought, I'll get there. Get where? Paris? Venice? Kraków? No, the sunset. And so I walk now, well aware that you cannot reach the sunset. Obviously, it was a dream of immortality.

Perhaps if there had been no effect at sundown, all history would have been different. Somebody once rightly told me that mankind would have invented something else, if only to torment itself.

Nothing's lovelier than the dog rose. Do you remember it, dear reader? My question isn't too impolite, for it's true that a great many people pass by a multitude of marvelous things standing near or moving along their path. Past trees, bushes, birds, the little faces of children following us with a glance somewhere near the threshold of a gate . . . A slender little red bird hops about every which way on a branch—do we see it? A duck tips its head forward into the water—do we notice how amusing and charming the movement is, do we laugh, do we look back to see what the duck is doing next?

It's gone! Where is it? It's swimming underwater . . . Just wait, it will surface in a moment. It has surfaced, flinging away with a single motion of its head such a quantity of shining drops that it's even hard to find a metaphor for them. But wait, wait—surfacing, it makes such movements with its head in order to shake off the water that it seems it's drying itself with the whole sky after a bath.

How rarely do we give our full attention to the world. It's for that reason that I allow myself to remind the reader how beautiful the dog rose is.

Its bushes are massive; one would have to link a dozen children in a chain to surround one. The trunk is invisible, but its ramifications are numerous—branches, branches, and more branches . . .

What really is the most beautiful thing I've seen on earth?

Once I wanted to answer that the most beautiful things are trees. And maybe they are. Some of them truly are beautiful. I remember a pine on some hill hurtling by in a train window. It was tipped slightly backward, which was magnificent in view of its height, and it was lit up by the sunset, not completely, but only at the crown where the trunk had turned a ruddy hue, while its needle-covered branches remained a deep green. The trunk reached slantingly into the sky like a ladder. The needle-covered branches, a whole wreath of them, shone dark against the blue sky and seemed to move within it, describing a circle.

The pine hurtled past forever somewhere in Lithuania not far from Vilnius, which I saw all of a sudden from atop the hill. I've remembered that tree ever since. Most likely it's still standing there on that hill, still tipped backward . . .

The birch really is a very beautiful tree. Born in the south, I had always regarded it with suspicion, even scorn, thinking more of tedious literary birches than of actual ones.

Some birches are very tall and thick. The white trunk, the bright, translucent foliage. The black transverse slits in the bark look like steamboats, like axes, like figures in a diagram. Sitting in the foliage are siskins, themselves small and green and resembling leaves. Once a birch on a knoll gazed at me like a woman who had separated the edges of the kerchief surrounding her face . . .

I should write a book about parting with the world.

I very often go far away by myself. And yet my link to a certain station remains unbroken. Does that mean I live within myself? How could that be? Do I really carry a whole charge of life within me? Is there really a complete conductor in me? A complete storage battery? Is my "I" all there is of my life? That couldn't be. Obviously, with every step I've taken since entering the world, I've been governed by my external environment; obviously, the sun, which continually keeps me in power, which keeps me connected, both sets me in motion and is my eternal charging station.

In the form of a dully shining circle, it breaks through a diffuse yet nearly impenetrable layer of cloud. It just barely breaks through, but look, shadows are still visible on the stones. Though barely discernible, my own shadow is still visible on the sidewalk, as are the shadow of a gate and, the main thing, even the shadows of some spring catkins dangling from a tree.

What then is the sun? There is nothing in my human life that could have been managed without the participation of the sun, be that participation overt or hidden, actual or metaphoric. Whatever I have done, wherever I have gone, whether asleep, awake, or in darkness, whether as a young man or an old one, I have always been on the tip of a sunbeam.

Notes

INTRODUCTION

1. The following account is based on *No Day without a Line*, on Olesha's remarks in *Sovetskie pisateli: avtobiografii* 3 (Moscow, 1966), on such autobiographical stories and sketches as "Human Material" (Chelovecheskii material, 1929) and "I Look into the Past" (Ia smotriu v proshloe, 1929), on conversations in Moscow in 1975 with his widow, Olga Suok, and on archival material then in her possession but now in that of the Russian State Archive for Literature and the Arts. Bibliographical data are from the checklist published in *Russkie-Sovetskie pisateli: prozaiki* 3 (Leningrad, 1959–66) and from the current card catalogue of the Russian National Library in St. Petersburg.

2. See Nabokov's *Speak, Memory: An Autobiography Revisited* (New York, 1966).

3. See the notes to the present edition for further identification of these groups and figures.

4. The quotation is from the "Moscow" chapter of the present edition.

5. See Ovchinnikov's untitled contribution to *Vospominaniia o Iurii Oleshe*, ed. O. Suok-Olesha and E. Pel'son (Moscow, 1975), 43–55, for an account of this period in Olesha's career.

6. See V. Kataev, "Vstrechi s Bulgakovym," and I. Ovchinnikov, "V redaktsii *Gudka*," in *Vospominaniia o Mikhaile Bulgakove*, ed. E. S. Bulgakova and S. A. Liandres (Moscow, 1988), 123–27 and 131–44, for descriptions of the lively atmosphere of that environment and of Olesha's distinctive place within it.

7. As quoted by M. O. Chudakova in her *Masterstvo Iuriia Oleshi* (Moscow, 1972), 7. Olesha's appreciation of Bulgakov's humor seems to have been reciprocated, judging by the latter's journal entry of July 21, 1924: "All the same, Olesha's interesting to talk to. He's sarcastic, witty." See Mikhail Bulgakov, *Dnevnik. Pis'ma, 1914–40*, ed. V. I. Losev (Moscow, 1997).

8. The issues here are obviously complex, but it should be kept in mind that the 1930s, as Lydia Ginzburg observed in a sage essay, were, despite their ever more dangerous accompaniment of arrests, show trials, and purges, still for many people a time of residual idealist commitment and creative ferment. See her *Chelovek za pis'mennym stolom* (Moscow, 1989), 305–19.

9. Nils Åke Nilsson, "Through the Wrong End of the Binoculars," in *Soviet Russian Writers: Essays in Criticism*, ed. Edward J. Brown (New York and London, 1973), 262.

10. Yu. K. Olesha, *Izbrannoe* (Moscow, 1974), 219.

11. See Yury Olesha, *Ni dnia bez strochki* (Moscow, 1965), and *Izbrannoe*, ed. O. Suok-Olesha (Moscow, 1974), the first volume with a preface by Victor Shklovsky and the second with notes by V. Badikov.

12. One should make a distinction between the diarylike material accumulated in Olesha's notebooks since the 1920s and the texts prepared by him expressly for publication in *No Day without a Line*, even though neither Russian edition of the book follows this distinction in practice. Many of the unpublished notebook writings of the 1920s and 1930s contained in Olesha's archive are now finding their way into print (a fact that allows us to better judge the provenance and the interrelationships of the fragments included in the first editions of *No Day without a Line*), and one hopes that they will eventually be combined with the extant collections in a new expanded edition of the notebooks. For the most impressive selection of early archival material published thus far, see Yury Olesha, "'My dolzhny ostavit' mnozhestvo svidetel'stv . . .': Dnevniki," ed. Violetta Gudkova, *Znamia* 10 (October 1996): 155–81.

13. See Yury Olesha, *Izbrannye sochineniia* (Moscow, 1956).

14. The preceding discussion of the preparation of Olesha's drafts for *No Day without a Line* derives from conversations with Olga Suok and Mikhail Gromov in Moscow in 1975. Readers interested in a complementary (if tendentious) discussion of the matter should consult A. Belinkov, *Sdacha i gibel' sovetskogo intelligenta: Iurii Olesha* (Madrid, 1976).

15. As quoted by Victor Shklovsky in his preface to the first edition of the book: *Ni dnia bez strochki* (Moscow, 1965), 5.

16. Elizabeth K. Beaujour, *The Invisible Land: A Study of the Artistic Imagination of Iurii Olesha* (New York, 1970), 176. She is quoting Olesha himself here: *Na literaturnom postu* 4–5 (February–March 1929): 120.

17. Lydia Ginzburg, *On Psychological Prose*, trans. and ed. Judson Rosengrant (Princeton, N.J., 1991), 7.

18. See Yury Olesha, *No Day without a Line*, trans. and ed. Judson Rosengrant (Ann Arbor, 1979).

19. As the critic and dramatist and Olesha's friend Alexander Gladkov wisely remarked in an excellent essay on Olesha, "It seems to me that it

would be wrong to regard the composition of the first edition of [*No Day without a Line*] as canonical, as established for all time." See his *Pozdnie vechera: Vospominaniia, stat'i, zametki*, ed. V. V. Zabronina (Moscow, 1986), 192.

CHILDHOOD

1. The Latin proverb "nulla dies sine linea," of which the title of Olesha's book in Russian and English is a direct translation, seems to have been first mentioned in the *Historia naturalis* of the Elder Pliny (23–79 C.E.).

2. Elizaveta Tarakhovskaya (E. Ia. Parnokh, 1891–1968) was a poet and author of socialist realist children's fiction and the sister of the better-known poet and translator Sophia Parnok (1885–1933).

3. Olesha probably means Sir John Herschel (1792–1871) of the distinguished family of British astronomers.

4. Until its conversion to the "New Style" Gregorian calendar in 1918, Russia employed (as the Russian Orthodox Church still does) the "Old Style" Julian calendar, which lagged behind the Gregorian by twelve days in the nineteenth century and thirteen in the twentieth. The serfs were emancipated by Alexander II in 1861.

5. Here as elsewhere "gymnasium" *(gimnaziia)* denotes the classically oriented European secondary school that was first established in systematic fashion in Russia at the beginning of the nineteenth century and would become, with its rigorous eight-year curriculum, the most common form of pre-university instruction until the 1917 revolution. Such schools were the exclusive province of boys until 1870, when comparable institutions were established for girls.

6. Olesha means the "Christmas Tree" chapter in *A Lone Sail Gleams* (Beleet parus odinokii, 1936), an autobiographical novel by Valentin Kataev (1897–1960) about childhood in Odessa around the time of the failed 1905 Russian revolution; and "Waltz with a Tear" (Val's so slezoi, 1941), a verse apostrophe to the Christmas tree by Boris Pasternak (1890–1960).

7. *The Children of Captain Grant* was an adaptation of Jules Verne's geographical epic *Les Enfants du capitaine Grant* (1867–68).

8. The Moscow Art Theater, where Chekhov's plays were first performed, was founded in 1898. Nicholas II was crowned czar in 1894.

9. The Russo-Japanese War was fought in 1904–5.

10. Tsushima Strait was the site of the May 27, 1905 battle in which the Japanese navy destroyed the Russian fleet; Chemulpo was the landing point in Korea of the Japanese First Army in action against the Russians.

11. The British engineer Robert Whitehead (1823–1905) invented the modern torpedo in 1866, providing it with a servomotor in 1876 and a gyro-

scope in 1896, refinements that gave it both frightening speed and accuracy for the day.

12. Mukden was the capital of Manchuria and site of the final battle (February 19–March 10, 1905) in the Russo-Japanese War; Lyaoyan was a city in southeastern Manchuria and site of one of the greatest battles in the Russo-Japanese War.

13. Roman Kondratenko (1857–1904) was killed in action in the defense of Port Arthur (Lü Shun) in China.

14. Nikolaevsky Boulevard, since renamed Primorsky, runs parallel to the waterfront in central Odessa and is headed by a semicircular assemblage of buildings in Russian neoclassical style dating from 1826 to 1829.

15. The crew of the battleship *Potyomkin* mutinied in June in support of striking workers in Odessa, where some two thousand people were killed and three thousand injured in the ensuing civil violence that marked the city's involvement in the abortive 1905 revolution.

16. *The Grainfield* (Niva) was an illustrated family weekly published in St. Petersburg from 1870 until 1918 with annual supplements of the works of Russian and European authors. It presented Russian social and political life in a conventionally patriotic light.

17. Grigory Vakulenchuk (born 1877), a leader of the *Potyomkin* mutiny and a Bolshevik, was killed on June 14, 1905. The mutiny and subsequent removal of Vakulenchuk's body to the port are powerfully portrayed in Sergei Eisenstein's classic expressionist film *The Battleship Potyomkin* (Bronenosets Potemkin, 1925) with its famous Odessa stairway sequence and its revolutionary romantic vision of liberated sailors in dignified conflict with cartoon oppressors. The film may be a source of Olesha's own account (see his mention of it in the story "A Stadium in Odessa" [Stadion v Odesse, 1936]), just as it may have influenced his image of the gunners on the battleship's deck, although in the latter instance he has (if you consider that the gunners would actually have been inside one of the battleship's turrets) substituted his own southern sunshine for the cinematographer Eduard Tisse's much starker chiaroscuro.

18. General Nikolai Kaulbars (1842–1906) was the governor-general of Odessa and thus the person principally charged with maintaining public order. Olesha identifies him in "A Stadium in Odessa" as responsible for the shooting from Stroganovsky Bridge of civilians fleeing the burning port—another scene depicted in Eisenstein's film.

19. The German colonists were immigrants invited by the Russian government beginning in the last third of the eighteeenth century to establish communities in southern Russia mainly along the Volga but also, in the nineteenth century, in the areas north, east, and west of Odessa. Since such colonists tended to be politically conservative, their communities provided relatively safe havens from social disorder.

20. Manheim (or Mangeim), now called Kamenka, is a town northwest of Odessa.

21. Arcadia is a resort district notable for its spas and sanatoriums on the south central shore of Odessa.

22. Olesha probably has in mind Chekhov's "In Low Spirits" (Ne v dukhe, 1884).

23. The reference is to the palace-museum (1828–46) of Count Mikhail Vorontsov in the resort town of Alupka on the southern shore of the Crimean peninsula.

24. *Le Serment du Jeu de paume* (1790) by Jacques-Louis David (1748–1825) depicted the 1789 oath at Versailles of the deputies of the third estate to remain in session until they had given France a republican constitution.

25. Piast was the legendary tenth-century peasant founder of the first Polish state, while Bolesław Chrobry (the Brave, 996–1025) and Bołeslaw Krzywousty (the Wry, 1085–1138) were kings of the Piast dynasty.

26. Ivan Krylov (1769–1844) was a popular satirist whose verse fables and bestiaries were originally published in 1806–41.

27. The reference is to the German romantic poet, novelist, and author of fairy tales, Wilhelm Hauff (1802–27).

28. *The Leper* (Trędowata, 1911) was an enormously popular novel by Helena Mniszek (1878–1943) about a woman ostracized after an illicit love affair.

29. *On the Silver Sphere* (Na srebrnym globie: Rekopis z ksiezyca, 1909) was the first volume in a trilogy of science-fiction novels by the Polish modernist poet Jerzy Żuławski (1874–1915).

30. Alexander Kuprin (1870–1938) was a neorealist prose writer. His naturalistic story "Seasickness" (Morskaia bolezn', 1908) concerns the rape of a young woman of radical political sympathies during a voyage from Odessa to Yalta. Contemporary critics objected to the story's depiction, verging on "pornography," of the "physiology of love."

31. Alexander Suvorov (1729–1800) was the Russian military commander during the Russo-Turkish War of 1768–74 and the French Revolutionary Wars and eventually supreme commander of the Russian army; André Masséna (1758–1817) was a general during the Revolutionary Wars and one of Napoleon's first commanders; Jacques Macdonald (1765–1840) was a French army officer who later became one of Napoleon's marshals.

32. Kulikovo Field is a large square and parade ground in Odessa.

33. Lanzheron (or Langeron) is a beach district on the main shore of Odessa.

34. The reference is to *Acrobat on a Ball* (Acrobate à la boule, 1905) in the Pushkin Museum in Moscow, although Olesha misremembers: the wrestler's back is a fleshy beige; it is his trunks that are blue.

35. E. S. Glavche (1871–1919) was the chief of the Male Outpatients Department of the Odessa Municipal Hospital from 1902 until 1917 and the founder of the first Soviet venereological clinic.

ODESSA

1. The allusions are to "Combray," the opening section or overture of *Swann's Way* (La Coté de chez Swann), the first volume of Marcel Proust's *In Search of Lost Time* (or *Remembrance of Things Past;* A la recherche du temps perdu, 1913–27).

2. Richelieu Gymnasium was named for Armand Richelieu (1766–1822), French émigré governor (1805–14) of the territory surrounding and including Odessa and founder of Richelieu Lycée (1817–65), the ancestral institution of both the gymnasium and the present-day Odessa State University. (See note 5 in "Childhood.")

3. Paul I (1745–1801) reigned from 1796; Odessa, which, as the Crimean Tatar citadel of Khadzhi-Bei (or Kachibei), dates at least to the early fifteenth century, was ceded to Russia by the Turks after the Russo-Turkish War of 1787–92.

4. Verdun-sur-Meuse is a city near Reims in northeastern France and the site of one of the bloodiest battles of the First World War. Yaroslav the Wise (978–1054) was grand prince of Kievan Rus from 1019; his daughter Anna became the second wife of Henri I (1031–60).

5. Lev Tolstoy was born in 1828 and died November 7 (20), 1910. Nikolai Nekrasov (1821–78) was an important poet and editor whose verse was notable for its technical accomplishment and social engagement. Sevastopol, a naval base on the Crimean Peninsula, was the scene of a series of hard-fought battles during the Crimean War (1853–56). Tolstoy took part in the fighting there as an artillery officer, and his grimly realistic stories "Sevastopol in December" (1855), "Sevastopol in May" (1855), and "Sevastopol in August" (1856) did much to undermine the romantic conception of war.

6. Max Linder (Gabriel-Maximilian Levielle, 1883–1925) was an internationally popular French comedian and screen actor who scripted and directed his own films (1906–25).

7. Alexei Pleshcheev (1825–93) was a civic poet and member, along with Dostoevsky, of the radical Petrashevsky Circle; Ivan Dmitriev (1760–1837) was a neoclassical poet; Antiokh Kantemir (1708–44) was a precursor of Russian neoclassicism known for his satires in syllabic verse; Apollon Maikov (1821–97) was a post-romantic poet noted for his imagery.

8. The patriotic "Who is He?" (Kto on?) was published in 1841.

9. The Maly Theater, founded in Moscow in 1757 and the home of Alexander Ostrovsky and traditional Russian drama, was known for its emphatic acting style. (See note 47 in "The Golden Shelf.")

10. According to the Table of Ranks instituted by Peter I in 1722 and remaining in force in some fashion until the 1917 revolution, everyone above a certain level in the three branches of state service (military, civil, and judicial) was assigned a rank and wore insignia indicating one of fourteen degrees of responsibility and seniority. Akimovich's rank of state counselor was fairly high, comparable to colonel in the military. It should be noted that most of the gymnasium teachers and staff mentioned by name in the text—not only Akimovich, but also Mayakovsky, Pytlyasinksy, Whitman (or Vitman), and the later-described athlete Bogemsky—all are identified in the 1911 Odessa city directory as members of the Richelieu faculty. They are not invented.

11. The Czech Sokol (or Falcon) gymnastic societies were in fact formed in 1862.

12. The White Guards were the coalition of anti-Bolshevik forces that took part in the civil war following the revolution (1918–20).

13. Nikolai Samokish-Sudkovsky (1860–1944) was a painter noted for his battle scenes; Victor Vasnetsov (1848–1926) was a Slavophile painter and member of the so-called Itinerant Society (Peredvizhniki) who favored folklore themes, including a famous rendering of folklore "Warriors" (Bogatyri, 1898).

14. Mikhail Vrubel (1856–1910) was a painter noted for his many portraits and his visionary canvases on Russian and European literary themes. (See note 16.)

15. The reference is to the fairy-tale realm depicted in Rimsky-Korsakov's opera *The Snow Maiden* (Snegurochka, 1881), based on the eponymous 1873 play by Alexander Ostrovsky. (See note 47 in "The Golden Shelf.") King Berendei was thus an archetype of sentimental depictions of "Old Russia," whether in opera or the handicrafts of "folk" art.

16. Vrubel's *The Daydream Princess* (Printsessa Greza, 1896) is an immense decorative canvas inspired by Edmond Rostand's play *The Faraway Princess* (La Princesse lointaine, 1896) about the quest of twelfth-century troubadours for a perfect woman. It hangs in the Tretyakov Gallery in Moscow.

17. The Latvian Division was a Red Army unit consisting almost entirely of workers.

18. The reference is to Count Alexei Ignatiev (1877–1954), whose memoir of military life, *Fifty Years in the Service* (Piatdesiat' let v stroiu), was published in 1941–44.

19. The allusion is to Gustave Doré (1833–83), the prolific French painter and book illustrator, and to his splendidly lurid renderings of Old Testament scenes.

20. Olesha means the noblemen of republican inclination who fought against Napoleon after the French invasion of Russia in 1812 and who later carried out the failed December 1825 insurrection against the czar—figures

at once romantic, patriotic, and progressive. Borodino was the site near Moscow of the decisive defeat of Napoleon by General Kutuzov in 1812.

21. Jan Kubelík (1880–1940) was a Czech virtuoso and composer who performed internationally to great acclaim from 1898.

22. Mandelstam's memoir of childhood and youth, *The Noise of Time* (Shum vremeni), was published in 1925, although, along with the rest of his legacy, it was suppressed at the time Olesha was writing.

23. Olesha is alluding to the similarity of "Kubelík" and *kulebiaka,* a savory pastry, and to the fact that, for a Russian, the violinist's name appears to end in a diminutive suffix.

24. A. G. Arnold was the stage name of the circus director A. G. Barsky (1897–1969).

25. Bolshoy Fontan is a resort community in the Arcadia district of Odessa.

26. The Italian tenor Enrico Caruso (1873–1921) was the most famous opera singer of his day. Canio's aria is the bravura piece that concludes Act I of Leoncavallo's *Pagliacci* (1892).

27. Kuyalnitsky Estuary is a large, narrow inlet of the Black Sea extending some twenty-eight kilometers north of Odessa.

28. The reference is to the battle for the Bulgarian town of Shipka during the Russo-Turkish War of 1877–78.

29. Ivan Bunin (1870–1953), a major prose writer and poet who emigrated to the West after the 1917 revolution, received the Nobel Prize in 1933, the first Russian writer to be so honored.

30. Georgy Shengeli (1894–1956) was a poet, critic, translator, and verse theorist.

31. Olesha slightly misquotes Shengeli's poem "In the distance a meltingly topaz river . . ." (Vdali rasplavlenno-topazovaia reka . . .).

32. Igor Severyanin was the pseudonym of the ego-futurist poet and translator I. V. Lotaryov (1887–1941).

33. Valery Bryusov (1873–1924) was an influential symbolist poet and critic.

34. The line, from Shengeli's "Verses of Falk" (Stikhi Fal'ka), actually reads, "In the silence of confessionals" (V tishi ispovedalen).

35. The reference is to Severyanin's lyric "It Was by the Sea" (Eto bylo u moria, 1910) and contains an embedded quotation from the poem.

36. Alexander Kerensky (1881–1970) was the head of the Provisional Government that took power in Russia after the February 1917 revolution deposing Nicholas II and that retained it until the Bolshevik putsch the following November (or October in the Old Style).

37. Maximilian Voloshin (1877–1932) was a symbolist poet and watercolorist best known for his poems about the revolution. The lines are a slightly inaccurate quotation from "The Taking of the Bastille" (Vziatie Bastilii, 1917).

38. Nikolai Grigoriev (1894–1919) was a leader of anti-Bolshevik Cossack detachments in the Ukraine who temporarily joined forces with the Red Army in 1918, when his troops briefly occupied Odessa.

39. The quotation, with a slight variation, is from "Dmetrius-Imperator" (1917) about the so-called false Dmitry (1591–1613), a pretender to the Russian throne who claimed to be the heir apparent of Ivan IV, the Terrible. The poem suggests a parallel between the early-seventeenth-century events and those of 1917.

40. Raymond Poincaré (1860–1934), president of France from 1913 until 1920, was the French chief of state during the modest allied intervention against the Soviet regime in 1918. The failure of that intervention seems in fact to have had little effect on his government, which at the time was chiefly concerned with concluding the war against Germany.

41. Evno Azef (1869–1918), a figure of almost mythic reputation, was at once a Socialist Revolutionary terrorist and an employee of the political police.

42. Eduard Bagritsky (E. G. Dziubin, 1895–1934) was an Odessa poet associated in the 1920s with the Divide (Pereval) group of prose writers and poets and with the constructivists, an offshoot of futurism. He and Olesha were eventually married to sisters and remained close until Bagritsky's death from pulmonary disease.

43. The reference is to Gogol's romantic tale "Taras Bulba" (1835).

44. The Constituent Assembly, an elected parliamentary body convened for the first and last time on January 18, 1918, was chaired by the Socialist Revolutionary leader Victor Chernov (1873–1952). It was not supported by the Bolsheviks and was therefore forcibly dissolved by guards under the command of the anarchist sailor Anatoly Zheleznyakov (1895–1919). *The Bluebird of Happiness* (L'Oiseau bleu, 1909) is a play by Maurice Maeterlinck (1862–1949), the Belgian symbolist poet and Nobel Prize winner (1911).

45. General Anton Denikin (1872–1947) was one of the leaders of anti-Bolshevik White Guard forces during the civil war.

46. *The Road to Calvary* (Khozhdenie po mukam, 1921–40) by Alexei Tolstoy (1883–1945) is a trilogy about the 1917 revolution.

47. Olesha's fanciful simile seems to be an allusion to the painting *The Abduction of Europa* (Pokhishchenie Evropy, 1910) by Valentin Serov (1865–1911) in the Tretyakov Gallery.

48. The reference is to Gogol's fantastical tale "Viy" (1835).

49. Olesha's earliest publication, the poem "Clarimonda," appeared in 1915 in the Odessa newspaper *The Southern Herald* (Iuzhnyi vestnik).

50. The group Olesha appears to be referring to, the youthful membership of the Odessa literary circle the Green Lamp, would have included, besides Bagritsky and Olesha, such subsequently well-known writers and

poets as Valentin Kataev, his brother Evgeny Petrov (E. P. Kataev, 1903–42), Ilya Ilf (I. A. Fainzil'berg, 1897–1937), and Adalis (Adelina Efron, 1900–69).

51. The allusion is to the so-called Extraordinary Commission (Chrezvychainaia komissiia) for Combatting Counterrevolution and Sabotage (1917–22), precursor of the NKVD and KGB.

MOSCOW

1. Sukharev Tower, built by Peter I in 1692–1701 to honor a regiment that had supported his accession to the throne in 1689 and then to serve as the premises of his Mathematical and Navigational School, stood on Sukharev Square (or Kolkhoz Square during the Soviet period) until it was razed by the Moscow City Soviet in 1934 to improve traffic flow.

2. The NEP, or New Economic Policy, was introduced in March 1921 as a temporary measure for restoring the devastated Soviet economy after the civil war. It permitted a partial return to private enterprise.

3. The great German mathematician and philosopher Gottfried Leibniz advised Peter on a number of matters, including establishment of the first Russian academy of sciences.

4. The Red Gate (Krasnye vorota) was one of four triumphal arches built for the coronation in 1742 of Peter's daughter, the Empress Elizaveta Petrovna (1709–61). Originally made of wood, it was refashioned in masonry in 1753–57 and stood on Lermontov Square (or Red Gate Square) until it was pulled down in 1928 to ease traffic movement.

5. The *Whistle* (Gudok), the principal Soviet and now Russian transportation trade newspaper, has been published continuously in Moscow since 1917. Its staff in the 1920s included several writers who would emerge as the best of their generation: Mikhail Bulgakov and Olesha's fellow Odessans Ilya Ilf, Evgeny Petrov, and Valentin Kataev. Olesha began working for the paper in 1922, finally ending his relationship with it some ten years later.

6. "A Poem about a Captain in Love" (Poema o vliublennom kapitane) was published in the paper's December 15, 1922 issue.

7. The figures are from Mayakovsky's long poem *A Cloud in Pants* (Oblako v shtanakh, 1914–15).

8. The lines are from the poem "Theaters" (Teatry, 1913) and refer to the French lithographer and portraitist Eugène Carrière (1849–1906).

9. Vsevolod Meyerhold (1874–1940), the great experimental theater, opera, and film director, was responsible, until his torture and murder by the Soviet political police, for many brilliant productions of works by classic Russian authors and by contemporary Soviet writers, including plays by Mayakovsky and Olesha. The severe, socially engaged "nihilist" Bazarov is the main character of Turgenev's novel *Fathers and Sons* (1862), an adaptation of which was planned for 1929.

10. Mayakovsky made three movies in 1918 in which he played leading roles and for which he wrote the screenplays: the commissioned adaptations "Not Born for Money" (Ne dlia deneg rodivshiisia) and "The Young Lady and the Hoodlum" (Barishnia i khuligan), based respectively on Jack London's *Martin Eden* and Edmondo de Amicis' *Cuore,* and the original expressionist fantasy "In the Grip of the Movies" (Zakovannaia fil'moi), costarring Lilya Brik as a ballerina fascinated by the new art of cinema. A fourth movie, "The Pursuit of Glory" (Pogonia za slavoi, 1913), based on Mayakovsky's first screenplay, was produced without his participation.

11. *150,000,000* (1919) is a frankly propagandistic poem in parodied folk epic style celebrating the Russian "masses" (the title is a population figure) and depicting a simple folklore warrior in mock combat with the archcapitalist Woodrow Wilson.

12. Sergei Esenin (1895–1925), an enormously popular lyric poet of peasant origin and a notoriously bohemian mode of life who was allied with the imagists (or imaginists), hanged himself shortly after the breakup of his brief marriage to the American choreographer and dancer Isadora Duncan.

13. Fyodor Shalyapin (or Chaliapine, 1873–1938) was a celebrated Russian basso best known for his roles in French and Russian opera and for his song recitals.

14. "Brooklyn Bridge" (Bruklinskii most, 1925) is a paean to modern technology inspired by Mayakovsky's three-month visit to the United States and Mexico in 1925.

15. "A Comedy with a Murder" (Komediia s ubiistvom) apparently never got beyond the planning stages.

16. Mayakovsky was punning: the word for "beggar" in Russian is *nishchii,* very similar in pronunciation to the name of the German philosopher. The work in question was Olesha's projected but never finished autobiographical novel, fragments of the first chapter of which were published as "Notes of a Writer" (Zapiski pisatelia, 1930; reprinted as "In the World" [V mire]).

17. The allusions are to Pushkin's "The Bronze Horseman" (Mednyi vsadnik, 1833) and "The Feast of Peter the Great" (Pir Petra velikogo, 1836), and to Lermontov's "Alone I come out onto the road" (Vykhozhu odin ia na dorogu, 1841).

18. The allusions are to "A Person" (Chelovek, 1916–17) and "Brooklyn Bridge." (See note 14.)

19. The allusion is to Mayakovsky's "At the Top of My Voice" (Vo ves' golos, 1929–30).

20. Iosif Utkin (1903–44) was a poet primarily known for his verse describing the effect of the 1917 revolution on provincial Jewish life.

21. The metaphor is from "Unfinished" (Neokonchennoe, 1928–29).

22. Sir Austen Chamberlain (1863–1937), a member of Lloyd George's war cabinet and in the official Soviet view an enemy of the Soviet Union, seems to have been a favorite target of Mayakovsky's and appears in such poems of his as "On a World Scale" (V mirovom masshtabe), "Lev Tolstoy and Vanya Dyldin," and "Christmas Greetings" (Rozhdestvenskie pozhelaniia), all published in 1926.

23. Mayakovsky lived in a *ménage à trois* with the formalist critic Osip Brik (1888–1945) and his wife Lilya (1891–1978) from 1915 until his suicide in 1930. (See note 10.)

24. Ivan Slonov (1882–1945) was a distinguished Russian actor, director, and pedagogue.

25. The exchange is between Polonious and Hamlet: Act II, Scene ii.

26. Ilya Ilf, a close friend of Olesha's from his youth (see note 50 in "Odessa"), was the coauthor with Evgeny Petrov of the classic comic novels *The Twelve Chairs* (Dvenadtsat' stul'ev, 1928) and *The Golden Calf* (Zolotoi telenok, 1931), as well as the travel memoir *One-storied America* (Odnoetazhnaia Amerika, 1936), describing their six-month car trip across the United States in 1935–36.

27. "The Black Man" (Chernyi chelovek), a longish meditation on melancholia and alcoholism, was published in 1925.

28. "The Iron Mirgorod" (Zheleznyi Mirgorod, a title adapted from that of Gogol's 1835 collection of tales and alluding thereby to New York's essential provinciality) was published in *Izvestiia* in 1923 in the August 22 and September 16 issues.

29. Anatoly Marienhof (or Mariengof, 1897–1962) was a novelist, poet, and dramatist. His memoiristic *Novel without Falsehood* (Roman bez vran'ia, 1926) is about Esenin and the imagist school, of which Marienhof was a principal theoretician.

30. Anna Nikritina (1900–1982), Marienhof's wife, played the principal role of Suok in the 1930 Leningrad Bolshoy Drama Theater production of Olesha's adaptation of his popular fantasy novel for children, *The Three Fat Men* (Tri tolstiaka, 1928).

31. The Cuban grandmaster José Capablanca (1888–1942) was world chess champion from 1921 until his 1927 defeat by the Russian-French grandmaster Alexandre Alekhine (1892–1946).

32. The lines are from Mandelstam's "Europe" (Evropa, 1914). Mandelstam speaks of the above-mentioned fur coat in his essay "The Fur Coat" (Shuba, 1922).

33. Akhmatova (1889–1966) was in fact born in Bolshoy Fontan, now part of Odessa.

34. Natan Altman (1899–1970), a Russian painter influenced by cubism, executed his famous portrait of Akhmatova in 1915.

35. The lines are from "Half-turned, O sadness . . ." (Vpoloborota, o pechal' . . . , 1914).

36. The reference is to words spoken by Malcolm (Act IV, Scene iii), although Olesha is quoting from Akhmatova's version of the play, or at least from his memory of their conversation.

37. Konstantin Stanislavsky (1863–1938), the great director of Chekhov and progenitor of "method" acting, founded the Moscow Art Theater in 1898 with the director and actor Vladimir Nemirovich-Danchenko (1858–1943).

38. Olesha's own adaptation of *The Three Fat Men* was produced by Stanislavky in 1930.

39. Boris Erdman (1899–1960), the brother of the dramatist and screenwriter Nikolai Erdman (1902–70), was a theatrical designer long associated with the Moscow Art Theater who designed their 1930 production of *The Three Fat Men.* Mikhail Bulgakov, best known for his brilliant *Master and Margarita* (1929–40), was associated with the Moscow Art Theater as a resident playwright from 1925 until 1936.

40. Klavdia Elanskaya (1898–1972) was a distinguished actress and a permanent member of the Moscow Art Theater from 1924.

41. Olesha's only original play, *The List of Assets* (Spisok blagodeianii), was first staged by Meyerhold in his theater in 1931.

42. The reference is to the Icelandic novelist and dramatist Halldór Laxness (H. K. Gudjónsson, 1902–98), who received the Nobel Prize in 1955. Feilan Ó. Feilan is the main character in his play *The Silver Moon* (Silfurtúnglid, 1954), which Olesha helped adapt for the Russian stage as *The Sold Lullaby* (Prodannaia kolybel'naia, translated by V. Morozova, 1955).

43. The phrase may be found in Part 2, Chapter 9, of Olesha's brilliant short novel *Envy* (Zavist', 1927), generally regarded as his masterwork. Olesha passed the Second World War in Central Asia in Ashkhabad in what is now Turkmenistan.

44. *The Conspiracy of Feelings* (Zagovor chuvst), Olesha's stage adaptation of *Envy,* was produced at the Vakhtangov Theater in 1929.

45. A. P. Sergeenko (1886–1961) was the author of *Stories about L. N. Tolstoy: From Memories* (Rasskazy o L. N. Tolstom: iz vospominanii; in serial publication from 1911, first separate edition, 1978). V. G. Chertkov (1854–1936) was a friend, confidant, and associate of Tolstoy and the editor of his complete collected works.

46. Yasnaya Polyana is the name of Tolstoy's working estate (now a museum) south of Moscow near the city of Tula.

47. The reference is to *Kabale und Liebe* (1783) by Friedrich Schiller (1759–1805).

48. The legend of Kitezh (or Kitej), celebrated in Rimsky-Korsakov's opera "The Tale of the Invisible City of Kitezh and the Maiden Fevronia" (1907), concerns a city said to have descended to the bottom of a lake during the first Mongol invasion of Kievan Rus in the thirteenth century. Kitezh is thus a symbol of the integrity and indomitability of Russian culture.

49. The allusion is to Heine's *Elemental Spirits* (Elementargeister, 1835–37). A literal rendering of *krasnoludki* would be "beautiful little folk."

50. The reference is to Olesha's stepson, who committed suicide as an adolescent in 1939. Sergei Merkurov (1881–1952) was a Russian sculptor famous for his monumental statues of Soviet leaders.

51. Andrei Bely (B. N. Bugaev, 1880–1934) was a leading symbolist poet, novelist, critic, and verse theorist; his influential novel *Petersburg* (Peterburg, 1916) is considered by many to be a masterpiece of Russian modernism.

52. Mikhail Zoshchenko (1895–1958), a prose writer associated with the antidoctrinaire Serapion Brothers in the 1920s who is best known for his extraordinary comic stories, develops many of the views and theories attributed to him by Olesha in his *Youth Restored* (Vozvrashchennaia molodost', 1933).

53. The catastrophe was the notorious 1946 "Decree" of the Central Committee of the Communist Party "On the magazines *Star* [Zvezda] and *Leningrad*," which singled out the "ideologically harmful" poetry and prose of Akhmatova and Zoshchenko for abuse, stigmatizing their work as pernicious and "alien to Soviet literature." As a consequence, both writers were immediately removed from positions of influence and authority (Zoshchenko had been a member of the editorial board of *Star*, for example), ostracized, rendered unpublishable, and therefore effectively silenced until well after Stalin's death in 1953.

54. Alexander Fadeev (A. A. Bulyga, 1901–56), a socialist-realist novelist best known for his *Young Guard* (Molodaia gvardiia, 1945), was a powerful literary politician and functionary, most notably as a leader of the Russian Association of Proletarian Writers (1928–32) and then as the chairman of the Soviet Writers' Union (1946–54). Evidently tormented by his role in the betrayal and persecution of other writers during his tenure as chairman of the Writers' Union and concerned that the Twentieth Party Congress's repudiation of Stalinism in 1956 would lead to his own public humiliation, he shot himself.

55. Olesha seems to mean Rembrandt, though he appears to have confused Rembrandt's *Danaë* (1636) with one of Titian's renderings, which, unlike Rembrandt's, does depict a shower of gold coins.

56. The great *Journal* of the romantic painter Eugène Delacroix (1798–1863), kept from 1822 until his death, was published in 1893–95. Olesha has in mind the entry for May 18, 1850.

57. Catherine II (1729–96), czarina from 1762 and an enthusiastic patron of literature and the arts, gave sustained material support to the work of the Encyclopedist Denis Diderot (1713–84), whose library she eventually purchased and who briefly resided in St. Petersburg at her invitation (1773–74).

58. The figure may be found in Pasternak's long poem "The Year 1905" (Deviat'sot piatyi god, 1925–27).

59. The comparison is made in Book VI of the *Odyssey*, although it in fact pertains to the transformation of Odysseus himself by Nausicaa and her maids.

60. Nikolai Morozov (1854–1946), revolutionary activist, populist scholar, and author of works on the history of religion and culture, as well as on chemistry, physics, astronomy, and mathematics, was incarcerated in Schlüsselburg Fortress on Lake Ladoga near St. Petersburg from 1882 until 1905 for his role in the assassination of Alexander II. Prince Dmitry Mirsky (D. S. Sviatopolk-Mirsky, 1890–1939) was a brilliant literary historian and critic whose classic English-language *History of Russian Literature* (1926) remains unsurpassed in any language. He left for London in 1921 following the civil war but returned to the Soviet Union in 1932. He was briefly arrested in 1935 after an article critical of a novel by Alexander Fadeev (see note 54) and then arrested again in 1937. He perished in the Gulag.

61. The allusion is to Mayakovsky's piece on "Mexico" in his collection of travel essays, *My Discovery of America* (Moe otkrytie Ameriki, 1926).

62. The first reference is to Benjamin Franklin's *Autobiography*, although, perhaps because of an error in the Russian translation, Olesha actually misrepresents Franklin's tone and intent. The expression *ça ira* was the oft-repeated refrain of a song that by virtue of its immense popularity effectively became the anthem of the French Revolution.

63. Paul Barras (1755–1829) was a prominent Jacobin and Convention member and a leader of the 1794 coup d'état that deposed Robespierre.

64. Evgeny Tarle (1875–1955), a prolific historian and member of the Soviet Academy of Sciences, early authored such works as *The Working Class in France in the Revolutionary Era* (Rabochii klass vo Frantsii v epokhu revoliutsii, 1909) but soon concentrated on the revolution itself. He eventually received several Stalin prizes in recognition of his efforts.

65. Adolphe Thiers (1797–1877), François-Auguste Mignet (1796–1884), and Louis Blanc (1811–82) were historians of liberal and, in the case of Blanc, socialist orientation.

66. Jean-Baptiste Kléber (1753–1800) joined the French National Guard in 1789 and distinguished himself in the Revolutionary Wars. In 1798 he accompanied Napoleon to Egypt, where, after leading a successful campaign against the Turks, he was killed by a Turkish fanatic.

67. See *Napoleon: His Court and Family* (Memoires de Madame la duchesse d'Abrantes; ou souvenirs historiques sur Napoléon, 1831) by Laure Junot, duchesse d'Abrantes (1784–1838).

68. See Stendhal's *Life of Napoleon* (Vie de Napoléon, 1876).

69. See *Napoléon* (1912) by the philosopher, critic, and historian Taine (1828–93).

70. The Italian neoclassical sculptor Antonio Canova (1757–1822) produced his bust of Napoleon from life in 1802.

71. Johann Gottfried von Herder (1744–1803) was, of course, not only a poet but also a philosopher, critic, and theologian who was early acquainted with Goethe and who exerted a strong influence on the subsquent romantic movement.

72. The czarist minister and diplomat Count Sergei Witte (1849–1915) published his *Memoirs* (Vospominaniia) in 1911. Alexander III (1845–94) was czar from 1881, while Wilhelm II (1859–1941) was emperor of Germany and king of Prussia from 1888 until 1918.

73. Vasily Shkvarkin (1894–1967) was a Russian dramatist best known for his historical plays and comedies. The term *Zuck* (or *tsuk* in Russian) is of German derivation and literally means a "yank" or "pull," as of (metaphorical) reins.

74. The reference is to Michelangelo's marble of David (1501–4), originally placed in front of the Palazzo Vecchio on the Piazza della Signoria in Florence.

75. Conte Giovanni Pico della Mirandola (1463–94), the Italian neoplatonic philosopher and humanist noted for his attempt to reconcile Christianity and Greek philosophy, was a resident of Florence and for many people of his age an epitome of the Renaissance man.

76. The reference is to the Polish Catholic canon and astronomer Nicolaus Copernicus (Mikolaj Kópernik, 1473–1543).

77. Girolamo Savonarola (1452–98), the Italian religious reformer and a member of the Dominican order, ruled Florence from 1494 until he was excommunicated in 1497. That rule was ruthless in its call for a regeneration of spiritual and moral values and its devotion to asceticism. Sandro Botticelli (1444–1510), perhaps best known for his scallop-shell "Birth of Venus" (c. 1480), was a Florentine painter of neoplatonic sympathies who produced many other mythological and religious pictures remarkable for their delicacy of color and line.

78. Johannes Kepler (1571–1630), the German astronomer and mathematician and precursor of celestial mechanics, published his *Commentaries on the Motions of Mars* in 1609 and his *Harmony of the Worlds* in 1619, the two works in which he first enunciated his three laws of planetary motion.

79. Albrecht von Wallenstein (1583–1634) was an imperial general in the Thirty Years' War and later a military commander in service to the Holy Roman Emperor, Ferdinand II.

80. *Eureka: A Prose Poem,* Poe's speculative investigation of "the material and spiritual universe," was published in 1848.

THE GOLDEN SHELF

1. See Percy Bysshe Shelley, "Notes on Sculptures in Rome and Florence" (1819).

2. The reference is to *War and Peace,* Book Twelve.

3. The reference is to the *Paradiso,* Canto 17.

4. The references are to the *Inferno,* Cantos 8 and 18, respectively.

5. The preceding is a rather loose rendering of the *Inferno,* Canto 21.

6. The reference is to the *Purgatorio,* Canto 10, although Olesha errs in certain details: Dante's scene concerns the Emperor Trajan, not Titus Flavius, and the bas-relief depicts an act of humility rather than mercy.

7. The reference is to the *Purgatorio,* Canto 2.

8. The description is a conflation of Cantos 29 and 31 of the *Purgatorio.*

9. The description of Limbo and its inhabitants is in the *Inferno,* Canto 4.

10. Mikhail Lozinsky (1886–1955), the great poet-translator not only of Dante and Shakespeare but also of Cervantes, Molière, Corneille, and Goethe, published his version of *La divina commedia* in 1939–45—the "great feat of his life," as his fellow acmeist Anna Akhmatova put it.

11. Olesha presumably means Wilde's self-justifying *De Profundis* (1905).

12. Wilde discusses Dante in Part II of his dialogue "The Critic as Artist" (1891).

13. Boris Livanov (1904–92) was a Russian stage and screen actor who was associated with the Moscow Art Theater from 1924. He played one of the three fat men in the 1930 Moscow Art Theater production of Olesha's adaptation of his eponymous tale.

14. Mikhailo Lomonosov (1711–65), the great polymath and inspirer of Russian neoclassical culture, was a scientist, poet, literary theorist, artist, and historian.

15. The reference is to Pierre Corneille's tragedy *Le Cid* (1637).

16. The allusion is to Chaplin's film *Monsieur Verdoux* (1947), the screenplay of which was translated into Russian in 1948.

17. Sergei Gerasimov (1906–85) was a director, producer, playwright, and cinema theorist who was perhaps best known for his film versions of Fadeev's *The Young Guard* (produced in 1948) and Sholokhov's *The Quiet Don* (produced in 1957–58). (See note 54 in "Moscow" and note 17 in "The Extraordinary Intersection.")

18. The quotation is from "Of Idleness" (De l'Oisiveté, 1572–74). The translation is by Donald M. Frame: *The Complete Essays of Montaigne* (1958).

19. The St. Bartholemew's Day Massacre denotes the systematic assassination of French Protestants by Counter-Reformation factions on August 24, 1572.

20. Ioann (or Ivan) IV, the Terrible (1530–84), was czar from 1547, while Boris Godunov (1552–1605) ruled from 1598. Both reigns were marked by unusual brutality.

21. Lamoral, Count of Egmont (1522–68), a Flemish nobleman and knight of the Golden Fleece, was beheaded in Brussels after protesting the persecution of Protestants in the Low Countries.

22. The citations may be found in "Our feelings reach out beyond us" (Nos affections s'emportent au dela de nous, 1572–74).

23. The lines are from "We now move off a little . . ." (My teper' ukhodim ponemnogu . . . , 1924).

24. The reference is to the essay "Of Cato the Younger" (Du Jeune Caton, 1572–74), although Olesha is slightly in error: there are five Latin poets in Montaigne's competition.

25. The line is from "Europe." (See note 32 in "Moscow.")

26. It was in fact Xerxes who "wrote a challenge to Mount Athos." See "How the soul discharges its passions" (Comme l'âme descharge ses passions, 1572–74).

27. The discussion concerns Goethe's epistolary novel *The Sorrows of Young Werther* (Die Leiden des jungen Werthers, 1774). The last line is an inexact quotation from Pasternak's poem "The trembling piano will lick the foam from its lips . . ." (Roial' drozhashchii penu s gub oblizhet . . . , 1918) in his cycle "The Rupture" (Razryv).

28. The writer, journalist, publisher, and memoirist Alexander Herzen (1812–70) lived in London between 1852 and 1864, establishing his influential émigré press there.

29. Sofia Andreevna Behrs (or Bers, 1844–1919) was Tolstoy's wife.

30. The reference is to "Gogol in Rome in the Summer of 1841" (N. V. Gogol' v Rime letom 1841 goda, 1857) by Pavel Annenkov (1812–87).

31. Sergei Aksakov (1791–1859) was a theater critic and memoirist best known for his fictionalized family and autobiographical narratives, *A Family Chronicle* (Semeinaia khronika, 1856) and *The Childhood Years of the Bagrov Grandson* (Detskie gody Bagrova-vnuka, 1856). His sons, Konstantin (1817–60) and Ivan (1823–86), were Slavophile journalists.

32. Herzen worked on his vast historical memoir *My Past and Thoughts* (Byloe i dumy) from 1852 until 1868. It is an acknowledged and well-studied masterpiece of Russian prose.

33. The scene occurs in *War and Peace,* Book 4.

34. Prince Alexander Shakhovskoy (1777–1846), a prolific playwright best known for his verse comedies, describes Napoleon's 1812 occupation of Moscow in his *Moscow and Paris in the Years 1812 and 1814* (Moskva i Parizh v 1812 i 1814 godakh, 1830).

35. Nikolai Chernyshevsky (1828–89) was a radical journalist, political thinker, literary critic, novelist, and revolutionary who is best remembered today for his influential novel *What Is to Be Done?* (Chto delat'?, 1863).

36. Olesha would seem to have in mind Tolstoy's "The Raid" (Nabeg, 1853), although the image itself is more a matter of his own vivid imaginative response than of Tolstoy's actual description.

37. "The Living Relic" (Zhivye moshchi, 1873) was included in the final version of Turgenev's great story cycle *A Sportsman's Sketches* (Zapiski okhotnika, 1847–74).

38. The lines are from Scene 3 of "The Stone Guest" (Kamennyi gost', 1830).

39. The reference is to Lermontov. (See note 17 in "Moscow.")

40. Karl Bryullov (1799–1852), Pushkin's coeval, was a Russian neoclassical painter whose work was marked by emergent realistic and psychological features.

41. The reference is to the great symbolist poet Alexander Blok (1880–1921).

42. The line is from "Whether I walk along noisy streets" (Brozhu li ia vdol' ulits shumnykh, 1829): "I pust' u grobovogo vkhoda."

43. The lines occur in "Fragments of Onegin's Journey" (Otryvki iz puteshestviia Onegina, 1825–30). Olesha's analysis is based on the pervasive voiceless-voiced opposition of the sounds [f] and [v]. *Orphé* (or *Orfé*) thus corresponds to *orvé,* which read backward produces the element *evro* in the Russian word for Europe: *Evropa.*

44. The academic sculptor Ivan Vitali (1794–1855) executed his bust of Nicholas I in 1855. Mikhail Glinka (1804–57), the acknowledged founder of Russian classical music, is perhaps best known for his operas *A Life for the Czar* (Ivan Susanin, 1836) and *Ruslan and Ludmila* (1842), the first based on a play by Alexander Shakhovskoy (see note 34) and the second on a narrative poem by Pushkin.

45. The lines belong to the lyric "I would repeat: 'When I shall . . .'" (Ia povtorial: 'Kogda ia budu . . . ,' 1864) by the lyric poet Afanasy Fet (A. A. Shenshin, 1829–92).

46. Olesha means the 1882 portrait of Fet by Ilya Repin (1844–1930) in the Tretyakov Gallery.

47. Alexander Ostrovsky (1823–86), perhaps the finest Russian playwright of the nineteenth century, is best remembered today for *The Storm* (Groza, 1860). *The Last Victim* (Posledniaia zhertva) was written in 1878.

48. Ivan Goncharov (1812–91), best known for the realist classic *Oblomov* (1859), published his first novel, *A Common Story* (Obyknovennaia istoriia), in 1847 and the travel memoir *The Frigate Pallada* (Fregat "Pallada") in 1855–57. The emergence of modern Russian prose is sometimes dated from the publications of Gogol and the natural school in the 1840s.

49. Olesha means the *Memoirs* (Vospominania, 1889) of Avdotya Panaeva (A. V. Golovacheva, 1820–93), a writer and the wife first of Ivan Panaev, then of Nekrasov. (See note 52.)

50. The jurist Anatoly Koni (1844–1927) speaks of Turgenev in his collection of memoirs *On Life's Path* (Na zhiznennom puti, 1912–29).

51. Nikolai Dobrolyubov (1836–61) was a radical journalist, publicist, and literary critic.

52. Ivan Panaev (1812–62) was a writer and, from 1847 to 1851, coeditor with Nekrasov of the literary journal *The Contemporary* (Sovremennik). His *Literary Memoirs* (Literaturnye vospominaniia) was published posthumously in 1888.

53. Alexander Mikhailov (Alexander Sheller, 1838–1900) was a magazine editor, poet, translator, and prolific if minor novelist.

54. The distinguished actress and director Aleksandra Remizova (1905–89) staged Olesha's adaptation of *The Idiot* in 1957, although his initial work on the project was actually done in the fall and winter of 1955–56.

55. Emmanuil Kazakevich (1913–62), a Russian novelist and short story writer whose first efforts in the 1920s were in Yiddish, was a friend of Olesha's and the owner of a particularly fine library. He won the Stalin Prize in 1950 for *Spring on the Oder* (Vesna na Odere, 1949).

56. Princess V. D. Obolenskaya wrote to Dostoevsky in December 6, 1871, regarding her adaptation of the novel, and he replied on January 20, 1872, conveying his gallant response to her praise and granting her permission to proceed. He expressed doubt, however, about the feasibility of the project, given that the novel's "epic form will never find a corresponding dramatic one," a view that proved well founded, since the adaptation was never completed.

57. Nikolai Vilyam-Vilmont (Nikolai Vilmont, 1901–86) was a Russian literary historian, critic, and translator specializing in German literature.

58. Nikolai Akimov (1901–68) was a director and theatrical designer.

59. The reference is to Gogol's fantastical Petersburg tale "Nevskii prospekt" (1835).

60. Antonio Pigafetta (ca. 1480–ca. 1534) was the author *Magellan's Voyage around the World* (Primo viaggio intorno al globo terracqueo, 1555), regarding the 1519–22 expedition.

61. Though largely accurate, Olesha's account, presumably by way of sharpening his essential point, still confuses a few particulars and the actual sequence of events in Twain's novel.

62. The Gun Club figures in Jules Verne's *From the Earth to the Moon* (De la Terre à la lune, 1864).

63. The prominent actors Victor (1879–1939) and Marius Petipa (1850–1919) were sons of the celebrated French-Russian dancer and choreographer Marius Petipa (1818–1910).

64. Tatyana Shchepkina-Kupernik (1874–1952) is known for her translations of such plays by Edmond Rostand (1868–1918) as *The Eaglet* (L'Aiglon, 1900), *Cyrano de Bergerac* (1897), and *The Faraway Princess,* as well as for versions of the comedies of Molière and Shakespeare. (See note 16 in "Odessa.")

65. Olesha's juvenile comedy in verse has not survived.

66. See *Macbeth,* Act III, Scene iv.

67. Tolstoy's discussion of Shakespeare may be found in his sometimes perverse *What Is Art?* (Chto takoe iskusstvo, 1898).

68. The reference is to E. T. A. Hoffmann's tale "The Golden Pot" (Der goldene Topf, 1814).

69. "Hoffmann" (Gofman), Herzen's debut piece, was published in 1836.

70. The allusion is to Hoffmann's "Ritter Gluck" (1809), although Olesha misremembers. The opera the composer listens to is not *Iphigénie en Aulide* but *Iphigénie en Tauride.*

71. The story is, of course, "The Black Cat," although Olesha mistakes some of the particulars and, as is his habit, supplies a few details of his own. Dostoevsky published translations of "The Black Cat" (1843), "The Tell-Tale Heart" (1843), and "The Devil in the Belfry" (1839) in the first issue of his literary journal *Time* (Vremia, 1860), with a preface in which he compared Poe and Hoffmann.

72. The text concerns Chapter 14, "The Giddy Bridge," of H. G. Wells's 1901 science fiction classic. Olesha (or perhaps Wells's Russian translator) errs in a detail: Cavor and Bedford use the chains they have been bound with to attack the Selenites; there is nothing on the ground.

73. H. G. Wells met with Lenin in Petrograd in 1920 and then, fourteen years later, with Stalin in Moscow.

74. The movie version of *The Invisible Man,* starring Claude Rains, was produced in 1933 with a screenplay by the playwright R. C. Sherriff. Because of a misunderstanding of the English term "navvy" in the Russian translation of the tale in Olesha's personal library, his own text has the Invisible Man felled by "sailors" on a beach.

75. Olesha means Lev Tolstoy and his early story "Notes of a Billiard Marker" (Zapiski markera, 1853–55). *The Circle of Reading* (Krug chteniia, 1906–7) was a publication made up of excerpts from Tolstoy's own works and those of other writers. Its purpose was the dissemination of his moral and religious philosophy.

76. Captain Nemo is prominent in Verne's *Twenty Thousand Leagues under the Sea* (Vingt mille lieues sou les mers, 1869), while Paganel and Ayrton appear in *The Children of Captain Grant.* (See note 7 in "Childhood" and note 62, this chapter.)

77. Lev Nikulin (1891–1967) was a poet, journalist, novelist, biographer, memoirist, and playwright. His historical novel *True Sons of Russia* (Rossii vernye syny, 1950) received the Stalin prize in 1952.

78. Honoré-Gabriel Mirabeau (1749–91), the great revolutionary statesman and orator, is perhaps best known as a writer for his almost day-to-day account of the revolution, *Letters from Count Mirabeau to His Electors* (Lettres du compte Mirabeau à ses commettants, 1789). He was a man of repellent ugliness, with a swollen face scarred from smallpox.

79. Olesha probably means Chaplin's film *A King in New York* (1957). The mentioned Picasso exhibit took place in Moscow in the fall of 1956.

80. Werner Krauss and Conrad Veidt costarred in Robert Weine's classic *The Cabinet of Dr. Caligari* (1919). Veidt went on to featured roles in Hollywood, most notably in *The Thief of Baghdad* (1940) and *Casablanca* (1942). Mary Pickford (Gladys Smith, 1893–1979) was a leading silent film star of Canadian origin. The Talmadge sisters, Constance (1898–1973) and Norma (1893/7–1957), were American silent film stars.

81. The story, actually a translation from the French, was published in 1910 in the fourth issue of *The World of Adventures* (Mir prikliuchenii) as "A Journey in Time" (Puteshestvie vo vremeni).

82. Alexander Grin (Alexander Grinevskii, 1880–1932) was a writer of romantic adventure fiction. The story in question is "The Vanished Sun" (Propavshee solntse, 1923).

83. Yuly Aikhenvald (or Eichenwald, 1872–1928), the author of *Silhouettes of Russian Writers* (Siluety russkikh pisatelei, 4th ed., 1923–29), was a sensitive and skillful impressionist critic who believed criticism should concern itself with purely aesthetic matters, in contrast to the emphasis on social utility that had been characteristic of most nineteenth-century Russian criticism since Belinsky. He was forced to emigrate in 1922.

84. *The Shining World* (Blistaiushchii mir) was actually published in *The Red Grainfield* (Krasnaia niva) in 1923.

85. The story is "Fire and Water" (Ogon' i voda, 1916).

86. The plays in question are *The Blind* (Les Aveugles, 1890) and probably *The Intruder* (L'Intruse, 1890). (See note 44 in "Odessa.")

87. See Konstantin Stanislavsky's memoir "Visiting Maeterlinck" in his *My Life in Art* (Moia zhizn' v iskusstve, 1928).

88. Franz Werfel (1890–1945), the Austrian novelist and poet, is considered the founder of Austrian expressionism; Leo Perutz (1884–1957) was a German novelist and dramatist born in Prague whose writings are characterized by a strong sense of the fantastic; Gustav Meyrink (1868–1932) was an Austrian writer with a fondness for fantasy and the grotesque.

89. The actress Vera Komissarzhevskaya (1864–1910) was celebrated for her roles in contemporary drama, especially the plays of Ibsen and Chekhov. She established her own theater in 1904.

90. The story in question is "Tonio Kröger" (1903).

91. George Bernard Shaw did visit Moscow in 1931, although Olesha (unless the passage is taken as a kind of visionary coda) is wrong about Mayakovsky's presence at the banquet, since the poet had committed suicide in 1930.

92. The science fiction and fantasy writer Karel Čapek (1890–1938) is probably best known for his play *R.U.R.* (1920), the source of the English word "robot."

93. Alexei Tolstoy published *Revolt of the Machines* (Bunt mashin) in 1924.

94. *War with the Salamanders* (or *War with the Newts*) was published in 1936.

95. Hemingway's *Selected Works* (Izbrannye sochineniia) was published in 1959.

96. The episode is from Hemingway's story "A Natural History of the Dead" (1938).

97. Jarosław Iwaszkiewicz (1894–1980) was a poet, novelist, and translator.

98. The figures may all be found in *Dead Souls* (1842).

99. The work in question is Bunin's "Night" (Noch', 17 September 1925).

100. The reference is to Bunin's classic tales *The Village* (Derevnia, 1910) and *Dry Valley* (Sukhodol, 1911).

101. The allusion is to the view of progress attributed to Chekhov by Kuprin in his short essay "In Memory of Chekhov" (Pamiati Chekhova, 1905), although Chekhov, according to Kuprin, thought the transformation of society would actually take three to four hundred years.

102. The references are to "Gospodin iz San-Frantsisko" (1915), "Lirnik Rodion" (1913), and "Zakhar Vorob'ev" (1912), respectively.

103. "The World of Art" was an avant-garde association formed in St. Petersburg in the 1890s for the propagation of modernist aesthetic views in all fields of art. It published a highly influential journal called *The World of Art* (Mir iskusstva, 1899–1904) edited by Sergei Diagilev and Alexander Benois that, in addition to articles on religious and philosophical themes, printed the works of symbolist writers.

104. "The Mire" (Tina) was published in 1886.

105. There are two paintings by Leonardo in the Hermitage Museum in St. Petersburg: the *Benois Madonna* (Madonna del fiore, 1478) and the *Madonna Litta* (c. 1490), the latter at one time of questioned authenticity but now accepted as his. It is the second work that Olesha appears to have in mind, although neither picture is in fact in an altar.

106. Olesha is describing the *Sistine Madonna* (1513), which is alluded to in Pushkin's love lyric "Her Eyes" (Ee glaza, 1828), the source of the quoted line. Olesha's assumption that the painting is called "Sistine" in reference to the chapel is actually incorrect; the picture in fact hangs in Dresden and its name derives from the presence in the composition of a portrait of Pope St. Sixtus II (Sisto II in Italian).

107. Olesha appears to have in mind the many views of Venice by Canaletto (1697–1768), but most notably his *Grand Canal toward the Rialto Bridge* (Il canal grande, presso il ponto di Rialto, c. 1723).

108. Olesha presumably means Poe's "The Assignation" (1834).

109. The references are to the Venetian masters Titian (1490–1576) and Giorgione (1478–1510) and to Titian's *Flora* (ca. 1520–22) and *Leda and the Swan* (ca. 1505–10), the latter attributed to Titian but perhaps produced by a third painter influenced by Giorgione.

110. The great neoclassical sculptor Fyodor Shubin (1740–1805) executed his bust of Catherine in 1789–90. It is in fact in the Russian Museum in St. Petersburg.

111. Vincent Van Gogh (1853–90) discusses *The Night Cafe* (1888) and the role of color in it in a letter to his brother Theo of September 9, 1888.

112. Velázquez (1599–1660) completed *The Surrender of Breda* (La Rendición de Breda o Las Lanzas) in 1634–35.

113. The reference is to *La Liberté guidant le peuple* (1830), which in fact concerns the French revolution of 1830. (See note 56 in "Moscow" in regard to Delacroix's *Journal.*)

114. The allusion is to the delirium of the wounded Andrei Bolkonsky in Tolstoy's depiction of the battle of Austerlitz in *War and Peace.* Tolstoy attacks the late, "deaf" Beethoven in his *What Is Art?*, condemning the Ninth Symphony for its "failure" to transmit "the highest religious feeling." (See note 67.)

115. The reference is to the crushing by Napoleon of the 1795 royalist insurrection, whose leaders had taken refuge in the church of Saint-Roch.

116. Olesha evidently means Stendhal's *Journal,* kept from 1801 until 1823 and published posthumously in 1888.

117. Olesha seems to mean Stendhal's views on the sensuous nature of music in his travel journal *Rome, Naples, and Florence* (1826).

118. The portrait of Rimsky would appear to be Serov's 1898 rendering of him and not the more dynamic 1893 effort by Repin.

119. The letter, dated July 11, 1891, was written to the Russian conductor and pianist and eventual Juilliard professor Alexander Ziloti (1863–1945).

120. Tolstoy cites Baudelaire prose fragment in *What Is Art?* (See note 67.)

121. The allusion concerns the boy Nikolenka's garbling of the Russian word for "Moravian" *(moravskii),* as it was used to denote the Protestant denomination of Hussite brethren from Moravia *(moravskie brat'ia),* and the adjective for "ant" *(murav'inyi).* The resulting portmanteau "ant brothers" *(muravskie brat'ia)* then became, in the private idiom of the Tolstoy boys, a symbol of universal brotherhood and happiness.

122. The term "metaphor" *(metafora)* has a somewhat broader meaning in Russian than it does in English and thus may sometimes stand for any verbal figure in which there is a direct transference of meaning, including, as should be clear from Olesha's allegory, the simile (the puddle is like a Gypsy woman) and the metonymy (the cherry is associated with sparrows).

123. The lines are from "The Bolshevik" (Bolshevik, 1921) by Vladimir Narbut (1888–1944). Narbut, whom Olesha had known in Odessa and Kharkov in 1920–22, headed the publishing house Land and Factory (Zemlia i fabrika, 1922–30), which issued the first editions of *Envy* and *The Three Fat Men.*

124. The vagabond Velimir Khlebnikov (1885–1922) was a leading futurist poet. The elephant comparison is from his "Menagerie" (Zverinets, 1909–11).

125. Olesha has in mind "V. V. Khlebnikov," an obituary by Mayakovsky published in the July–August 1922 issue of *Red Virgin Soil.*

126. See Khlebnikov's "Fragment from the Tablets of Destiny" (Otryvok iz Dosok sud'by, 1922). War Communism refers to the radical but failed attempt during the civil war to place the Soviet economy on a socialist basis.

127. The quotation is from "The Fall of Atlantis" (Gibel' Atlantidy, 1912).

128. The lines are from "War in a Mousetrap" (Voina v myshelovke, 1915–22) and refer to Vyacheslav Ivanov (1866–1949), a leading symbolist poet who combined masterful technique and a deep knowledge of the classical world.

129. Dmitry Petrovsky (1892–1955) was a poet and short-story writer and a disciple of Khlebnikov's.

130. Yakov Ukhsai (b. 1911), National Poet of the Chuvash Republic in 1950, wrote verse characterized by a whimsical sense of fantasy.

131. Jules Renard (1864–1910), a novelist associated with the symbolist movement, also published sketches of country life, including "A Family of Trees" (Une Famille des arbres), collected in *Natural Histories* (Histoires naturelles, 1896).

132. Alfred Brehm (1829–84) was a German zoologist and the author of the classic zoological reference work *The Life of Animals* (Tierleben, 1864–69), which was translated into Russian shortly after it appeared in Germany.

133. The Russian poet, playwright, and writer Ilya Selvinsky (1899–1968), associated with the constructivists in the 1920s, describes the tiger in the poem "A Tiger Hunt" (Okhota na tigra) in his collection *Poems of the Pacific* (Tikhookeanskie stikhi, 1932).

134. The story is Grin's "The Rat Catcher" (Krysolov, 1924). (See note 82.)

135. The Alhambra is the palace built by the Moors near Granada between 1230 and 1354, and now considered the finest example of Moorish architecture in Spain. The Registan is the decorative main plaza in Samarkand constructed at the end of the fourteenth century when the city, presently in Uzbekistan, was the capital of the Mongol empire of Tamerlane the Great.

THE EXTRAORDINARY INTERSECTION

1. Spassky (or Savior) Tower, built by the English architect Christopher Galloway in 1624–25 and situated on Red Square, is the main entrance to the Kremlin.

2. The story is "The Devil in the Belfry." (See note 71 in "The Golden Shelf.")

3. Olesha means the three terminals on Komsomol Square in northern Moscow: the Leningrad, the Yaroslavl (or Northern), and the Kazan.

4. The popular Leningrad party boss Sergei Kirov (b. 1886) was assassinated in 1934, probably at Stalin's behest.

5. Alexander Nikitenko (1803–77) was a literary critic, scholar, and censor and the author of a valuable posthumously published *Diary* (Dnevnik, 1882–92).

6. Lydia Seifullina (b. 1889) was a short-story writer and playwright best known for her studies of the effects of the revolution on the Siberian peasantry.

7. Vladimir Lidin (V. G. Gomberg, 1894–1979) was a short-story writer and novelist.

8. Vladimir Bill-Belotserkovsky (1885–1970) was a popular playwright.

9. Vsevolod Ivanov (1895–1963) was a prolific prose writer and dramatist who made his debut in the 1920s, when he was associated with the Serapion Brothers. (See note 52 in "Moscow.")

10. Sergei Martinson (1899–1984) was a stage and screen actor who had been associated with Meyerhold's theater in the 1920s, Mikhail Yanshin (1902–76) was an actor and director early associated with the Moscow Art Theater, and Maria Babanova (1900–83) was a celebrated actress who had studied with Komissarzhevskaya in the 1920s and been associated with Meyerhold's theater. The new stage adaptation of *The Three Fat Men* was done by I. S. Dobrovolsky (Moscow, 1959).

11. Aleksei Diky (1889–1955) was a distinguished director and film and stage actor who was associated with the Moscow Art Theater from 1910.

12. *The Good Hope* (Op Hoop van Zegen, 1901) was in fact by the Dutch novelist and playwright Herman Heijermans (1864–1924).

13. *The Three Fat Men* was eventually produced by Valentina and Zinaida Brumberg in 1963 as a forty-minute cartoon with a scenario by the critic, memoirist, and biographer Victor Shklovsky, a close friend of Olesha's (they were married to sisters) and an editor of *No Day without a Line.*

14. Abram Ioffe (1880–1960) was a prominent Soviet theoretical and research physicist.

15. Pavel Markov (1897–1980) was a director, critic, and theater historian associated with the Moscow Art Theater from 1925 to 1949 and with the Maly Theater from 1951 to 1955. Semyon Mezhinsky (1889–1978) was a distinguished stage and screen actor and theater critic associated with the Maly Theater from 1933 to 1959. Markov and Mezhinsky took part as director and principal actor, respectively, in the Maly Theater's 1955 production of Halldór Laxness's *The Silver Moon,* which Olesha helped to adapt. (See note 42 in "Moscow.")

16. Poe's definition may be found in *Eureka.* Pascal's definition, cited by Poe in *Eureka,* is no. 72 of his *Pensées.* (See note 80 in "Moscow.")

17. Mikhail Sholokhov (1905–84), a novelist and powerful Soviet political figure, is best known for his classic civil war epic *The Quiet Don* (Tikhii Don, 1928–40). The reference is to the short critical pieces published by Olesha in the 1950s and collected in his *Selected Writings* (Izbrannye sochnineniia, 1956). Most of them have been included in *No Day without a Line.*

18. The Blok allusion is most likely to his notebook entry of May 11–12 (24–25), 1910, regarding a similar attempt to view the comet, although Olesha may in fact mean his poem "The Comet" (Kometa, 1910).

19. Fyodor Gladkov (1883–1958) was a short-story writer and novelist whose revolutionary romantic *Cement* (Tsement, 1925) was one of the first attempts to write proletarian fiction.

20. Alexander Malyshkin (1892–1938) was a novelist, poet, and screenwriter known for his fiction about the civil war and later for his socialist realist writings. He perished in the Gulag.

21. Cheyne-Stokes respiration is characterized by the cyclic alternation of shallow rapid breathing and no breathing at all; it is named for the Irish physician William Stokes (1804–78) and his Scottish colleague James Cheyne.

22. The allusion is to Tolstoy's tale *The Death of Ivan Ilyich* (Smert' Ivana Il'icha, 1886).

23. Alexander Vertinsky (1889–1957) was a variety artist, actor, poet, and composer who lived and performed abroad from 1919 until his return to the Soviet Union in 1943. He may be best known for his version of the perennially popular song of the 1920s "By the Long Road" (Dorogoi dlinnoiu), rendered in English as "Those were the days."

24. The lines are in Vertinsky's "In the Moldavian Steppe" (V stepi moldavanskoi, 1925). Akkerman, now called Belgorod-Dnestrovsky, is on the border of Moldova (in what used to be Rumanian Bessarabia) and the southern Ukraine and thus close to Odessa and Russia.

25. Paolo Veronese (1528–88) was an Italian painter of the Venetian school whose works, including his landscapes, are notable for their rich color and extraordinary illusionism.